Breaking the Brass Ceiling

Breaking the Brass Ceiling

Women Police Chiefs and
Their Paths to the Top

DOROTHY MOSES SCHULZ

Westport, Connecticut
London

Library of Congress Cataloging-in-Publication Data

Schulz, Dorothy Moses.
    Breaking the brass ceiling : women police chiefs and their paths to the top /
by Dorothy Moses Schulz.
      p. cm.
    Includes bibliographical references and index.
    ISBN 0–275–98180–0 (alk. paper)
      1. Women police chiefs—United States. 2. Policewomen—United States.
3. Sex discrimination against women—United States. 4. Discrimination in law enforcement—
United States. I. Title.
HV8139.S33 2004
363.2′092′273—dc22   2004014775

British Library Cataloguing in Publication Data is available.

Library of Congress Catalog Card Number: 2004014775
ISBN: 0–275–98180–0

First published in 2004

Praeger Publishers, 88 Post Road West, Westport, CT 06881
An imprint of Greenwood Publishing Group, Inc.
www.praeger.com

Printed in the United States of America

The paper used in this book complies with the
Permanent Paper Standard issued by the National
Information Standards Organization (Z39.48–1984).

10 9 8 7 6 5 4 3

To my Dad, Henry Moses, a gentle man who was intensely proud that I was a journalist, a police captain, and, finally, a college professor. He was eager to see how this book would combine all those careers but, very sadly, he died shortly before it was completed.

Contents

Preface

This book really began in 1979, although I didn't know it. I was a captain in the Conrail Police Department, and I was taking courses that would ultimately result in my receiving a doctorate in American Studies from New York University in 1992. Yes, it took a long time, but that's another story for another book! Through a series of events, I delivered a paper on women in police supervisory ranks at the American Society of Criminology meeting in Philadelphia. The panel was concerned with a number of policing issues, and I was one of the few people there who was actively involved in policing and who did not yet possess a Ph.D. There was quite a bit of interest in my findings about what was then a very small number of women police supervisors, but this did not come close to matching the interest in me personally. It was obvious that most of the people I chatted with had never met a woman police manager—in fact, many had never met a woman police officer.

My career took many turns. By the time I was seriously considering a dissertation topic, the Conrail Police Department had been ordered by federal government mandate to divest itself of all but freight operations, and my colleagues and I who worked in New York City became part of a new agency, the Metro-North Commuter Railroad Police Department (subsequently renamed the MTA Police Department). In addition to my academic pursuits, I became active in the International Association of Women Police (IAWP), where I met many women like myself, who joined policing on an equal basis with our male colleagues. There were also many women who had started their careers as policewomen, with a completely different set of entry requirements and job descriptions, who were thrust onto patrol late in their careers. Some flourished, while others were not so sure this was an appropriate use of "womanpower" in policing.

I put on a back burner my interest in women police managers to write my dissertation on the history of women in policing, which was published in different form by Praeger in 1995, as *From Social Worker to Crime-fighter: Women in United States Policing*. I also began a new career on the faculty of John Jay College of Criminal Justice, a branch of the City University of New York. John Jay College is the only college in the country that is devoted solely to the study of criminal justice and related fields and it offers the widest possible range of academic achievement, from two-year associate's degrees to doctorates. I began to attend not only police conferences but also academic meetings. Most of my presentations were on women in policing, and I was struck by a wide gulf between what I heard at the academic meetings and what my women police colleagues and I had experienced. Almost all the discussions about women in policing focused on the problems women faced being accepted in a man's world. Discussions were overwhelmingly on stress, discriminatory treatment, and harassment.

Yet my friends and I loved being cops. That's not to say that problems didn't exist; we certainly weren't always welcomed with open arms, but when we met at police conferences or at each other's homes, we were more likely to share adventures than to engage in pity parties. Most of us thought what we did was exciting and adventurous. Most other women we met seemed to envy us. We certainly weren't cringing in any corners; we were quite pleased with ourselves and would more likely have been accused of swaggering.

When I shared these thoughts with friends who were still in policing, they agreed that it was time for someone to document their successes. *Breaking the Brass Ceiling* is that document. It joins a growing literature on women who are succeeding in fields in which they are a numerical minority but in which they are gaining in numbers and are moving up to visible, decision-making positions.

This work could not have been written without the active support of women in the law enforcement community. No book that relies on information provided by more than 200 women can be a solitary project. Women police chiefs and sheriffs working all across the United States completed surveys on their career paths, gave interviews, suggested other women who had particularly interesting careers, and answered countless e-mails to confirm information on their or other women's careers. These women are the CEOs of their agencies: chiefs of police and sheriffs who have reached the top of their profession. They are proud of themselves, and they believe it is time for more people to be aware that women can succeed in law enforcement and can have a voice in setting the national policing agenda.

I particularly want to thank the members of the International Association of Chiefs of Police's (IACP) Police Administration Committee for providing initial financial support. My deep gratitude goes to the members of the National Association of Women Law Enforcement Executives (NAWLEE), not only for financial support but also for acting as "test cases" for the questionnaires, for encouraging me to participate in their meetings, and for reinforcing my belief that theirs was a story that needed to be told. Many NAWLEE board members are among the chiefs quoted here, and my opportunity to interview a number of other chiefs for a column I write for the NAWLEE Website further enriched the material in this book. My NAWLEE column is aptly titled "View from the Top," and that is what I present here.

I have analyzed questionnaires, interviewed at length, spoken to casually, appeared on panels with, and exchanged e-mails and telephone calls with more than half of the women chiefs of police and sheriffs who have held office between 1998 and the completion of this book. That translates into more than 100 women police chiefs and 25 sheriffs. Although it may sound trite, they are the police managers of the twenty-first century and they are making the new—by sometimes breaking the old—rules for those who will follow, whether female or male.

For help in locating these women, I am indebted to many organizations, including the IAWP, NAWLEE, the IACP, the Hispanic American Police Command Officers Association (HAPCOA), the National Organization of Black Law Enforcement Executives (NOBLE), and the National Sheriffs' Association (NSA). The U.S. Bureau of Indian Affairs helped locate women who are tribal police chiefs.

I also received financial support and a reduction in my teaching responsibilities from the City University of New York PSC-CUNY Research Award Program. The time was invaluable when it came to transcribing interview tapes and entering and analyzing data from the surveys. The data portion of the project was aided immensely by Robert Panzarella, my John Jay College colleague, who helped me design the questionnaire and analyze the data.

Special thanks are due to each of the chiefs and sheriffs who took time to complete the questionnaires and to be interviewed. They belie the paramilitary proviso that one should never volunteer for extra work. Many of the women are where they are today because they are risk-takers, and they proved it by taking the risk to get involved in this project. Their interest reinforced my belief that the time was right for women in policing to expend greater efforts in looking forward. As a historian, I am forever reminding women in policing to stop thinking of themselves as new to the field; we've been here for more than 100 years. That being said, the last thirty of those years have been under totally different circumstances than the first seventy. Since the years after 1968, when integration of women onto patrol began quite tentatively, and throughout the 1970s, when it took root, the percentage of women in policing has steadily increased, as has the small but growing percentage of women supervisors and managers. Although it wasn't always easy, there comes a time when looking forward is more fruitful than remembering the bad times. That time is now!

Thanks to Suzanne I. Staszak-Silva at Praeger for taking a risk of her own: that the success stories of women police chiefs and sheriffs would appeal to readers outside the policing profession. She and the other editors at Praeger and the Greenwood Publishing Group understood that despite the many unique aspects of policing, the experiences of women managers in all fields have certain similarities, and need to be explored and documented.

In addition to those who supported the research, those who participated in it, those who listened to reports on its progress, and those who agreed to publish it, there are those who must live with it. Thanks to my Mom, who was certainly going through one of the most difficult periods in her life during the last stages of this book, but managed to have the presence of mind to provide me with the time for it to be completed. Special thanks to my husband, David, who for the second time in his life found his living space invaded by the physical evidence of research about women in policing. I'm sure he thought my first book would never move beyond papers on the living room floor; one can only guess what he thought about the second go-round.

Introduction:
A Note on Method
and Scope

This portrait of past and current women police chiefs and sheriffs will enhance the reader's knowledge of American policing and provide an understanding of both the pathways and the obstacles for women who seek to reach the top of one of the most quintessentially male professions in America. *Breaking the Brass Ceiling* presents a unique opportunity to hear from women who are challenging the boundaries of a historically male domain. It is a chance to look beyond the problems women face in these areas and to hear from those who have succeeded.

Breaking the Brass Ceiling is based primarily on data collected from questionnaires completed by women police chiefs and sheriffs in the winter of 2001 and on interviews conducted before and after that date. The questions traced the women's entry into policing, their upward mobility in police departments and sheriffs' department, and personal information about them. The responses were enlivened by the interviews and enhanced by documents provided by the women; by transcripts of phone conversations, e-mails, and presentations the women made at police conferences; by official department records; and by a variety of published sources. This portrait represents more than three years of research specifically for this book and more than two decades of research in the areas of policing about whichI have taught and written.

The collective portrait of the women who responded to the questionnaire is provided in Chapter 10. The questionnaire was developed specifically for this research with the assistance of women police chiefs. It contained thirty-seven questions, some of which had multiple parts. Some questions (termed close-ended) required checking either yes/no or selecting from specific choices. The women were asked about their assignments, their years on patrol, any significant jobs they held before entering law enforcement, and about their ages, education, and social status. Each chief or sheriff was asked whether she was the first sworn woman in any agency in which she had worked, and whether she was the first woman supervisor in her current agency. Open-ended questions left space for the chief or sheriff to describe her department or agency, the length of time she had been in her position, the career moves she had made before reaching her present position, and who had assisted or resisted her on the way to the top.

Most of the sheriffs were interviewed in the summer of 2001, and all were in office at the time; those featured in Chapter 8 were still in office in 2004. The chiefs were interviewed between 2000 and 2004; a few have retired and some have moved to other agencies, but this does not change their career paths. The end of 2003 and the early months of 2004 saw the selection of a large number of new women chiefs, particularly in big-city police departments, where they had previously been only in token numbers. These chiefs were contacted even though they had not completed questionnaires; their careers are explored in Chapter 9. Their career paths were strikingly similar to the women in smaller departments.

I conducted and transcribed each of the interviews; all were on the record. No chief or sheriff refused an interview, and none refused to answer any of the questions she was asked. The ease of obtaining interviews may have been based on my own career in policing. I knew many of the women before they were chief or sheriff, and I met many others through a variety of police associations. I knew what to ask, and the women were comfortable speaking to someone who was familiar with the issues. Interviews and questionnaire responses were enriched by tapes of the women's presentations at a variety of police conferences and by press coverage of their careers.

Among the factors that influenced selection for the interviews were size, location, and type of agency; length of time as chief or sheriff; whether a chief or sheriff was in the department in which she began her law enforcement career, or whether she had made strategic moves to position herself for the job of top cop; and whether she held any firsts, including but not limited to first woman in her department, first woman supervisor, or first woman in a nontraditional assignment, such as homicide, canine, motorcycle, or special weapons and tactics (SWAT).

Demographic information included age; race; level of education and major; prior work experience, including military service; years in policing; number of departments employed in before reaching chief or sheriff; marital status and whether the respondent's spouse or partner was in law enforcement; types of assignments; motivation to enter policing and to seek higher rank; and numbers and types of mentors inside or outside the department.

Each of the women individually and all of them as a group add to the growing literature on women in leadership positions. Being the first is never painless and is often painful. But the more society can learn about pioneering women in all professions, the easier it will be for future generations to move up more quickly. They will have greater confidence that their efforts to reach the top will be successful, and they will gain by their knowledge that they have every right and the privilege to aim for the highest levels of management, a right and a privilege that each of the women profiled in *Breaking the Brass Ceiling* has attained.

CHAPTER 1

How It All Began: What Is a Nice Girl Like You Doing in a Place Like This?

I was about eight year old. While riding my bike, I found a police badge. I went home and told my mom I wanted to be a policeman. She said I was a girl, so I couldn't be a man, and I certainly couldn't be a policeman.

—Chief Susan Riseling
University of Wisconsin, Madison, Police Department

Being a police officer was my dream.

—Chief Carolyn Hutchison
Carrboro, North Carolina, Police Department

I wanted to do something that was outside the norm for women.

—Chief Doris Conley
Lincoln City, Oregon, Police Department

I was divorced, I had two children, and I needed the money.

—Chief Donna Green
Oakland, Oregon, Police Department

My older sister was a trooper for Alaska and took me on a ride-along. I was hooked.

—Chief Denise Pentony
Shoreline, Washington, Police Department

Why do women become police officers? The answers are as varied as the women. Each of the chiefs arrived at her position from a slightly different background and brought with her different work experiences and different reasons for joining a police department. Although the women had different reasons for becoming police officers, most of their reasons are the same as the reasons that men become police officers. Some dreamed of being police officers, although many were not sure exactly why and how they came to have what for women was a nontraditional dream. Some had family or friends in law enforcement and received encouragement from them.

Virtually all wanted to help others, and many thought policing was a more exciting helping profession than such traditional women's jobs as teaching, nursing, or social work. Some wanted to enter a field that was overwhelmingly male, not, as some observers believed, to meet a husband, but because they knew it would mean higher salaries and better benefits. And for some, it was a lark, quite literally in response to a dare from a friend, a boss, or even a spouse. For most, it was some combination of these factors.

Why do so many people want to do know why a perfect stranger has selected a particular career? Every woman police officer can recall instances of being asked, either literally or in so many words: What is a nice girl like you doing in a job like this? The question can come from many sources. Sometimes it is someone at a social gathering. Sometimes it is the person to whom the woman gives a traffic summons. Sometimes it is the crime victim who finally figures out what is different about the police officer asking the questions or providing assistance. Sometimes it is another police officer or a supervisor.

For Chief Carolyn Hutchison, of Carrboro, North Carolina, the question came from the two chiefs who interviewed her for her first job: the chief who didn't hire her because he didn't think she'd stay, and the one who hired her reluctantly even though he, too, thought she'd leave quickly. One of the chiefs who started her career to follow a dream, Hutchison had just graduated from Duke University with a double major in sociology and Spanish. She had always wanted to be a police officer, but luckily the chief who hired her wasn't aware that the dream was not based on admiration for the police, but on negative encounters she had had with officers. Despite the chief's initial reluctance, he became her mentor, and although the department wasn't her first choice, "When the chief gave me a chance, I grabbed it, and I haven't been unhappy since."

Annetta Nunn, the first African-American woman to lead the Birmingham, Alabama, Police Department, also was motivated by what she saw and didn't like about the police. While Hutchison had a few personal run-ins with police, Nunn had observed police in her neighborhood who were protecting illegal activity. What both women shared was the belief that policing didn't have to be either insensitive or corrupt—sufficient motivation to form their career decisions.

Milwaukee, Wisconsin, Chief Nannette Hegerty dreamed of being a police officer in the days before women were on patrol. She remembered growing up in the 1960s and 1970s and seeing patrol cars in her neighborhood and thinking what a "neat job" it would be to ride around the city helping people. By 1976, the city was hiring women on an equal basis with men, and Hegerty was able to fulfill her dream.

Susan Riseling's dream was based on fate. While riding her bicycle, she found a police badge. She returned home with the badge in her pocket and, using the language of the times, told her mother that she wanted to be a policeman. Her mother explained that it was impossible for her to be a man, and therefore equally impossible to be a policeman. Although Riseling didn't argue, she decided to study criminal justice, but, with her mother's words in her mind, she opted for a career in college and university policing because she believed it would be more female-friendly. She was correct. Riseling, who was named chief of the University of Wisconsin at Madison's Police Department in 1991, had previously been the second in command at the State University of New York at Stony Brook's Police Department.

Some of the women were able to fulfill their dreams through internships or cadet programs that allowed them to work with their local police department in high school or in college. These programs were developed in the 1970s and 1980s primarily as a way to bring minority men into police agencies. In large cities, the programs often were open only to those who lived in specified neighborhoods, which usually assured that the majority of the applicants would be African-American or Hispanic. In smaller cities or in sheriffs' departments, the programs were sometimes also aimed at college students, providing them with a chance to earn college credits or funds toward their tuition bills. A number of the programs were structured to raise the standards of police applicants, who rarely were college-trained, by enticing college students into law enforcement careers after they graduated.

Many agencies also participated in police reserve programs, where local residents attended a police academy and worked, as volunteers or for pay, a certain number of hours a week or a month. In departments where reserve officers did not attend academies, they did clerical work, took reports, or provided extra eyes and ears for police officers at fairs, parades, or sporting events. In other jurisdictions, reserves were sworn police officers; they carried firearms and had arrest authority, and were really part-time employees, many of whom hoped to become regular, full-time police officers.

Although departments had not anticipated it, by the mid-1970s women began to apply for cadet and reserve officer positions. Many of the departments were reluctant to hire these young women, and rarely allowed them to do anything but clerical tasks. But even in these limited roles, some women were able to use the programs to establish their credibility and reinforce that they were serious about careers in policing. Particularly in small agencies, where hiring is often outside civil service rules, the women were able to impress the chiefs enough to be offered full-time positions when they became available. Patricia Medina, chief of the Rio Dell, California, Police Department, began her career as a police cadet. She had wanted to be a police officer since high school, and in 1976 the program opened the doors in her original department, where she was the first woman police officer and the first woman supervisor. After nineteen years in policing, Medina, one of only a handful of Hispanic-surnamed chiefs, had worked in four police departments, the last two as the chief.

Gwendolyn Boyd-Savage began her policing career as a public service aide with the Miami, Florida, Police Department, assisting police officers by taking reports from citizens. She used the position as a stepping-stone first to police officer and ultimately to three chiefs' positions, stopping along the way to serve as vice president of administrative services at Florida International University, her alma mater. One of the few African-American women to have led other than a large-city police department, Boyd-Savage had been nicknamed Hot Pants for her undercover arrests on the streets of Miami before becoming the department's first black female major and then its first female assistant chief. Prior to being named chief in North Miami, Florida, in 2002, Boyd-Savage had been chief in Prichard, Alabama, and Miramar, Florida. At the time of her selection in North Miami, Riviera Beach, Florida, was planning to offer her its vacant chief's position. Boyd-Savage was the first Florida police chief—male or female—with a doctorate, and she was the first African-American female police chief in North Miami, the fourth largest city in Miami–Dade County. Had she waited for the Riviera Beach job, she would have become the first black woman to head a police department in Palm Beach County.[1]

Vickie Peltzer, whose career with the Albuquerque, New Mexico, Police Department led to her becoming the chief of police at the University of Washington, benefited from a different type of cadet program. Peltzer was able to join the Albuquerque Police Department's Explorer Program in 1972, barely a year after it was opened to women. The program began with the Boy Scouts of America, and was open to Scouts between the ages of fourteen and sixteen. In 1971 the age limit was extended to twenty-one and women became eligible to participate. The program allows young people to assist police officers, to attend lectures on police topics, and to compete for a variety of college scholarships.

Peltzer recalled that she had big dreams and wanted it all, including the pay and benefits of policing. "I wanted a real career, excitement, helping people, interest in law enforcement, pay, benefits—all of it," she said, ticking the items off on her fingers.

Although she married and left Albuquerque, when she and her family returned in 1979, she was able to join the department as a police officer. During her twenty-year career there, she gained experience in patrol and administrative units, earned a master's degree in public administration, and received two civil service promotions to the rank of lieutenant. Seeing little opportunity to move higher in rank, she became one of almost seventy applicants for the position of chief at the University of Washington in Seattle, where she led a department of fifty police officers and a number of civilians responsible for public safety on the 640-acre campus. In 2002 she was elected president of the National Association of Women Law Enforcement Executives (NAWLEE), a group of mostly high-ranking women who provide networking and mentoring for women who aspire to become chiefs. Divorced for many years, she remarried in 2004 and has begun using her new name of Stormo.

Heather Fong, who in 2004 was named chief of the San Francisco Police Department, recalled that since the age requirement to be a police officer was twenty-one, she could only serve as a cadet when she joined at age eighteen, and that since women were not allowed on patrol, she had to stay in the office.

Colonel Anne Beers, head of the Minnesota State Patrol, and one of only two women to have led a state police agency, also was attracted by a cadet program that included a pre-entry academy. One of only three women officers at the time she joined the State Patrol, she was drawn to the independence and service aspects of policing. Beers's career has been history-making. Except for the rank of sergeant, she was the first woman to hold every rank in her agency, including lieutenant, captain, major, deputy chief, and chief.

Shirley Pierini, who in 2004 became the fifth woman president of the 33,000-member American Society of Industrial Security–International in its more than fifty-year history, recalled that before starting a career in private security, she had worked as a communications officer with the San Diego Police Department and as a reserve officer with the Imperial Beach, California, Police Department and then with the Washoe County (Nevada) Sheriff's Office. Family responsibilities made it difficult for her to remain in one place long enough for a policing career, but proved less of a problem in private industry, which enabled her to hold a number of management positions in corporate security and to take an active role with ASIS–International.[2]

These programs opened doors for the women, but the women were quick to see that departments viewed them as little more than typists and clerks. While male cadets were permitted to go out in the field with officers or were assigned to help in bureaus that were more active, the women often had to be content with filing reports or typing for middle-ranking officers in administrative jobs. Neither the women nor the men found this unusual, since the vast majority of women who worked in police departments before the 1970s, with the exception of the few sworn police-women, were employed in clerical roles.

A number of the chiefs who weren't cadets began their careers in police departments as clerks or as dispatchers in the communications section, where they answered telephone calls from the public and sent (dispatched) police officers to answer the public's requests for service. These jobs, which often entailed working nights and weekends just as the police officers did, generally paid less and had fewer fringe benefits (sick and vacation leave, pension accrual, or time off for education) than the officers' jobs. In many departments, dispatchers work alongside sworn officers and are supervised by sergeants or other sworn members of the department who also supervise police officers. Chief Barbara Childress, of Richmond Hills, Texas, one of the first women chiefs in the state and one of the few who has been chief for more than twenty years, began her career as a dispatcher. Another Texas chief, Nona Holoman, who was selected to lead the Seabrook Police Department in 2000, also began her career as dispatcher before becoming a police officer and moving up the ranks.

Evelyn Hicks, who in 1995 became the first African-American female chief in Florida, joined the Opa-Locka Police Department as a clerk-typist in 1973. At the time, she recalled, "it was a male-dominated department. There [was] a small percentage of blacks, but there were no female officers at all." It took her twenty years to advance from police officer to corporal, to sergeant, to acting patrol commander, and to commander of the department's criminal investigation and administration. Fiscal problems in Opa-Locka, a financially strapped Dade County community that until the 1950s was home to a U.S. Navy base and that is still trying to change its image from a crime-ridden "Baghdad of the South," resulted in Hicks and other officers being demoted in 1993. She decided to stay, and two years later was named chief, a position she held for approximately three years.[3]

Shirley Gifford, who in 2003 retired as chief of the Soldatin, Alaska, Police Department, spent most of her career in the Anchorage Police Department. She had recently completed a degree in criminal justice and was hired to type police reports. She realized she could do the job of police officer and asked to be sent to the police academy. Twenty-one years later, she gave up her Anchorage captain's bars to become a chief. She was one of a number of the chiefs who followed a time-honored career path set by many men: leaving a larger police department at middle management or higher rank to take over as chief in a smaller police department.

Chief Linda Davis began her career in the Winston-Salem, North Carolina, Police Department as a secretary. When she retired in 2004, for the second time, she had spent thirty-four years in the department, eighteen of them on patrol. She had been the department's first female patrol officer, sergeant, lieutenant, captain, assistant chief, and chief. She had originally retired as the assistant chief in 1998, but was soon asked to return as interim chief, and the following year the "acting" was removed from her title. When she retired for the second time, she said she thought it would be for good.

Lori Emmert, who in 2003 became the second female chief in Wyoming when she was selected to lead the Douglas Police Department, began her career in 1980 as a dispatcher and animal control officer. After six years, she was promoted to a records and communications supervisor before finally becoming a police officer in 1992. Things moved more quickly after that. In 2001, she was promoted to sergeant after earning an associate's degree from Eastern Wyoming College. She had been acting chief for less than two months when City Administrator Bobbi Fitzhugh selected her, noting with some understatement that she had "truly worked her way up through the ranks."[4]

Carol Williams of Montclair, New Jersey, who was named chief in 1994, was working in the civilian position of security specialist when her supervisor dared her to become a police officer. Accepting the challenge, she became her department's first woman officer, sergeant, lieutenant, and captain before being named only the second woman chief in the state. When the fifteen-year veteran was named chief, she was still the only woman in the department. Her sole motivation to become a police officer had been her supervisor's challenge. Glassboro's Patricia Kunchynski had become the first woman chief in New Jersey in 1987. She, too, had been the first woman in her department. By the time she retired in 2003, about a dozen women had been chiefs in the state. The overall percentage of women in policing in New Jersey is below the national average. This is because many of the small departments have no or only one or two women, but this has not prevented some of the women from rising to the top of their agency.

Fewer than a dozen women mentioned family or close friends as their motivation for becoming police officers. Of those who did, though, the family member differed; sometimes it was a father or brother, but for Chief

Denise Pentony, of Shoreline, Washington, it was accompanying a sister, an Alaska State Trooper, on a ride-along. Two others also mentioned older sisters who were already police officers. One, a chief in a small village of only 1,200 residents, was her department's only full-time officer. She supervised only three part-time police officers. She indicated that her former husband had also been a small-town chief, but, possibly to maintain some confidentiality in such a small community, she did not specify whether he had been chief of the department she now led.

Elizabeth (Betsy) Watson, who was the only woman to have been chief of two large municipal police departments (Houston from 1990 to 1992 and Austin from 1992 to 1997), was persuaded to try policing by her mother, who had been intrigued by the stories told by relatives who had been in the Philadelphia Police Department. Although Watson wasn't sure she wanted a police career, both she and her sister were pioneers, she as a chief and her sister as the first woman captain in the Harris County (Texas) Sheriff's Department.

Two of the university chiefs described fathers who had been in federal law enforcement, and one also mentioned that her sister, who been able to use funds from a law enforcement grant to complete her education, was a mentor to her. Another chief had actually planned to become an attorney, but the death of her father, a federal law enforcement officer, resulted in her having to put her plans on hold for both emotional and financial reasons. She switched to a criminal justice program, thinking she might go to law school later, but the municipal department in which she was interning gave an exam for police officer, and after taking it "on a whim," she decided to take the job when it was offered to her.

Others mentioned brothers, spouses, boyfriends, or friends, overwhelmingly male. That most of the chiefs referred to male relatives or friends reflected the years in which they entered policing, when the profession was only opening up to women on an equal basis with men. Although few of the chiefs were the first woman in their agency, women were not as prevalent in policing as they are today, so it is not surprising that most of the police officers the women knew were men.

The few mentions of mothers were also a reflection of the times. None of the chiefs had a mother who was a policewoman or police officer, but a few of the mothers were employed as civilians in police departments, mainly as dispatchers. They encouraged their daughters to apply for police positions when they became available in the mid-1970s. Vanessa Wall, chief at Middle Georgia College in Cochran, Georgia, who spent sixteen years in a municipal police department before becoming chief, recalled that her mother worked as a dispatcher and had been fascinated hearing the sheriff's deputies talk about their jobs.

"some college" without specifying a particular number of credits.[6] The figures have not changed greatly; although a few more departments require some college credits, they rarely require a degree.

Since many of the women chiefs already held degrees when they became police officers, they tended to be somewhat older than male recruits. This may have affected their progress through the ranks and may also have played a role in the assignments they selected or which they were given. Two studies have indicated differences among police officers based on age. One found that officers who were hired at older ages were less likely to have citizens' complaints lodged against them and were less likely to be assaulted. A number of departments in Oklahoma found that younger officers were more likely to engage in violent encounters with civilians than older officers.[7] Neither study took sex into account, since they were done when women were not assigned to patrol.

One group that advocates hiring and promoting greater numbers of women, the National Center for Women & Policing (NCWP), has argued that hiring more women would result in fewer brutality complaints within police departments. It based its analysis on the 1991 Christopher Commission report on the Los Angeles Police Department (LAPD) in the wake of the Rodney King videotape. The commission recommended hiring more women in order to reduce police brutality, based on its findings that of the 183 officers who each had more than four allegations of excessive force or improper tactics from 1986 to 1990, none were women. In its own study of the years 1990 to 1999, the NCWP found that the LAPD paid out $63.4 million in lawsuits that resulted from accusations that male officers used excessive force or were involved in sexual assaults or domestic violence incidents, while for the same years only $2.8 million was paid out for excessive force lawsuits involving female officers and no female officers were named in either sexual assault or domestic violence cases.[8]

Regardless of the women's ages, races, or types of departments in which they worked, it was a rare chief who did not at some point refer to the desire or ability to be of service to her community. Donna Waters, who worked in two departments before being named chief in Zebulon, North Carolina, said she "wanted to make a difference, but also didn't want a stereotypical job." Another of her motivations was to avoid being stuck behind a desk, something she said she is unable to avoid as the chief of a thirty-person department. For Gloria Parker Smith, police chief of the Jacksonville, Florida, Airport Authority, it was a combination of "family tradition and helping people."

Chief Donna Woods, whose official title was town marshal of North Judson, Indiana, wanted to help her small community remain safe. Her career proved that deferring a dream doesn't mean giving up on it. Woods, a mother of three when she was appointed marshal in the community of 2,500 in 1995, had wanted to become a police officer twenty years earlier, but became discouraged by the lack of opportunities for women.

After driving a school bus for a decade and seeing a woman hired as a North Judson police officer, Woods decided it wasn't too late. She and her husband had served as volunteers with the police reserve, he as a captain and she as an officer, but it was she who decided, in 1990, at age forty, to attend the police academy and try for a full-time job. She was the oldest recruit, and one of only six women in her 110-member class, she said, but was "determined to make it" even though many of her classmates were in their early twenties. After graduation, Woods joined her small department as a paid employee, was promoted to captain by the marshal, and when he resigned, the town council offered her the job. "I'm no Wonder Woman," she said at the time, "but I want the community to grow and be a good and safe place to raise a family." Despite having faced male chauvinism in her career and some skepticism from town residents as to whether she was really the right person for the position, Woods felt she had made the right decision.[9]

A former nurse who became a university police chief wanted to stay in a helping profession but wanted better pay and more security than nursing offered in 1969, so she became a deputy sheriff, retiring with the rank of assistant sheriff before fulfilling her desire to be a chief. Three chiefs had previously worked as emergency medical technicians. Each said she had been encouraged by the police officers she met in the course of her job to consider changing careers. A recurring theme among the women who were encouraged by officers was that the officers, sure their departments would be pressured into hiring women, were trying to recruit women they believed would be likely to succeed. One of these chiefs said she was never sure the men encouraged her because they liked her, because she was the lesser of the evils they thought they faced with women coming into the department, or because they believed she would do a good job since she was familiar with working odd hours and dealing with people in emergency situations. "You want to think they really wanted you as a co-worker," she added, "but then you have to admit they might just have thought you'd be better than someone who was afraid to go out at night and had never seen blood before."

Mary Muhlig, chief in Pine Knoll Shores, North Carolina, had been a physical education teacher. She said she already had been dealing with "problem students" and had spent so much time with the local police in the first city in which she worked that some of the officers urged her to join, even though there were "only five token females in the 400-person department." In addition to support from male officers, she said her biggest supporter was her mom, "even though she thought I'd lost my mind." Muhlig, who spent four years in the Navy before becoming a police officer in 1978, is one of a handful of chiefs with a doctorate and also one of the few women who had been a chief prior to taking over the twelve-person Pine Knoll Shores department.

Juliet De La Cruz, one of only three Hispanic-surnamed women who were identified as chiefs, left a career as an elementary school teacher to become a police officer in 1987. Although she was drawn to public service, she was also looking for "excitement and unpredictability." She left a county police department to take the position of police director at Georgia Perimeter College in Clarkston when she realized she could do a better job than most of the supervisors for whom she had worked. Having earned bachelor's and master's degrees, she didn't want to give up her career in law enforcement but wanted to continue her education, and she felt it would be easier to do with a college police department.

There are also women who were "accidental" police officers: those who chose the career because it was available or on a lark, but who at some point decided to stay and then to excel. Probably the best known of these was Atlanta's Beverly Harvard, who became a cop to win a $100 bet with her husband. By the time she retired more than twenty years later, she had become the first African-American woman to lead a major-city police department. Others accepted dares from a variety of challengers. Leslye Ann Bass, chief of the Louisiana State University Health Services Center Police in New Orleans, was actually trying to prove to a male friend that she could *not* pass the test, but when she was proven wrong, she became a harbor police officer and, she said, "lived happily ever after."

Mary F. Rabadeau was teaching eighth grade in a parochial school in 1977 when the Elizabeth, New Jersey, Police Department advertised that women were eligible to take the police exam. A male teacher walked into the lounge with applications for his female colleagues, and she decided to give it a try. She passed the written exam but expected to fail the physical, recalling that she wasn't dedicated to the idea of becoming a police officer but that she'd stick it out "until they said no." The "no" never came; in 1978 she and four others became the first women to join the department. In 1992, having reached the civil service rank of captain, she was appointed director of the 321-member department, the first woman to lead a large department in the state. When she was named director, she said, the major difference from teaching was that in policing she carried a gun while helping people or telling them what to do. In 1995 she became one of the few women to head a second police agency, after she was recruited to become chief of the New Jersey Transit Police Department, a smaller agency but one with jurisdiction in New Jersey and New York. She retired in 2002.

A university chief who had spent thirteen years in a sheriff's department before becoming chief had possibly the least motivation, admitting, only upon the promise of anonymity, that she "needed a job and was only practicing interviewing, so that when my dream job came along, I'd know what to say. But when the work seemed interesting and they flattered me by actually recruiting me, I guessed that I had nothing to lose. I've done very well for a career that was meant to be short-term. My current department, where I'm the chief, also actively recruited me, which is why I now tell others not to turn down opportunities, because you never know where they will lead."

EQUAL PAY FOR EQUAL WORK

The chiefs who spoke specifically about policing in terms of salary, job benefits, and security tended to be older or to have been in the field longer. These women, many of them divorced and the sole support of their families, were drawn to policing because they could earn more money doing "men's work" than they could doing "women's work." Although fewer of the younger chiefs raised this issue, it was most likely because they took it for granted that male and female police officers would receive equal pay based on union-negotiated contracts and civil service guarantees.

This assumption is not shared by most women in the labor force. A 1997 survey by the American Federation of Labor and Congress of Industrial Organization's (AFL-CIO) Working Women's Department found that equal pay was the top concern of working women. Although union officials had expected women to complain about an absence of child care in the workplace, this ranked far below benefits that are provided routinely by all but the smallest police and sheriffs' departments. The women, many of whom were in the "pink-collar" clerical jobs from which noncollege-educated women in policing are often drawn, cited as their most important concerns equal pay for equal work; secure and affordable health insurance; paid sick leave for themselves; pension and retirement benefits; protection from layoffs and downsizing; and paid leave to care for ill family members.[10] Policing provides virtually all of these, and salary and benefits for women and men are identical.

Smith, the Jacksonville airport chief, chose a career in policing because it would not be boring, but also because it offered "equal pay for equal work." At close to sixty years of age, she was the most senior woman in terms of age and years in policing. She had worked as a teacher's aide and a secretary, and had joined the workforce at a time when high-paying jobs for women were harder to find than they are today. This may explain the large number of career moves she had made since 1976; the airport authority was her fourth law enforcement agency.

Diana Borer, chief in Tilden, Nebraska, said that as important as it was "to make a difference in other people's lives, I also needed to make a difference in my own life. I was divorced, the single parent of two boys, and I needed to make money to support us. A good friend in my first agency encouraged me to apply because the job had a better future than the place I was working as an office manager." Now remarried, the chief described her then fiancé as one of those who later motivated her to consider changing agencies to become a chief. "That, and getting tired of working nights," she said, only partially in jest.

Bev Ecklund, director of the University of Minnesota at Duluth police, one of the few chiefs who had worked in the separate title of policewoman (rather than police officer), wanted to serve the public, wanted excitement, and also wanted "job stability, good pay, and good benefits." Originally hired by a municipal police department, she remained for twenty-seven years before being recruited in the late 1990s to become the police director at the university from which she had graduated years earlier.

Ann Glavin, who became one of the youngest chiefs ever when she was named chief at the Massachusetts Institute of Technology in 1987, wanted to be a teacher but discovered in 1975 that there was a "glut of teachers and no jobs." At the same time, she wanted a challenge, didn't want to work behind a desk, and wanted to "brave a man's world." After a dozen years, all of them at MIT, Glavin was only thirty-four when she was named chief. She had been her department's first woman officer and the first female graduate of the police academy she attended, and she was the first woman chief at a major university police department. She was also the first woman member of the Massachusetts Chiefs of Police Association. She recalled that when she was hired, "jealous wives didn't want me patrolling with their husbands," and that her supervisor insisted that she be picked up every night from her remote beat on the campus by a squad car, because he thought it was too dangerous for her to walk back to headquarters—although he did not think it was too dangerous for her to patrol alone.[11]

A founding member and a past president of NAWLEE, Glavin, who has a bachelor's degree in government from Wheaton College and a master's in education from Boston University, remained chief for thirteen years before accepting a promotion that took her out of direct supervision of the police department. She soon found that she missed policing, and she and her husband moved across the country so that she could accept the job of chief of police and director of public safety at California State University in Northridge.

Glavin's comments about the wives of male colleagues were typical of those of many of the chiefs who entered policing in the mid-1970s. When women were first assigned to patrol with male officers, some of the fiercest opponents to their presence were officers' wives. In many cities, including New York, wives actually took to the streets, protesting that women officers would place their husbands in mortal danger because of their small size and perceived inability to provide adequate protection and backup in an emergency. Although some wives might really have felt this way, since police officers are well-known for assuring their families that they face minimal danger on the streets, a hidden agenda may have been the fear that their husbands would become romantically involved with their new co-workers. Since the men had never before worked around women in sizable numbers or as equals, and because it was thought that the women had entered policing primarily because it was a male-dominated field that would provide them with marriage proposals, it is likely that jealousy played a larger role than fear. It also appeared at the time that many of the protests were orchestrated by police unions, which generally fought against equal hiring and assignment of women.

The earliest television portrayals of women police officers supported the vision of them as helpless temptresses. The better known of the shows, *Policewoman*, featured the leggy Angie Dickinson as Sergeant Suzanne "Pepper" Anderson of the Los Angeles Police Department (LAPD). Dickinson answered her doorbell's ring draped in little more than a towel on virtually every episode of the show, which ran from 1974 to 1978. Her legs were considered so exceptional that they stood the test of time. In 2003 Britney Spears posed in *Esquire* magazine in a takeoff on one of Dickinson's classic poses. Another show, *Get Christy Love*, ran for only a year, from 1974 to 1975, and was in the style of action adventure movies aimed at African-American audiences that came to be labeled "blaxploitation" films. It featured Teresa Graves, whose bosses tried to keep her away from the big cases. Yet she managed each week to flaunt her good looks, big pocketbooks, and karate moves, and to serve notice on the bad guys that "You're under arrest, Sugah." Both shows sought mileage from the sex appeal of a woman with a gun. Dickinson became a pinup poster queen, but Graves's career flagged; she died on October 10, 2002.

Although a number of the chiefs said that television had influenced their interest in a policing career, few mentioned these shows, referring more frequently to either *The Mod Squad* or *The Rookies*. These shows, which aired from 1968 to 1973 and from 1972 to 1976, respectively, featured young police officers who worked in teams, and each team included one woman. Most of the chiefs were already in policing by the time *Hill Street Blues* (1981 to 1987) and *Cagney and Lacey* (1982 to 1988), two shows with more realistic portrayals of policing and women's roles, were telecast.

MEN'S WORK, WOMEN'S WORK

Although the concerns of some of the older women chiefs with "pay opportunities" and "a better future" may not resonate quite as strongly with younger women, those who began their job searches in the 1960s and 1970s will understand why this was so important. It was a time when women's careers were limited to traditional women's work. For women with a college degree, women's work was primarily teaching, nursing, social work, or youth counseling—the traditional women's helping professions. For women without a college degree, it was primarily secretarial or clerical work.

Although they didn't realize it, the chiefs who as young girls dreamed of police careers were atypical. Even today, occupational segregation on the basis of sex is common. One of the major reasons that women continue to earn about 75 cents for every dollar earned by men is that women are clustered in jobs that are considered "women's work," and that almost always pay less than jobs that are considered "men's work." Like many jobs that are assumed to require physical strength, courage, and heroism, and are performed outdoors with little direct supervision, policing has always been considered a man's job. On the other hand, women's jobs have come to be defined as those that require attention to detail and close supervision (often by men in higher ranks), and that are expressive, meaning that they rely on women's supposedly inborn qualities of patience and caring, emotions associated with motherhood and child rearing.

Based on these beliefs, men are encouraged to become police officers, airline pilots, firefighters, mechanics, and physicians, while women are encouraged to become social workers, nurses, teachers, librarians, and secretaries. Research on job selection has shown that those who dream of careers outside sex typing have a difficult time. Not only does the work world segregate jobs by sex, but parents, schools, guidance counselors, and the media send messages about what is an appropriate dream for members of each sex. Friends and classmates, even in early childhood, also reinforce sex stereotypes, ostracizing those who don't conform to appropriate behavior.[12] This is why Susan Riseling's mother told her she couldn't be a policeman and why Nannette Hegerty didn't think she could have the "neat job" of riding around Milwaukee in a patrol car.

When a friend seems shocked that a man plans to become an elementary school teacher or a woman plans to become a police officer, the friend is adhering to gender stereotypes that the man will be doing women's work and the woman will be doing men's work. Not only are the candidates defying society, they are seen as defying nature, since those who accept these stereotypes often believe that the traits for either type of job are determined by one's sex.

Women actually have a wider range of gender-acceptable behavior than men do. Girls still play with dolls and dress up in their mother's clothing, but they may also climb trees, play sports, and engage in tomboyish behavior. Boys have fewer choices. A boy who plays with dolls might be called a wimp or a sissy; a boy who dresses in his mom's or sister's outfits may have his sexuality seriously questioned. Fewer people today would raise eyebrows at a girl who wanted to be a police officer, a lawyer, or a doctor than at a boy who wanted to be an elementary school teacher, a nurse, or a homemaker. This greater range of freedom for women can also be seen in clothing. Today it is acceptable for women to wear trousers to school, to work, and to many social events; despite a few halfhearted attempts by the fashion industry, it is unlikely men will go to the same places in dresses or skirts anytime soon.

Yet the workplace continues to be segregated on the basis of sex. In 2001, the U.S. Census Bureau found that very few jobs were close to 50 percent men and women, that most jobs continued to be heavily sex-typed, and that jobs that were filled primarily by women continued to pay far less than jobs filled primarily by men. A few examples will suffice. Four of the highest-paying jobs included in the survey were lawyer, pharmacist, physician, and electrical engineer. The percentages of male employees in these fields were, respectively, 66, 58, 67, and 91. Median annual earnings (defined as half of the workers making more and half less) ranged from $72,696 for the physicians to $61,040 for the engineers. The three highest-paid traditionally women's jobs were registered nurse, elementary school teacher, and social worker. The percentages of women working in these fields and the salaries were nurse, 91 percent, $43,108; elementary school teacher, 81 percent, $38,480, and social worker, 70 percent, $33,488. Even though those fields require at least a bachelor's degree and most police departments still require no more than a high school diploma, the median salary for police officers was $40,664 and 87 percent of the workforce was still male. The closest women's job to policing in terms of educational requirements would be secretary or receptionist, where the employees were 99 and 98 percent women, and the salaries were almost half those of police officers: $24,700 and $20,852, respectively.[13]

Gender stereotypes also reinforce that men are more committed to their work and generally more ambitious for professional recognition. This is often attributed not only to stereotypes but also to the realities of the workplace. Economists have speculated that women, because they know they will take career breaks to marry and raise their families, enter fields where breaks are less damaging to a career. Thus, again, teaching, nursing, and a variety of fields where there is more planned time off or where it is easier to take a leave of absence and resume a career without losing momentum have been viewed as women's work. Some economists say this is why these fields traditionally pay less than men's work, but another theory is that the work women do is undervalued solely because it is done by women, who have less status in society.

In the 1970s and 1980s there was much talk about "comparable worth," which tried to evaluate the worth of jobs that were traditionally done by women and those done by men. The thought was that once men's jobs and women's jobs were deemed comparable, the salaries could be equalized. Thus, a janitor (usually a man) and a file clerk (usually a woman) could have their salaries and benefits equalized. Most of these attempts did not get very far, and in most cities, the jobs that men do continue to pay more than those women do. Many people believe that police officers and firefighters are being better compensated for the danger of their work or the nights and weekends they work, but if that were true, trash collectors, chauffeurs, and laborers would not earn more than secretaries, clerks, and child care workers, which they do in most government pay scales.

In all but a very few cities, police officers and firefighters earn higher salaries and can retire at younger ages than teachers and social workers. The women who selected careers in policing were aware of this. A study in 1993 of the reasons men and women joined the LAPD found that the primary motivation for women was salary. The women knew that their pay as police officers would be far better than what they had been able to earn in their previous jobs. While security was the major reason men claimed to have become police officers, followed by service, the major reason for women of all races was salary, followed by security and excitement. Service was a close fourth.[14]

PRESTIGE TRANSLATES INTO DOLLARS

The women who said they became police officers because they needed to make a better salary than they could in women's professions were on to something. Not only does men's work usually pay better, but it tends to be higher in prestige. Most of the discussion about changing the workplace is about women entering men's fields, not the other way around, because women are seen as gaining economic clout and prestige by entering traditional men's occupations, while men are seen as losing both when they enter traditional women's occupations. In one of the few studies of men doing "women's work," Christine L. Williams found that the numbers of men in librarianship and social work declined between 1975 and 1990, while the number of men in nursing doubled in the decade between 1980 and 1990. She found, though, that men who "cross over" into work that is nontraditional for their sex must defend their seriousness of purpose and, often, their masculinity. Despite this, they are likely to be welcomed into the field by their female co-workers, who believe the presence of men will raise the status of the profession. Williams also found that, contrary to the "glass ceiling" discrimination that women face in men's fields, the men are able to take advantage of a "glass escalator," getting promoted into management and administration more quickly than their female colleagues.[15] The reason for this was the assumption by top management that men wanted to move into administration, but Williams also suggested that male managers were more comfortable working with other men.

Studies that compare why men and women enter particular professions are viewed as important for women's credibility. If women and men enter a field for the same reasons, the theory argues, they should be taken equally seriously and should be given equal opportunity to experience all aspects of the job. One study that compared men's and women's motivations to become police officers found that their major reasons were identical, except that the order of importance was slightly reversed. The four top choices were helping people, job security, fighting crime, and the excitement of the job.[16] The first two were exactly the same for men and women; the second two were reversed—men selected fighting crime third and excitement fourth, whereas women reversed the order. The major differences were the level of support they had received from family and friends and, even more specifically, the support—or absence of it—they had received from within the profession.

A similar survey of more than 500 women officers working in departments in nine states found that the two reasons most often selected for becoming a police officer were the desire to help people and the attraction of a nontraditional career. The third-highest choice was a desire for job security. Some of these women had been in policing since 1963, but almost 60 percent had been hired since 1980. Just over half the women had more than six years of service, but only one, forty-three years old, was a chief. Again choosing from a range of answers, the least selected choice was "recruited by police department," indicating the reluctance of many police departments to hire women.[17]

Possibly because the women chiefs were older than the women in either of these surveys, their reasons were more varied than those of the younger women, fewer of whom indicated that policing was "a dream" or that they were looking for a higher salary than they could earn elsewhere. Having achieved leadership positions, the chiefs may also have been confident enough to answer honestly rather than provide scripted replies. Some of the differences, particularly among the older chiefs, no doubt reflected the more limited career opportunities available to women in the 1970s than now.

Women in policing are not the only ones whose career options have expanded since the 1970s. Like women chiefs and sheriffs, women in other professions have risen to the top. Despite the outward symbols of policing—the uniform, the gun, and the badge—many of the issues facing women chiefs and sheriffs are no different from those facing other women CEOs.

CHAPTER 2

Women in Nontraditional Professions: Law Enforcement Is Big Business

I would be disappointed if my promotion was looked at as a gender issue.

—Colonel Anne Beers
Chief, Minnesota State Patrol

I thought, why should I help somebody else? I can do this.

—Sheriff Beth Arthur
Arlington County (Virginia) Sheriff's Department

Whether Christopher or Christine, I'm the best person for the job.

—Chief Chris Ziemba
Cheektowaga, New York, Police Department

It's about the job, not the gender. My role is to be the best chief for Bloomfield.

—Chief Betsy Hard
Bloomfield, Connecticut, Police Department

As a chief, I've had to address issues of rapid growth, cultural diversity, and crime. Those are more important to my community than my sex.

—Chief Mary Ann Viverette
Gaithersburg, Maryland, Police Department

Women police chiefs? Women sheriffs? Are you serious?
A few years ago question marks and embarrassed smiles would have greeted any mention of women police chiefs or sheriffs. Even today, many police executives, criminal justice researchers, and scholars tracing

women's upward mobility are unable to name even one woman who fits either of these descriptions. But that is changing, for 2003 was a strong year for women in the top echelons of law enforcement; more were appointed chiefs or were elected sheriffs than in any other single year. Appointments of women chiefs continued in 2004; by the early months of the year, women led four of the fifty largest police departments (Detroit, San Francisco, Boston, Milwaukee), and a fifth was chief in Birmingham, Alabama, one of the sixty largest departments in the nation. In addition, a record number of women were named to lead smaller departments, and women continued to make substantial progress as chiefs of college and university police departments.

The approximately 200 women chiefs of police and 30 women sheriffs in the United States in 2004 were only about 1 percent of the law enforcement chief executives in the nation, but they were beginning to emerge from the obscurity of small departments to lead not only large police departments but also some of the nation's largest sheriffs' departments. The first woman elected to a vice presidency of the International Association of Chiefs of Police (IACP), Gaithersburg, Maryland's, Mary Ann Viverette, will, if she remains a chief until 2006, become the 19,000-member organization's first woman president in its more than 100-year history.

Women had been elected to some of the largest sheriffs' departments in the nation. Laurie Smith, sheriff of Santa Clara County (California), managed an office of 1,600 sworn and 300 nonsworn officers. Margo Frasier, sheriff of Travis County (Texas), had more than 1,300 sworn and nonsworn members of her department. Jackie Barrett, sheriff of Fulton County (Georgia), led a department of almost 800 sworn officers. In Fulton County, deputies do not answer citizens' calls for police service; they are responsible for jail operations, court security, and process serving. Beth Lundy, sheriff of Calcasieu Parish (Louisiana, where counties are called parishes), in October 1999 defeated an entrenched incumbent to become the only woman sheriff in the state and the first to have been elected to office. Terms of office are somewhat different in Louisiana than elsewhere in the country; Lundy took over on July 1, 2000, overseeing a department of more than 800 full-time employees, about 25 percent of whom responded to calls for service, while the others were assigned to investigative tasks, jail operations, court security, and process serving. Lundy, who had campaigned as a change agent, chose not to run for reelection, and stepped down on June 30, 2004.

At the end of 2003, the swearing in of chiefs Ella Bully-Cummings in Detroit and Nannette Hegerty in Milwaukee within a period of two weeks represented a major step for women in top management. Not only were they leading, respectively, the sixth and eighteenth largest police departments in the nation, but their selections came in a year in which a number of other women chiefs were appointed in small cities and at campus police departments throughout the country. These events were followed quickly in early 2004 by selection of Kathleen O'Toole as Boston's police commissioner and Heather Fong as San Francisco's police chief. Each of these women was selected to lead the department in which she had started her policing career, although all but Fong had left the department at some time to pursue other opportunities.

Other women who were named chiefs in the departments in which they began their careers were Annetta Nunn, who was the highest-ranking woman in the Birmingham, Alabama, Police Department at the time she was named chief, and Beverly Lennen in Santa Fe, New Mexico. Nunn began her career in 1980, primarily because the department was operating under a U.S. Department of Justice (DOJ) consent decree mandating that it hire women and African-Americans. Lennen became a police officer in 1984 following the death of her first husband, a sheriff's deputy who was killed in 1980 while responding to a domestic dispute. She remarried and, as is the case with a number of the women chiefs, her husband is retired from the department she was selected to lead.

One of the more surprising appointments was Pam Cap, who had sued the Calumet City, Illinois, Police Department three times between 1995 and 2002 after being passed over for promotions. In May 2003 the twenty-year veteran officer was named chief of the department. Cap, like most of today's women chiefs, did not want to dwell on her sex. "I realize," she told the *Daily Southtown*, "that a female police chief is a rare thing, and I'm extremely proud I've attained this personal goal, but it's not something I want to dwell longer on. I just want people to base their decision on my job performance, my communication skills and my concern for Calumet City and its residents and business owners." Cap, who at the time of her appointment was completing a graduate degree in law enforcement administration, pledged that the department would be more aggressive both in its community policing and its tactical units, warning gangs, drug dealers, and prostitutes that they would be able to tell when the tactical units had been reorganized.[1] Portland, Oregon's, Penny Harrington, the first woman chief of a major-city police department, had sued her agency numerous times before her selection as chief in 1985, but women who have brought lawsuits have rarely made it to the very top, although some have won promotions to lower ranks, particularly sergeant or lieutenant.

A number of women followed what has often been a successful route to the top for male chiefs: serving as acting chief before winning the position on a permanent basis. Among these were Lori A. Emmert, a twenty-two-year veteran of the Douglas, Wyoming, Police Department, and Lisa M. Maruzo-Bolduc, a twenty-three-year veteran of the Willimantic, Connecticut, Police Department, who had been filling in for the town's longtime chief during his lengthy illness. Emmert, who joined the department in 1980 as a dispatcher and animal control officer before becoming a police officer in 1992, became the second woman chief in the state. In 2001, Peggy Parker, a twenty-one-year veteran of the Jackson, Wyoming, Police Department, was promoted from interim chief to chief. The department, with twenty-three officers, had considered consolidating with the Teton County Sheriff's Department after its chief was killed in an accident, but decided instead to remain a separate department and give Parker the opportunity to implement some of the recommendations of the report by an outside consultant. The impetus for consolidation was to save money in the community of only about 10,000 people. But residents decided that they and the approximately 100,000 tourists who visit annually would be better served by continuing to fund their local police department.

A number of the new women chiefs had competed in national searches to move from management-level positions in their original agencies to become chiefs in their new departments. One, Betsy Hard, became the first female chief in Connecticut in November 2002, when she was selected chief in Bloomfield. She was a twenty-year veteran of the Santa Monica, California, Police Department who had retired as a lieutenant commanding about eighty officers and civilian employees and handling an almost $4 million budget. In Bloomfield, Hard, a Massachusetts native whose husband was a retired Santa Monica captain and whose two children would be continuing school in Connecticut, took charge of a department with approximately fifty officers and an annual budget of over $5 million. Prior to Hard's selection, Connecticut's only experience with a female chief had been the fifteen months that Deborah Barrows served as acting chief in Hartford. Barrows, who took over a troubled department, was unable to make any improvements, and in July 2000 was returned to her civil service rank of captain.[2] The Hartford department, one of the largest in the state, had been plagued with internal problems; Barrows was replaced by another acting chief, who was replaced by a permanent chief, but by 2004 the city was searching for another new police chief.

Another woman who moved from one department to another was Deborah E. Linden, a commander with the Santa Barbara (California) County Sheriff's Department, who became chief of the San Luis Obispo, California, Police Department. In 1999 another sheriff's department commander had relocated to become a chief. Donna Green, who at the time she was named chief in Oakland, Oregon, was a fifty-four-year-old grandmother of five, had retired in 1995 after twenty-six years with the Alameda County (California) Sheriff's Department. She was second in command to the sheriff, managing almost 300 employees and a $22 million budget. She and her husband, who was retired from the Oakland, California, Police Department and the Federal Bureau of Investigation, had been vacationing in Oakland, Oregon, an 850-person community, when she learned the one-person department needed a chief, so she decided to apply. Her husband planned to stay retired.[3]

In a unique nod to the dual-career family, there was even a husband-and-wife chief combination. No, it was not the ultimate form of job sharing. Kathy and Ray Samuels became chiefs in two neighboring California communities. The Samuelses, who had been married for twenty-five years at the time of their selections, met while working for the Vallejo, California, Police Department, he as a police officer and she as a dispatcher. Kathy left Vallejo and worked as an officer with the Contra Costa County Sheriff's Department and briefly, in the 1980s, as an officer in San Ramon, the community in which she became chief on May 31, 2003. Within two months, Ray, a captain in the Newark, California, Police Department, was named its chief.[4]

Women also continued to make gains in university policing, an area that has become a successful route for them to reach executive status. New university chiefs included Heather Coogan, who became chief of the University of Denver Auraria Campus, and Liz Woolen, chief of the University of Oklahoma Police Department at Norman. Janeith Glenn-Davis, the highest-ranking woman in the Oakland, California, Police Department, was named director of public safety at the California State University campus in Hayward. Glenn-Davis, a seventeen-year veteran in Oakland, had graduated from Cal State–Hayward in 1984.

Prior to the appointments of women as big-city chiefs in 2003 and 2004, there had been a flurry of selections of women chiefs in 2002, although none in departments anywhere near the size of Detroit, San Francisco, Boston, Milwaukee, or Birmingham. Lynne Johnson, once dubbed Palo Alto's "Goddess with a Gun," who in 1975 was the eighth woman hired by the department, in May 2002 became its chief. She was the seventh woman nonuniversity chief in California. There are also two women sheriffs in California out of a total of fifty-eight.[5] Susan Jones, a lieutenant with the Concord, California, Police Department, was named chief in Healdsburg, California; Diana Soratino was named chief of the Cape May, New Jersey, Police Department; and Bernadette DiPino, who became acting chief of the Ocean City, Maryland, Police Department when the incumbent chief retired in July 2002, was also named chief. A fourteen-year veteran of the department, she came from a law enforcement family; both her father and grandfather were members of the Baltimore City, Maryland, Police Department, and a great-grandfather was a New York City police officer. Each is the first of her sex to lead her department.

In the only documented instance of a woman chief replacing an immediate predecessor who was also a woman, Linda L. Black, who retired after twenty-one years with the Evanston, Illinois, Police Department in November 2001, became chief of the Delaware, Ohio, Police Department. The forty-officer department, serving a community of about 30,000 people, was previously led by Kathy Lieski, who retired after twenty-three years with the department. Black, the only woman among the thirty-six applicants for the position, didn't feel at all like a stranger; her parents and four sisters lived in the area.[6] Two small communities have had two women police chiefs. The southern Illinois village of Buckner had a woman chief, Lydia Overturf, in 1921, and another woman chief, Brenda Burke, from 1996 to 1998; and in Minneloa, Florida, Sue Wegner was chief from 1979 to 1981, and Jane Newcomb was chief from 1994 to 1995.

STARTING A NEW CENTURY ON A HIGH NOTE

A number of appointments in 2000 and 2001 seemed to herald a twenty-first-century outlook toward women chiefs, with a number of selections pointing forward. In 2000, Nona Holoman, who in 1978 was the first woman officer in the Seabrook, Texas, Police Department, became the thirty-person department's first woman chief. She was sworn in by Judge Joe Pirtle, who had been the town's mayor when Holoman, who previously worked as a dispatcher, became a police officer. Pirtle recalled that he had received criticism then, "but none since."[7] Holoman joined the department as a dispatcher and was forced to leave after completing the police academy because Seabrook would not allow her to work as a patrol officer until the chief she replaced had rehired her and later promoted her to lieutenant. In 1989, the woman who had originally had trouble finding a job as a police officer had broadened her perspective on policing issues as president of the Texas Municipal Police Association, a hybrid labor organization and lobbying group that promotes police professionalism through training, political action, and communication among Texas police agencies and police officers.

Pam Westlake, who was named chief of the Elkhart, Indiana, Police Department in 2001, had also begun her career as a dispatcher. After working dispatch for the county sheriff's department, the only job open to women, she joined the Elkhart department in 1981. In a highly unusual move, Elkhart's mayor, Dave Miller, promoted Westlake from second in command to chief and announced at the same time that the incumbent chief, Larry Kasa, would remain with the department as Westlake's assistant chief. Everyone, including Westlake and Kasa, were surprised by the move, but Westlake, who became the first woman chief in the state, played down the significance of the change, noting that she did not look at herself as male or female, but as a police officer, saying also that becoming the chief "was just another position."[8]

When Gwen Deurell was named chief in Canterbury, New Hampshire, in 2001, she joined Pauline Q. Field, Lyme's chief, who was appointed in 2000, as the only two women full-time chiefs in the state. There were also two female part-time chiefs. Although Deurell, a former Air Force law enforcement canine officer who spent five years as a New Hampshire State Police patrol officer and investigator and two years as a motor vehicle inspector, is full-time, her department is composed solely of part-time officers. Her inspiration for seeking the position came from her former husband, who advised her that town officials were looking for a chief.

Federal law enforcement moved more slowly than municipal, university, and even state policing. It wasn't until 2003 that Karen P. Tandy, who was named director of the Drug Enforcement Administration (DEA), became the first woman to head a major federal law enforcement agency. Tandy, an experienced federal drug prosecutor, was an associate deputy attorney general and director of the Organized Crime Drug Enforcement Task Force at the time of her appointment. The nomination by President George W. Bush of Michele M. Leonhart as Tandy's deputy is also an important first. Leonhart, a career DEA special agent who was in charge of its Los Angeles field office, was the first woman in her agency to come from the agent's rank to a top management position. Previously, a few women rose from special agents to high-level management positions in the FBI. Although it sounds higher-ranking than police officer, special agent is the entry-level title in federal law enforcement agencies, making Leonhart's elevation the equivalent of a police officer becoming the second in command after having been in charge of a division or bureau as a midranking officer.

Progress has also been slow for women in state police agencies, the last to employ them and still the most hierarchical and authoritarian in training and demeanor of all American law enforcement agencies. Only two women have headed state agencies; one, Annette Sandberg, retired from the Washington State Patrol at the end of 2002, and only one,

Colonel Anne Beers, chief of the Minnesota State Patrol, remained in 2004.

Sandberg was not the only woman chief whose retirement made news. Among those whose careers ended were Mesa, Arizona, Chief Jan Strauss, who was the only woman chief in the state when she retired in November 2002. She recalled having spent most of her career as a detective working with young victims—an assignment that was once typical of those for which women were selected. One of her few regrets, she said, was that less than 10 percent of Mesa's officers were women, a situation she hoped to influence by teaching criminal justice at a local college and encouraging women to go into law enforcement. One of the ways she would do this was by pointing out that in the 1970s "you'd have been lucky to see a female sergeant, but today women are able to move into high-ranking positions and young women should take advantage of these career opportunities." Strauss had raised an important issue; no matter who is chief, if women do not apply for police positions, their presence will not increase, regardless of the sex of the chief.

Western law enforcement lost another woman leader when Broken Arrow, Oklahoma, Chief Carolyn Kusler followed through on her promise to retire after five years as chief. Saying that she stayed to see the start of one of her pet projects, construction of a new Justice Center, Kusler, a former major with the Tulsa Police Department, retired in early 2003. A Tulsa native who began her career in policing as a patrol officer in 1974, Kusler refused attempts to make a fuss when she was selected as Broken Arrow's chief in 1997. "There have been other female chiefs throughout the country; it's really not groundbreaking," she said then, as if she had anticipated that one of her last acts in Broken Arrow would be the ceremony breaking ground for the Justice Center she worked so hard to bring to fruition.[9]

MORE WOMEN MEANS LESS ATTENTION

The increased presence of women in the top ranks of law enforcement has resulted in less attention being paid to them. The women view this change as positive, believing that it indicates they are no longer curiosities. Previous media coverage of the selection of a woman police chief or the election of a woman sheriff had a certain (wo)man-bites-dog quality, even a sense of incredulity. None miss the hoopla that surrounded earlier appointments or the obligatory press conference in which a city official—usually the mayor or city manager—would assure citizens that the new chief had not been selected because of her sex, but had been chosen solely because she was the best candidate for the job. The chief would then quickly change the subject, usually concentrating on changes she wanted to bring to her agency. If she was particularly daring, she might allow that her sex could be an asset in such areas as community relations or a less rigid management style, but since this might be viewed as a weakness (or might not fit her personality), she would likely avoid drawing attention to her sex. An enterprising reporter might note how many other women chiefs there were in the state, usually a number in the single digits.

Because sheriffs are elected, women candidates have been forced to confront these dilemmas of style and presentation much earlier in the selection process. The candidates' opponents would have made sure to raise the issue of sex during the campaign—sometimes subtly, sometimes not. They might have called her by her nickname, as happened to Chester County (Pennsylvania) Sheriff Carolyn "Bunny" Welsh in 1999. Republican Party leaders reluctantly supported her campaign after advising her that they did not think the county was ready for a woman sheriff. Despite this less-than-wholehearted support, Welsh ignored advice to drop her longtime nickname "Bunny" from her campaign literature. She argued that the people who would vote for her knew her by that name.

Welsh received the endorsement of the Chester County Police Chiefs Association and won with about 60 percent of the vote, becoming the only woman—although not the first woman—of the sixty-seven sheriffs in the state. Norma Jean Santore had held the post in Fayette County from 1982 until 1999. And Ann A. Osborne, who in 1997 was elected by Delaware County voters to a ten-year term on the Court of Common Pleas, had been appointed in 1991 to complete her predecessor's term and in 1992 had been elected to her own four-year term as sheriff. Unlike Osborne, an attorney, Welsh professed to have no further political ambitions.

Being called "Bunny" was mild compared to what happened to Carmella Jones when she ran for sheriff of the small Panhandle county of Armstrong (Texas) in 1994. As if to reinforce the commonly held notion that Texas politics can get down and dirty, her opponent kept telling the voters that the position of sheriff called for a candidate with balls. His tactics backfired. Residents, 22 percent of whom were over sixty-five years of age and were more concerned about service than traditional crimefighting, kept handing candidate Jones paper bags containing two tennis balls, or two Ping Pong™ balls, or whatever balls they had, telling her that now she had some balls, too.[10]

Jones won and continued to win, remaining sheriff until 2003, after which she went to work for the Texas Association of Counties as a law

enforcement specialist and adviser. Proving that she might not have
needed those paper bags, Jones initially received criticism when she purchased a one-ton, diesel pickup truck for her department. As if anticipat-
ing Welsh's decision to stress her management and budgetary skills, Jones
was able to counter the argument that she was buying a toy for her deputies by illustrating cost savings based on fuel prices, longevity, and fewer
repairs due to wear and tear. "I told them," she said, "that if they were
looking for your typical sheriff, they had the wrong gal." She argued that
one of the county's most serious problems was the high rate of arrests of
young drivers charged with driving while intoxicated (DWI). Despite the
age of the county's residents and its ban on liquor sales, its location between Amarillo and a popular lake, which the sheriff described as "the
only body of water in the area," made the county a drive-through for
young people, and the pickup proved useful for mounting radar without
rocks and tumbleweed getting in the way.

Race can also be an issue; and not just in the South. When Fulton
County's Jackie Barrett in 1992 became the nation's first black woman
elected to the position of sheriff, she called it "just an extra piece of the
puzzle; we'd had a black sheriff in Fulton County but had never had a
woman, so for me the larger issue was gender." That being said, Barrett
recalled that Georgia still had its share of "those stereotypical movie and
television Southern sheriffs, with the drawls and the bellies, so my election probably did surprise a number of folks."

By the end of 1999, nine African-American women had served or were
still active as sheriffs, but not all commentators were color-blind.[11] When
Andrea Cabral was sworn in on November 29, 2002, as the first female
sheriff in Massachusetts, she also became only the second black person
to hold the office. Like Barrett, she was not a cop, but she faced obstacles
more pointed than that. She had not been elected, but had been appointed by the unpopular acting governor, Jane Swift, to serve until the
end of 2004. Cabral is a lawyer who had begun her career as a prosecutor sixteen years earlier, as a staff attorney at the sheriff's department she
was appointed to lead. Although no one questioned her competence, one
Democratic political consultant reminded the *Boston Globe* that "she's a
woman sheriff, and that's unusual. She's a black person running in the
entire Suffolk County—not just Boston—and that's unusual."[12] Equally
unusual, Cabral is a black Republican in a predominantly white and
Democratic county. Cabral, who was single and had never held political
office, changed her party affiliation to Democratic and in 2004 won 60
percent of the primary vote against a white male challenger. Without
Republican opposition, she is assured a six-year term in office, the
statndard full term for sheriffs in Massachusetts.

AFTER THIRTY YEARS OF EQUALITY,
STILL "UNUSUAL"

In 2004, it has been just about thirty years since women gained legal equality in police and sheriffs' departments. Prior to the 1970s, women's roles in policing were limited, their titles were different from men's titles, and they were barred from competing for promotion on an equal basis with men. Why, then, despite thirty years of such equality, are women at the top still unusual? Simply put: Legal equality doesn't always equal actual equality. Women have always faced obstacles entering the law enforcement profession. Probably no public service occupation in the United States except firefighting is more closely identified with masculinity and masculine stereotypes than policing.

Ironically, the law enforcement establishment was not eager to abide by the legal equality mandated in 1972 by Title VII of the 1964 Civil Rights Act. But despite lawsuits and foot-dragging by police and sheriffs' departments, women gained equal access to all police assignments. They also won the right to compete on an equal basis with men for promotion to ranks that provide the types of experience needed to become a police chief or a sheriff. It has been long enough for the current chiefs and sheriffs to have started and ended their careers under rules for hiring, assignment, and promotion that make no distinctions based on sex.

As in so many fields in which women are a minority of the workforce, even those who have reached the top of their profession are still expected to prove their worth and defend their positions on a regular basis. The effort and the time involved in this can discourage women from trying to crack the brass ceiling, but those newest to the field may bring different expectations and worldviews to their situations. While in other industries employees may refer to "bosses" or "managers," in law enforcement it is common for those bosses or managers to be known collectively as "the brass"—yet another reminder not only of the paramilitary trappings of the police but also of how visible symbols are a constant cue to one's place in the organization.

A police chief may report to a mayor, a city manager, a civilian oversight board made up of politicians, an airport manager, or a college president, but a sheriff virtually always reports to the electorate. By the time a woman is named a chief, she has probably spent most of her working life in policing. She is most likely a careerist who started at the lowest rank of police officer and moved up through the ranks at some agency—not necessarily the one she now leads. For most of the chiefs, early promotions to sergeant, lieutenant, and captain came via civil service tests. For some, the promotion process to chief may have been the first in which their résumés, personalities, and leadership qualities played a role in their selection.

Sheriffs, on the other hand, are politicians in addition to managers. To become a sheriff, a candidate must convince voters in the county that he or she is the best person for the job. Sometimes this means running against the incumbent; other times it means facing an opponent who also has decided that the incumbent's decision not to run for re-election has created an opportunity to run and win. Each of the women sheriffs—whether she ran against an incumbent or not—ran against a man, and that man always made reference, open or veiled, to her sex. Yet none of the women sheriffs—even those who did not have prior law enforcement careers—ever considered running for any other office, and only one of the women sheriffs said she might consider running for anything else.

Very little has been written about male or female police chiefs, and even less attention has been paid to sheriffs. This may be because, as elected officials, sheriffs are seen as outside the policing mainstream, or it may be because criminal justice researchers tend to focus on large, urban police departments. Also, since many sheriffs are less involved with patrolling their county than they are in maintaining their county's jails, observers are not sure whether to include them with police or corrections. Whatever the reason, despite the recent attention focused on women elected officials, not one book or study mentions sheriffs.

The absence of attention to police managers—male or female—is surprising. Even today, when concerns about terrorism have led to an expansion of the roles of federal law enforcement agencies into local events, it is local police chiefs and sheriffs and state police officials who bear the primary responsibility for police activity in the United States. The power is awesome; even in the smallest agencies, law enforcement executives retain the power to arrest and to deny citizens their liberties, and to oversee the work of others entrusted with the same powers. Police are the only public servants who are empowered not only to detain citizens and deny them their liberty, but also, under certain circumstances, to take their lives.

In 1909, Leonard F. Fuld, one of the first sociologists and management experts to study policing, observed that "the character of the city government as a whole is judged by the character of the police administration."[13] Most mayors seem to believe this is true, since the choice of police chief is usually made first in any new administration and is likely to receive the most scrutiny. It remains a mystery why, even when policing strategies are discussed in the media or by politicians, so little attention is paid to the background or personality of the chief, and how he or she might or might not influence the direction of the agency.

What is the primary role of the chief or the sheriff? Do citizens want a "top cop," with a certain swagger and the desire to catch crooks, or do they want a business-oriented CEO, who will manage resources wisely and keep the public informed? The cops themselves want a boss who was "a good cop"—which to them means someone who could be trusted on patrol and who now can be trusted to back them up if they make mistakes and who will support their union's attempts to win them better salaries and benefits. This is not always what the politicians or voters selecting the chief or sheriff had in mind.

Thus, even before taking the oath of office, the chief or sheriff may be faced with contradictory roles, particularly if the department has recently experienced scandal and is still in the cleaning-up phase or if budgetary constraints will mean having to do more while spending less money. These multiple roles of representing officers, the appointing officials, the voters, and the rule of law can be particularly difficult when a chief or sheriff has risen through the ranks of her department and must now institute policies she knows will meet with unhappiness from at least some of those who have a stake in how the agency is managed. Both Detroit's Bully-Cummings and Milwaukee's Hegerty followed unpopular chiefs and took over agencies under federal oversight for a variety of civil rights violations. Boston's O'Toole faced labor disputes involving all three of the department's police unions, an investigation into the department's lax handling of post–Super Bowl disturbances in February 2004, and planning for the Democratic National Convention in the summer of 2004. San Francisco's Heather Fong had to contend with the aftermath of a scandal that had resulted in the indictment of a number of senior officers and the departure of her predecessor. Many chiefs in smaller cities also took over in the wake of controversies but because the cities were smaller, media coverage of the problems remained strictly local.

Chiefs and sheriffs are faced with these dilemmas because policing, despite the myths created by television and the movies, qualifies as big business. It qualifies as big business in the amounts of money it consumes, the numbers of people it employs, and the fact that the salaries paid to police officers and sheriffs' officers (usually called deputies) are among the highest in government employment. Although they may complain bitterly about their wages and conditions of employment, officers and deputies, particularly where they are covered by civil service, a union, or both, usually earn higher salaries and have better health benefits and retirement plans than others working for the jurisdiction. With the possible exception of education, policing is usually the single largest item in any municipal government's budget.

More and more police managers are aware of this, stressing their educational credentials and their motivational and management skills over their rough-and-tumble assignments. Mayors are starting to take notice, but the notion that policing is a business has not really pierced the public's consciousness, no doubt in part due to movie and television shows that continue to focus on handcuffs and car chases over budgets and bottom lines. Even shows that focus on hospital emergency rooms sometimes show administrators grappling with management issues, but it is a rare television cop show where anyone above a lieutenant or captain is portrayed as having any role in the life of the police department or its rank-and-file members. While it is true that hardly anyone would want to watch a chief pushing papers instead of watching a detective running through the streets to catch a bad guy, this image reinforces the view that policing is a game of cops and robbers rather than a multimillion (even billion) dollar industry.

How big a business is policing? Although most police departments in the United States are small, in the year 2000, almost 800,000 people were employed as full-time sworn police officers in about 18,000 different departments throughout the country. The total operating budgets for all these departments was $36,692,534,000. Personnel costs were the largest part of virtually all police departments' budgets, with departments serving populations of over 25,000 spending between $83,500 and $90,000 per sworn officer, and small departments (serving populations up to 24,999) spending between $42,300 and just over $72,000 per sworn officer. Not all of this is salary; some of it is the cost of generous fringe benefits, primarily health benefits, sick leave, and retirement after twenty or twenty-five years, often at half pay or more. The average cost of operating a local police department in 2000 was $179 per resident, with the highest cost ($262 per resident) in cities of more than 1 million people.[14]

Included in the 18,000 police agencies are approximately 3,000 sheriffs' departments, most of which are led by a sheriff who is elected on a countywide basis. The District of Columbia, Alaska, and Hawaii have never had sheriffs; Connecticut voted in 2000 to do away with the position. The sheriffs' departments employed about 165,000 of the 800,000 full-time police officers nationwide, plus an additional 10,300 part-time officers and more than 141,500 civilians, the majority of whom are full-time employees. Although many sheriffs' departments are not covered by civil service and salaries are often lower than in police departments, operating costs per sworn officer are much higher. Costs average almost $108,000 for all agencies, from a low of $66,900 for sheriffs' departments serving counties of under 10,000 to a high of just over $160,000 for counties of 1 million or more.[15]

In some counties, sheriffs' deputies are assigned to provide patrols and to investigate crimes, exactly as police officers do. This is in addition to their responsibilities for performing legal functions for the county and local courts, including delivering court and other legal papers (often called "process serving"), taking individuals into custody for the courts, providing physical security in court buildings and for judges, and operating the county jail. In many counties, though, deputies are assigned primarily or solely to court functions and jail operations. Although individual jails may be small, the total number of inmates is not. At the end of 2002, local or county jails housed 665,475 people, one-third of the slightly more than 2 million people incarcerated in state and federal penal institutions.[16]

In addition to the political and organizational power women police chiefs and sheriffs wield, they are responsible for budgets that rival those of many private companies, but they are rarely compared with private-sector managers. Because there are so few women at the very top of their professions, it is interesting to look at women law enforcement CEOs as part of the emerging cadre of women who wield power in a number of fields. This is also important because, throughout the business and academic worlds, much has been written about the glass ceiling, the invisible barrier that women have seemed to be unable to crack to get to the very top of their professions. The discussions might be about the small number of women CEOs of companies ranked anywhere from the Fortune 50 to the Fortune 500, or about the small percentage of women full professors or college presidents, or about the inability of women to fill the anchor seat on network evening news programs. Whatever the profession, women, with rare exceptions, seem to get near the top but never quite to it, and the women who are profiled either are still grasping for the brass ring or have decided that the efforts to continue on the carousel are not worth the rewards.

WOMEN IN THE BUSINESS OF POLICING

Counting the actual number of women in the business of policing is more difficult than it should be. The large number of police departments in the nation, and the fact that three-quarters of them employ fewer than twenty-five police officers, make it almost impossible to know at any given time how many women are actually employed as police officers. In the early 1970s, many departments had no female officers and most large departments limited policewomen to between 1 and 2 percent of the patrol force. In 2000, women constituted about 11 percent of all police officers but fewer than 7 percent of state police officers. Sheriffs' departments historically had slightly higher percentages of women because only women deputies were permitted to work in women's jails. They limited the number of women, however, by often using civilian matrons in women's jails. Also, since the number of women housed in the jails is smaller than the number of men, even sheriffs' departments that employed women deputies often needed only a few.

Because there are about 18,000 police agencies, percentages can be misleading. Generally, the percentages of women are higher in the largest police departments, but even here both the percentages and the actual numbers can vary widely. A few examples will be illustrative. The largest police department in the nation, the New York City Police Department (NYPD), in 2000 had about 40,000 officers; by 2003 the number had fallen to about 37,000. In 2000, 15.5 percent of sworn personnel in all ranks (about 6,500) were women. This is the largest *number* of women in any department, but it is not the largest percentage. The second largest police department, the Chicago Police Department, in 2000 had a much larger *percentage* of women (21.3) but, with a full-time staff of about 13,500 officers, there were fewer than 3,000 women.

The number of women in a department depends on many variables, including not only the department's recruitment policies but also local economic conditions that may or may not make policing an attractive career for men or women. A number of large Midwestern cities, including the two with women chiefs, Detroit and Milwaukee, have residency requirements, which can affect recruitment. The Cleveland Police Department, which had a woman interim chief from August 2001 to February 2002, also had a residency requirement. There have been no studies as to whether residency requirements influence the percentages of women, but there are indications—although not studied either—that they do affect the percentages of minority applicants, particularly, of course, in cities where the minority population is high.

There is also little indication that the selection of a woman chief is influenced by the percentage of women in the department. This is evidenced by the four major cities with women CEOs. Thus, the Detroit Police Department, the sixth largest in the nation in 2000, with about 4,000 officers, was that year 25 percent female (about 1,000 women). The same year, Milwaukee, the eighteenth largest department, with about 2,000 officers, was slightly more than 16 percent female (about 320 women). Both departments had increased their percentage of women in the decade from 1990 to 2000; in Detroit, from 20 to just over 25 percent, and in Milwaukee, from 8.6 to 16.3 percent. In 2000, 15.5 percent of

San Francisco's 2,520 sworn officers were women, and about 13 percent of Boston's 2,164 sworn personnel were women. The percentage increase in female officers between 1990 and 2002 was smaller in both these cities than in Detroit and Milwaukee; in Boston, women's presence in the department increased from 8.4 to 13 percent, and in San Francisco it increased from just over 11 percent to 15.5 percent.[17] It is equally difficult to equate the numbers of women in small agencies with their progress through the ranks. A number of women chiefs in departments with between 50 and 100 police officers were the only women in their department during some or all of their tenure as chief.

Estimating the number of women in supervisory or management ranks below chief is even more difficult. Although departments are asked by the federal government to provide information on the numbers of women and minority officers they employ, they are not asked to provide ranks or assignments. Since 1997, the National Center for Women & Policing (NCWP) has attempted to estimate the percentages of women in various ranks through distribution of a questionnaire to a random sample of law enforcement agencies.

In 2001, the NCWP mailed its survey to 360 agencies that were identified in 1997 by the U.S. Department of Justice's Bureau of Justice Statistics as having 100 or more sworn officers. Based on 257 responses (ten from agencies with fewer than 100 officers), including 20 state-level agencies, 59 county agencies, and 168 municipal agencies, the NCWP estimated that women accounted for 12.7 percent of all sworn officers in agencies with more than 100 officers and 8.1 percent of all sworn officers (including agencies of fewer than 100 officers). Based on the agencies of more than 100 officers, the NCWP estimated that women held 9.6 percent of supervisory positions (defined as sergeant and lieutenant or their equivalent) and 7.3 percent of top command positions (defined as captain, major, commander, deputy chief, and chief or an equivalent position that may have a different title in some agencies).[18] Since the numbers were weighted by the researchers, using a formula that took into account the proportions of agencies of a particular size and type in the larger population, the figures were more an estimate than a census. San Francisco, Boston, and Milwaukee did not respond to the survey, but Detroit did. The department reported that 25.7 percent of its 1,085 women were in line operations (police officers and probably detectives), and that 27.28 percent of supervisory positions and 17.39 percent of top command positions were filled by women.

The tallies may mean even less in small departments. In 2000, the Santa Fe, New Mexico, Police Department had 142 sworn officers, 13 of whom were women, and women made up almost 17 percent of top commanders.

In early 2003, Beverly Lennen was named chief, which would tend to support the view that having women in top command results in more women chiefs. Yet, also in 2000, the Cheektowaga, New York, Police Department had 132 sworn officers, only six of whom were women and none of whom were in top command. But in March 2002, the only female lieutenant, Christine Ziemba, was named chief, becoming the first woman chief in western New York State. Similarly, in 2000, the San Mateo, California, Police Department had 107 sworn officers, 11 of whom were women, and women made up almost 20 percent of top command. But when the department chose Susan Manheimer as its chief, she did not come from within its own ranks, but from a midlevel command rank (captain) in the San Francisco Police Department.

Even though policing is highly localized, many departments conduct national searches to select a chief. One need not already be a chief to apply, but generally, except in the smallest departments, an applicant must be at least in a supervisory rank. Thus, what the numbers of women in these ranks may indicate is how many women are potentially available to be considered for chiefs' positions, but the numbers give no idea of how many are interested in such positions, would be willing to relocate for available positions, or are not currently in police departments but would be serious candidates for chiefs' positions, as was Boston's O'Toole.

The numbers from individual departments do help to compare the progress of women in policing with other fields. Despite the relatively small number of women chiefs, women in policing are doing as well or better in reaching executive-level positions than women in other traditionally male fields.

It has been said that power is an aphrodisiac, but for women it is also elusive. In the fall of 2003, *Fortune* magazine's Top 50 deemed Oprah Winfrey the seventh most powerful woman in American business in 2002. Here, where the definition of powerful was based on financial data, the women ranked above Oprah were less famous but were all successful businesswomen. Hewlett-Packard's Carleton S. (Carly) Fiorina, the then fifty-year-old chairman and CEO of a $72 billion company, was selected as the most powerful woman in American business. Others who ranked ahead of Oprah, all between their mid-forties and mid-fifties (similar to the ages of most of the women law enforcement CEOs), included, in order of selection, Meg Whitman, president and CEO of eBay; Andrea Jung, chairman and CEO of Avon Products; Anne Mulcahy, chairman and CEO of Xerox; Marjorie Magner, chairman and CEO of Citigroup's Global Consumer Group; and Karen Katen, executive vice president of global pharmaceuticals at Pfizer.

Indicating how difficult it is to quantify power, Oprah was the only woman on the list whose name would be recognized beyond her industry. Just as power and fame are not always related, neither are power and money. Fiorina ranked fourth on the list of top-paid women in 2003, behind Pat Russo, chairman and CEO of Lucent Technologies; Susan Decker, chief financial officer and executive vice president for finance and administration of Yahoo; and eBay's Whitman. Possibly measuring a different form of equality, Martha Stewart, the well-known home fashion authority and entrepreneur, was missing from the list, a victim of the securities trading investigation that was still unfolding when the list was formulated. In another form of equality that Stewart would rather have avoided, she was one of very few women to have lost power via a personal scandal rather than professional missteps by her or her company. On March 5, 2004, a jury found Stewart guilty of conspiracy, obstruction of justice, and making false statements in conjunction with a securities trading case involving almost 4,000 shares of ImClone Systems stock that she sold on December 27, 2001, based on information from her stock broker that the company's founder and chairman had sold a portion of his own shares.

Women have had as hard a time reaching the boardroom as the executive offices. Despite the few high-profile women whose names dot the business sections of many newspapers, only 5 percent of top positions at Fortune 500 companies were held by women in 1998. According to Catalyst, a nonprofit research and advisory group that has monitored women's progress in a number of professions since the 1980s, the numbers were not expected to change radically in the new century. Catalyst estimated in 2000 that about 13 percent of corporate officers, few of whom are CEOs in Fortune 500 companies, would be women. By the end of 2003, women held slightly more than 13.5 percent of corporate board seats, an increase of a little more than 1 percent over the results of a similar 2001 study.[19]

DIFFERENT PROFESSIONS, SIMILAR CONCERNS

Despite their many differences, women in nontraditional roles have many things in common. Most have had to overcome gender stereotypes that they were too emotional or too sensitive for the job they sought, or that they would leave prematurely to marry and raise a family. New York State Supreme Court Judge Leslie Crocker Snyder's life was threatened when she presided over a number of murder and drug trials in New York City. Upon her retirement in 2003, at age sixty-one, she recalled that when she had begged legendary District Attorney Frank S. Hogan to allow her to become the first woman assigned to the homicide division in 1968, he told her she would "need a note from her husband" before he would allow her to do that.[20] Although she was never sure whether he was kidding, she did eventually get into the division. When Linda A. Fairstein, who became a top prosecutor in the same office, joined the staff four years after Snyder, there were only 7 women among the 170 prosecutors. By the time Fairstein retired in 2001, she was one of the nation's best-known sex crimes prosecutors, an advocate for rape law reform, and a best-selling author—and had stayed long enough to see the prosecutorial staff of 600 become about half female.[21]

Even in fields where they predominate, women seem to have trouble reaching the top. In 2000, women represented 75 percent of all non-college teachers, but few were school superintendents. The pattern of women leading school districts is surprisingly similar to police departments, where, until 2003, women had been named to the top positions overwhelmingly in small jurisdictions. Women school superintendents were clustered in small agencies, primarily in rural districts of under 300 students. In such districts, the superintendents, like the chiefs in departments of fewer than fifty sworn officers, wore many hats and had few administrators to whom to delegate tasks. The close relationships that these school superintendents must maintain with the school board lead to high levels of stress, resulting in these "starter-districts" often being extremely unfavorable places for a woman to begin her career as a school superintendent.[22]

This did not seem to be the case for the police chiefs; most were content in their department and only a few seemed eager to "trade up" to a larger department. A few, though, had already "traded up" to larger departments or to departments that represented a better career fit, thus reinforcing the distinction between the police chiefs and the sheriffs. Police chiefs, like school superintendents, can be either insiders or outsiders—they may rise through the ranks of the department or school district, or they may be recruited from outside the agency. At least one of the women chiefs is now serving in her fourth agency.

Chiefs, depending on personal or family preference, were able to move about the country as jobs became available or, as in the case of a number of the university chiefs, were able to apply for positions that did not always require a physical relocation. Sheriffs, though, who are elected officials, can rarely run without roots in the county, even if those roots are not specifically in policing. The issue of "place" is important, since there are indications that women school superintendents are more location-bound because of their spouses' positions and that they appear to apply for few positions outside their district or geographic area.[23] This is less an issue for women chiefs, many of whose spouses have also been in law enforcement and who are often retired after twenty years of service, making them able to relocate just at the time a high-ranking woman would be considering a position as a chief.

WHAT DOES A CHIEF OR SHERIFF LOOK LIKE?

Another issue for women in power is having their credibility questioned. Female doctors are mistaken for nurses; women executives are presumed to be secretaries. Each of the women chiefs and sheriffs had been told at least once that she did not look like a chief or a sheriff. For those whose careers spanned all ranks, it was likely that each was selected for some assignments because she didn't "look the part," and for that reason could go into a bar, or a hotel, or a home because no one would suspect that she was there to gather evidence or to fulfill some law enforcement function. This is particularly true for those who were the first woman in their department, the first woman supervisor, or the first woman to hold command-level rank (usually captain or above). Today's women chiefs and sheriffs are the first to lead their departments; all have stories to tell that may seem laughable but that reinforced their uniqueness and could have hampered their effectiveness.

Gwendolyn Boyd-Savage had been a chief in two other communities prior to her 2002 selection by North Miami, Florida. She also had gained the nickname Hot Pants for her undercover work. Similarly, Palo Alto's Lynne Johnson, the "Goddess with a Gun," had worked undercover as a masseuse. Richmond Hill, Texas, Chief Barbara Childress recalled that people had once asked her whether she preferred to be called "Mrs. Childress" or "Chief," a question she doubted would have been asked of a man.[24]

More of the chiefs reported working in traditional women's assignments than in elite, specialized areas such as homicide, hostage negotiations, special weapons and tactics (SWAT), or as physical trainers or firearms instructors. But there were exceptions: Gaithersburg's chief, Mary Ann Viverette, had been a motorcycle officer; Jeanne Miller, the chief in Reynoldsburg, Ohio, who had started her career in the Detroit Police Department, had worked in the major case squad and in commercial auto theft; and Minnetonka, Minnesota, chief Joy Rikala, who had worked for three agencies in the state in her more than twenty-five-year career, had worked in organized crime and homicide units. No women, though, mentioned having worked in SWAT or similar heavy weapons or high-impact, tactical units.

None of the women are Amazons. No one meeting them individually or as a group would be particularly struck by their size or their toughness. Although a few are model-tall and obviously spend some time in the gym, most are of average height and a few, like their male colleagues, have midsection bulge. A few are petite. As Vicky Peltzer, who stands about 5'2" and left the Albuquerque, New Mexico, Police Department to become chief of the University of Washington Police Department, said: "I'm small, I've always been small, and it's too late for me to grow." If an observer were particularly astute, she might notice many short, sensible hair styles and the absence of frou-frou jewelry, especially large bracelets or dangling earrings, but these are less fashion statements than the habits that come from spending years in uniform and adhering to stringent grooming standards based on a desire for uniformity and a need to meet safety concerns.

The women—individually and collectively—are not that different from other women who have broken through to the top of their profession. They are mostly between the ages of forty-five and fifty-five, are well-educated and well-spoken, and exude a level of confidence that is in keeping with the image of a top manager. Although each of the women has a unique story to tell, there are interesting patterns to their careers that may provide a road map for others hoping to become CEOs. Both the chiefs and the sheriffs followed a surprisingly long tradition of women in law enforcement management positions.

CHAPTER 3

The Road to the Chief's Chair: Early Trailblazers and the Long Climb to the Top

She was poor, but she was tough; she had to be; she did what she had to do to provide for her family. Today we'd call her a single mother.
—Mildred Fitzgerrell describing her grandmother,
Chief Lydia (Leida or Lizzie) Overturf
Buckner, Illinois, Police Department (1920–1921)

I was no quitter, and made a success of my undertaking.
—Commissioner Kate Shelley Wilder
Fargo, North Dakota, Police Department (1919–1921)

I broke up bar fights without lifting a finger. All I had to do was outthink the suspects.
—Chief Sue Wegner
Minneloa, Florida, Police Department (1979–1981)

I went from a cotton patch to police chief.
—Chief Beulah Lott
Magee, Mississippi, Police Department (1980–1981)

To some, I'm Chief Hess, to others I'm Sally, and to others I'm still Mrs. Hess's daughter.
—Chief Sally Hess
Burton, Ohio, Police Department (1987–1989)

When John Mallory, mayor of the small community of Buckner, Illinois, appointed Lydia Overturf his police chief sometime in 1920, the gamblers laughed, the drunks snorted, and his wife thought he'd lost his mind.

Despite indications that her appointment may have cost him the election in 1921, it was probably the best decision he ever made. Chief Overturf (also sometimes known as Leida or Lizzie) was a local woman who gained a reputation for arresting the gamblers and rousting the drunks. Overturf was a poor, twice-divorced working woman who took in laundry before she was police chief and ran a small hotel to support her six children before, during, and after she served as chief in the 300-person village.

A poor, mining community, in 2004 Buckner was home to fewer than 500 residents. It and the two nearby villages of Benton and West Franklin are remembered for a mining disaster in 1951 that claimed the lives of 119 men. Known as "the Christmas Disaster," the explosion in New Orient Coal Mine No. 2 occurred on the evening of December 21, the last shift before the mine was to close for Christmas. About 250 men had reported for work at what was the largest mine shaft in the country; of those in the direct area of the blast, only one survived. The incident, which led to congressional action in 1952 to strengthen the Coal Mine Health and Safety Act by giving federal inspectors the authority to close mines they determined to be unsafe, has remained the defining event of Franklin County and speaks to the hardscrabble nature of the area, one in which Overturf seemed to have fit right in.

"She was poor, like everybody here, and she was tough, also like everybody here, but she did what she had to do to provide for her family," Mildred Fitzgerrell recalled. Although a number of people in Buckner and the communities around it remembered stories about a woman police chief in the 1920s, only Fitzgerrell, Overturf's ninety-one-year-old granddaughter, remembered any details of her life, and referred to her repeatedly as "my grandmother." Fitzgerrell, born near Buckner in the equally small town of Sesser, Illinois, is the widow of Illinois State Representative Wayne Fitzgerrell, for whom an area state park is named.

According to a local newspaper, Overturf had been appointed by Mayor Mallory after local women complained about gambling in town and about the police department's failure to do anything about it. Although the gamblers initially rejoiced at the appointment, Overturf, a big woman who weighed about 200 pounds, took her job seriously. One of her first official acts was to club a drunk over the head and drag him off to jail. Succeeding at what the paper called "running her bluff," Overturf was able to convince the gamblers she meant business, and the problem seemed to abate.[1]

At the time of her selection there had been local rumors that Overturf had been appointed by Mayor Mallory to help her support herself and her three children after her husband was killed in a mine accident. Considering the importance of mining in the area, the story seemed plausible, and two of Mallory's children—his son Robert, who was mayor from 1972 to 1984, and a daughter, who did not remember Overturf but recalled her mother's outrage at the inappropriateness of a woman police chief—said they had heard the story frequently. Regardless of its popularity, Fitzgerrell said the story was a myth. She recalled that neither of Overturf's two husbands had worked in the mines; her first husband, Fitzgerrell's grandfather, had worked in a tavern and had deserted her and their two sons and a daughter. She later remarried and had three more sons. "Today we'd call her a single mother," Fitzgerrell said. "Her first husband left her, and she divorced her second husband, a farmer. She always had to work. I remember one of her boys saying she took in washing and ironing, and he often delivered the clothes later."

Indications are that Overturf kept Buckner's small jail full. The town, like many poor, rural mining communities, was tough. Helen Mallory Overturf, the first mayor's daughter, who said she didn't know if she was related to the chief, remembered that no one questioned Chief Overturf's toughness. "She wasn't afraid of anybody," she said. Reinforcing this view, numerous stories, including some in the local papers, recorded how Overturf had regularly marched into the many taverns to quell disturbances at any time of the day or night. She was also known to ensure that her prisoners got a good breakfast from her boardinghouse before being placed on the train to Benton, where the county jail was located. The younger Mayor Mallory, Robert, remembered that even during his tenure, one of the three biggest problems was complaints about taverns and the fights and other activities that took place in them.

Despite her successes at improving law and order in the community, Overturf's sex was an issue. There were predictions that Mallory's decision not to run for re-election would mean the end of Overturf's career. Fitzgerrell could not recall these details, but confirmed that Overturf gave up the chief's position to run her small boardinghouse and hotel, where many traveling salesmen stayed and where local residents often stopped in for the family-style dinners she cooked and served. Fitzgerrell had vivid memories of the hotel because many of the salesmen provided Overturf with woolen fabric they sold. "My mother used to make me dresses from it, and I hated it, because it was always scratchy," she said.

Overturf had been a local celebrity in her day, mostly due to her willingness to swing her billy club to assure doubters that she was really the police chief. As part of her patrol, Overturf went each night to meet the train that went from Christopher to Benton, stopping at Buckner's small station. "People would try to sit on the side of the train where the platform was so they could see her out there, with her club, every night," Fitzgerrell related. One local historian said Overturf had been known to break up bar fights regularly, and wasn't surprised that she had organized a posse and pursed the gambling bandits in a wild chase and shoot-out that brought her to the attention of the *New York Times*. But, indicating how fleeting fame can be, particularly in a small community for a woman who lacked both social standing and financial comfort, when in 1925 the Zeigler city council appointed Sara Laundsbury, a widow, as an inspector of weights and measures, she was described as possibly the first policewoman in Franklin County, if not throughout southern Illinois.

Reinforcing that fact can be stranger than fiction, Buckner has actually had two women police chiefs. From December 1996 to July 1998, Buckner's police department was again led by a woman when Brenda Burke served as its part-time chief, supervising two part-time officers. Burke, who had lived in Buckner before moving to the slightly larger community of West Frankfort, was hired by a woman mayor, Jesse Oyston, and then fired by Oyston when the two failed to agree on a number of issues. At the time of her selection as chief, Burke was working for the Franklin County Sheriff's Department as a deputy. She disliked her assignment in the courthouse and wanted to work patrol, so she applied for the position in Buckner to get experience doing "real policing." Her intention was to make herself more marketable to larger departments in the area, but when she was offered the twenty-four-hour-a-week job of chief, she grabbed it. Many in the community remembered her as an active officer, one who was particularly involved with the local children, but, like Overturf, not afraid to break up a fight when necessary. After leaving the chief's position, Burke, unlike Overturf, remained in law enforcement as an officer in the Benton Police Department.

Newspaper articles mentioned a woman police chief in Milford, Ohio, in 1914, but local records contradict this. Although references to Dolly Spenser allude to her having been better educated than Overturf and more prominent locally, the references to gamblers taking over the small town raise a question of whether secondary reports might have somehow confused the two women. Even if she was not Milford's police chief, Dolly Spenser had a pioneering role as a probation officer and mayoral candidate. According to some, Milford, a community of about 1,500 people in which gambling was a problem, had turned to Spenser, the "general adjuster of...social problems," to act as its chief for about two years. She was said to have stopped the illegal activities after she "went after the boys and took them out of the gambling joints to her own home," where they were joined by their parents. These raids ended the problem, and Spenser kept the chief's position until a new mayor took office.[2] An article in the *Columbus Evening Dispatch* on February 28, 1921, supported Spenser's role as chief and, under a photo of "Aunt Dolly" braiding a rag rug, the paper reported that she had been so successful that she was expected to be "unanimously elected mayor at least in part because she had the endorsement of both parties and was running unopposed." But other records do not support this. Spenser is listed by the Milford County Historical Society as a juvenile court probation officer who never held public office. A history of the Milford area described her as prominent in social service and civic work, and confirmed only that she was an unsuccessful candidate for mayor in 1921.[3]

A few other small communities are mentioned in feminist publications as having had female police chiefs or commissioners, but only one of these women, Kate Shelley Wilder, was actually in charge of a police department. The lives and careers of Overturf and Wilder could not be more different. While Overturf was a poor woman who was not afraid to use her fists or her club, Wilder came from a prominent family, was married to an attorney, and had been active in Progressive Era women's reform groups.[4]

Wilder's tenure as police commissioner of Fargo, North Dakota, began in 1919, when she became the first woman to serve on Fargo's city commission and the first woman in the state elected to a citywide position. Wilder was an early leader of the North Dakota League of Women Voters who was active in women's suffrage campaigns, and her assignment gave her "entire direction of her department." In 1974, the *Fargo Forum* confirmed her role, calling her the first female police commissioner in the nation.[5]

Wilder's selection was not a fluke. She had for many years been active in the Florence Crittenden Circle, and she was a member of the national board of directors of the Woman's Christian Temperance Union (WCTU). Both these groups were early and active supporters of policewomen. In 1909, members of the the Grand Forks chapter of the Crittenden Circle, concerned over conditions involving transient men and local women, had advocated giving women police powers to stem female delinquency. In May 1910, the Crittenden Circle successfully lobbied the city council to pass an ordinance creating a position for a police matron. This was four months before the Los Angeles Police Department appointed Alice Stebbins Wells as the first woman in the United States to be called a policewoman. By 1915, Fargo also employed a policewoman, making it and Grand Forks among the smallest of the nation's towns to employ women in their police departments.

Both the Crittenden Circle and the WCTU were instrumental in the appointments of matrons and then policewomen around the nation. Founded in 1874, the WCTU, although best known as a temperance group, became involved in many reform areas and was an important source for the recruitment and training of women activists. Frances Willard, elected president of the national WCTU in 1879, used the doctrine of women's sphere—women caring for women—to encourage WTCU members to get involved in such emerging social and political issues as care of incarcerated women, the need for women's prisons, the need for matrons and policewomen to assist women and girls who came into contact with the police, suffrage, and the establishment of kindergartens. She believed that women's sphere was not just the home, but all public facilities utilized by women. The public sector, she told her supporters, was no different from the home, where women cared for other women, for children, and for those unable to care for themselves.

Willard transformed the WCTU into one of the most powerful women's groups in the nation. She depended on women like Wilder to lobby for civic reforms, including, in the nineteenth century, the employment of police matrons and then, in the twentieth century, the employment of policewomen, who were more likely than matrons to have powers of arrest. The Crittenden Circle had similar concerns. It was founded in 1892 by Charles Crittenden after he attended a WCTU convention and agreed to finance its homes for unwed mothers.

Wilder, who was born in Meadville, Pennsylvania, on January 23, 1876, had moved to Fargo with her parents on January 1, 1902, but the family soon moved again, to Grand Forks, where she grew up and graduated from Grand Forks High School in 1893. As the daughter of a financially comfortable lawyer and the wife of an Easterner who had graduated from Tufts College near Boston and was prominent statewide in the insurance business, Wilder was typical of the women supporters of policewomen. Most of them were native-born, well-educated, upper-middle-class or middle-class women who were members of Protestant churches, and who were active in civic and political groups in their communities. They were part of what has come to be called the first feminist movement because many were in favor of women's suffrage and of increasing women's presence and influence in public institutions.

These activist women did not advocate equality by today's definition; in fact, they favored separate institutions for women that would be run by women on behalf of women. This is how they came to spearhead the movement for women's prisons, for matrons and policewomen caring for women and children, and for related areas such as home economics and public health, in which they envisioned women like themselves influencing the lives of other women. These women were in the vanguard of the Progressive movement, which lasted from roughly 1890 to 1920. These years saw a vast expansion of government services, particularly in urban areas and in institutions involving young people and single women. The period overlapped the creation of the modern criminal justice system, including formalizing police departments, establishing juvenile courts, and developing probation officer and parole officer as separate professions. Progressive Era women were able to influence those portions of the agenda that involved care or custody of other women, particularly the juvenile courts, women's prisons, and creation of matrons' and police-women's positions in jails and police departments.

The influence of these Progressive Era women was stronger in corrections than in policing, since it was easier to establish the need for women-only institutions. As early as the 1820s, Quaker women had entered penal institutions to provide Bible training and sewing skills to incarcerated women. Even earlier, Mary Weed had been named principal keeper of the Walnut Street Jail in Philadelphia in 1793. The women who volunteered in these institutions were concerned about the deplorable conditions that existed, including drunkenness and sexual contact between inmates and between inmates and keepers.

These concerns led to paid positions for women who cared for female inmates. By the 1870s, three states—New York in 1839, Indiana in 1873, and Massachusetts in 1877—had established separate women's prisons. This led to positions of authority for a number of women whose careers were influenced by the doctrine of separate spheres. The Indiana Reformatory Institution for Women and Girls was not only the first totally independent women's prison (New York's was located separately on the grounds of a men's prison), but also the first to be run by an entirely female staff under a female superintendent. That superintendent, Rhoda Sloan Coffin, a Quaker whose husband was the only male staff member at the institution, was the first woman CEO in what would eventually come to be called the criminal justice system. Other prominent women also obtained high-level positions in corrections. Clara Barton served as superintendent of the Massachusetts Reformatory Prison for Women in 1882. Kate Barnard was the first woman in the country to win statewide elective office, as the first commissioner of charities and corrections in Oklahoma in 1907. She served two terms, until 1914. And Katherine Bement Davis was superintendent of the Bedford Hills women's prison in New York State from 1901 to 1904, and later New York City's commissioner of corrections from 1914 to 1915, before she became active in suffrage campaigns.

This heritage of women in corrections management continued: Oklahoma Corrections Commissioner Mabel Bassett, who served from 1922 to 1946; Mary Bell Harris, who became the first superintendent of the federal women's prison at Alderson, West Virginia, in 1927 and remained in charge for sixteen years; and Dr. Miriam Van Waters, who was

superintendent of the Massachusetts Reformatory for Women from 1932
to 1957. Louisiana appointed a female corrections commissioner in 1972;
three states (Maine, New Jersey, and California) had female directors of
their state prison systems in the 1980s; and another three states (Alaska
and North and South Dakota) and Puerto Rico had women commissioners of corrections in the 1990s. Also by the 1990s, a number of women
had been wardens of men's prisons.

Wilder was typical of the Progressive Era women whose influence had
led to these positions for women. She was American-born, middle to
upper-middle class, a member of the Congregational Church, and active
in numerous women's and civic associations. In addition to the WCTU
and Crittenden Circle, she belonged to the Daughters of the American
Revolution (DAR), Pioneer Daughters, and the Eastern Star. By the time
of her marriage in 1901, Wilder had been a clerk in the Register of Deeds
office in Grand Forks County, and she was also a teacher. When she and
her husband moved to Fargo in 1902, she continued her involvement in
civic affairs. She was a member of the Republican Party, but in 1913 she
chaired the women's division of the North Dakota Progressive Party.

Wilder's activities were chronicled in the Fargo press, and at least one
story she told from her childhood may have been an indication of how
she persevered in a nontraditional role. Describing her first "job," trying
to sell books to neighbors when she was a preteen, she recalled that when
she admitted she was scared to approach neighbors, she overcame her fear
after a younger brother called her a quitter. After serving as police commissioner for about two years, Wilder was named health commissioner,
but she was defeated in her bid for re-election in 1923. She was by then
the mother of one daughter and had at least one grandchild. Still not a
quitter, despite her defeat she remained active in civil and temperance
activities. In 1933 Wilder was selected as president of the board of directors of the national WCTU. She lived in Fargo until 1940, when, by
then a widow, she returned to Grand Forks to live with her daughter's
family. She died in 1946, at the age of seventy. No other woman was
elected a Fargo city commissioner until 1952.

In yet another odd twist of fiction echoing fact, Fargo did get another
female police chief in 1996, the fictional and very pregnant Marge
Gunderson. Gunderson, played by Frances McDormand in an Oscar-
winning role, investigated and cleared three murders in the Joel and Ethan
Coen movie *Fargo* after Jerry Lundegaard (played by William H. Macy),
a nerdy car salesman in a financial jam, hired two men to kidnap his wife
so he could get his rich father-in-law to pay ransom. After a police officer and two innocent people were killed, Marge investigated and cleared
the three murders in the frozen reaches of Fargo. A big part of the humor

stemmed from the notion of a pregnant police chief, as Marge waddled around, making offbeat observations about life in the rural hinterland. Even this was not as fictional as the Coen brothers might have believed, since in 1990 Elizabeth (Betsy) Watson had been the real-life pregnant police chief of Houston.

In 1997, North Dakota finally got another real female chief, this time in Bismarck, when, on February 1, Deborah Ness, one of the first women police officers in the state, was named chief of the seventy-eight-officer department, which included four women officers. Ness had been one of the first three women hired as patrol officers in Minot, North Dakota, in 1974. After reaching the rank of captain, she was selected as Bismarck's chief when the incumbent retired. An instructor in the Minot State College's criminal justice program, like many of the chiefs appointed since the mid-1990s, she had both bachelor's and master's degrees.[6] Ness also became an unfortunate pioneer. Two years after being named chief, she was diagnosed with breast cancer. She returned to work only five days after her radical mastectomy and then underwent chemotherapy. She counseled other breast cancer survivors, including sharing with them the story of the windy day her wig flew off while she was assisting one of her officers at an accident scene. She has continued to serve as Bismarck's chief.[7]

Other than Overturf and Wilder, the only woman who could be confirmed as having been in charge of a police department prior to the 1970s had the title but only a very limited role in managing the agency. Florence Grall, a mother of six, was appointed safety director of Lorain, Ohio, in 1926 by the mayor—her husband, William. She was an interim replacement due to the mayor's unhappiness with the incumbent, and she was appointed specifically to hear charges against a lieutenant whom the mayor sought to remove. Grall, who like Wilder was active in women's groups, told the *Cincinnati Post* that she could give her new position only two hours a day. This was, she said, referring to her husband and children, because she had "several reasons for spending the rest of her time at home."[8] Unlike Wilder, Grall had not shown any interest in police issues, and to the extent that she acted as safety director, it was solely to facilitate the changes her husband wanted to make in the department.

MODERN WOMEN CHIEFS EMERGE

Sue Wegner, who in August 1979 was named chief of police of Minneola, Florida, may have been the first of those who could be called modern women chiefs. These are women who had chosen careers in policing and who, with only one exception, had worked in police departments in ranks lower than chief. Although many had come into policing as civilians, all had become eligible for sworn officers' positions in the 1970s, and many had been the first or only female officer in their department.

Wegner, one of the first women in Florida to attend a police academy with male officers, was older and smaller than her fellow students. She had taken advantage of Florida's "alternate route" training, which permits a police candidate to attend an academy without the support of a police department and then to begin searching for a job after becoming certified as a police officer. At the time, few states recognized this path. Although this type of entry has now been approved in a larger number of states, it is still uncommon. In most states, police officers are hired by a department and are then sent to a police academy, which generally bars from attendance those who are not already employed. The advantage of the alternate route to the candidate is that he or she need not have been hired by a police department, but, by attending the academy at his or her own expense, may become more desirable to a department with vacant positions. The advantage to the department is the financial saving of not having to pay an officer to attend the academy.

Despite Wegner's ability to begin working immediately, she had trouble finding an agency willing to employ her for patrol work. She was reluctant to attribute this to her age (over thirty), her small stature (5′2″ and 112 pounds), or her sex, but presumed that one or all played a role. The six-person Minneloa department was the only one that would hire her. Wegner later told one of the women with whom she had attended the academy that she believed any cop should be in top physical condition. But, presaging what many women who followed her into policing would say, she also noted that she had broken up many a bar fight without having to lift a finger, primarily by outthinking the suspects.

Wegner was the senior officer when she was named chief by City Manager Richard Waters, who said she was far from the only candidate for the position, but that he had selected her specifically because she had come up through the ranks of the department. Recently divorced from her husband of seventeen years and attending college, Wegner was faced with a rising crime rate and a shrinking budget. By the time she left in 1981, she had remarried and changed her name to Hogan. Indicating how small a community it was, Wegner had been on a first-name basis with almost everyone in the town, including those who, she said, referred to her as their "lady chief."[9] Minneloa had a second woman chief, Jane Newcomb, who was in charge from 1994 to 1995, when the department was disbanded and policing responsibilities were turned over to the Lake County Sheriff's Department.

Donna Hansen, another Florida chief, had a rockier tenure than either Wegner or Newcomb. A twenty-year veteran of the Metro–Dade Police Department when she was named chief in Fort Myers in 1991, she was only forty-three years old, and she may have tried to change the department too quickly. She developed the motto "Unity, Pride, and Commitment," and promptly emblazoned it on the department's vehicles. By 1995, the unity was gone; she left the 140-person department in April after a public falling-out with Mayor Wilbur Smith. Although she denied being forced out, neither she nor the mayor would say anything other than that they had differences in their management styles.[10] Hansen may have been ahead of her time; she worked with a local television station to promote a "most wanted" show that might have brought more publicity than the mayor wanted.

Mississippi appointed its first woman chief in 1980. Beulah Lott, of the Magee, Mississippi, Police Department, began her career in the department as a dispatcher. Like many of the chiefs who would come after her, she was looking for a better job. She had been supervising a Laundromat™ and was offered a job by Paul Kennedy, the chief she would later replace. She was reluctant, less interested in a policing career than in any other job that paid more and had a better future; but after her husband urged her to take the job, she relented. Thinking she probably wouldn't stay very long, she soon took on the added responsibilities of records officer and, at a time when there were no mandatory training requirements in the state, she was promoted to sergeant. She recalled that her friends were in shock, unable to imagine her as a police officer, let alone as a supervisor. She served twice as interim chief before the town board voted to return to a system in which the police chief was an elected official. Lott won a special election in April 1980 that assured her position until the next city election in May 1981.

Although Lott had been undecided when she was first offered the chief's position on an acting basis, by the time of the election she felt confident she could run and win. "I felt the chief's shoes would be big ones to fill," she said, "but, just like when I first took the dispatcher's job, the pay was more than I was earning, and I had already done most of the jobs in the department, so I figured, what did I have to lose?" She was also encouraged by her husband and children. Lott, alternately known as the chief or the city marshal, was well known in the community. She recalled that she was called out frequently at night, but that she loved the job and the excitement; nevertheless, she declined to run again, because by 1981 her husband was ill and she was unable to remain on call twenty-four hours a day, seven days a week. Reducing herself in rank to sergeant, she stayed with the nine-member department until early 1985, when she retired. During her time as chief, the only other woman in the department was the radio dispatcher who had replaced her.

Discussing the racial tensions that existed in many small Southern communities at the time, Lott recalled that friends were concerned that a white woman would not be accepted as the police chief by the African-American community, but she found that as long as she treated people fairly, she had no problems with men or women of either race. "Cops have problems with people because they can get ugly," she said, remembering how she told her "boys" (the police officers who worked for her) that there was no need to knock people around to get them to listen to you. A widow teaching Sunday school, she said she was encouraged by the increasing number of women in policing, especially in high ranks. "I put three boys through college as a police officer. I broke in the dispatcher who replaced me, an African-American woman who is also a widow and who has also been promoted. Women need to work together," she concluded.[11]

One of the early modern women chiefs was the first of only two women chiefs who have died in the line of duty. Coalinga, California, Chief Luella Kay Holloway was killed on January 3, 1980, in a plane crash while returning home from a state training meeting. Holloway, who, according to a current member of her department, held a leadership position in the state's Commission on Peace Officers Standards and Training (POST), was returning from a meeting in Sacramento when the Cessna 172 in which she was flying crashed due to poor weather conditions. She was traveling with her husband, a California Highway Patrol officer. Although few in the department recalled her career, despite budgetary constraints and the loss of officers due to downsizing, the department honored Holloway and two other officers during 2004 ceremonies in conjunction with National Police Memorial Week, held annually in early May.[12]

More recently, in August 1998, Chloe (Frankie) Stanton, the forty-three-year-old chief in the small town of Bradshaw, West Virginia, was shot and killed in her office, in front of her niece and nephew, who happened to be visiting her that day. Stanton had been chief in the 400-person community about 120 miles southwest of Charleston for just over a year. She had arrested Charlie Vance, a sixty-one-year-old man she had known all her life, after he rode into town on horseback and caused a disturbance in a local drugstore, apparently because he was intoxicated. Stanton took him to the small police station, where she confiscated a gun from him but was unaware that he was also carrying a derringer in a fanny pack. He pulled out this second gun and shot the chief, without warning, while she was either making or answering a telephone call.[13]

By the mid-1980s, the numbers of women chiefs began to increase slowly. In 1988, the International Association of Women Police (IAWP) was able to locate about thirty of the fewer than fifty women chiefs in office at that time. Virtually all led small departments (the largest had twenty-eight sworn officers) in small communities (the largest with a population of 35,000). The overwhelming majority were chiefs in the community in which they had started their police career, and many were natives or had grown up in that community. Of the twelve who responded to an informal IAWP survey, two had been chief for more than seven years, many had been the first woman in their department, ten were still the only woman officer in their department, and most were the first or only woman chief in their state. Seven were married (two to police officers), and four had children.[14]

A number of small Midwestern communities were among the first to employ women chiefs, including Burton, Ohio; Hinsdale, Illinois; Union City, Michigan; and Benson and Biwabik, Minnesota. Sally Hess was only twenty-five at the time of her promotion to chief in 1987 in Burton, Ohio, a village of about 1,400 residents roughly an hour east of Cleveland. Hess, who was the youngest police chief in Ohio, had been mentored by her predecessor. When he resigned to take a federal job, he recommended that she be appointed to take his place in charge of three full-time and six part-time officers. Hess had been with the department as either a full-time or a part-time officer for about three years and had also worked in other local law enforcement agencies. A village native, she had graduated from high school in Burton and was only a semester shy of a degree in education from Kent State University. She recalled that the chief had more concerns about her age than about her sex.[15]

Her youth, Hess said, was evident in comments about her from residents and the varied ways in which people greeted her. "To some, I'm Chief Hess, to others I'm Sally, and to others I'm still Mrs. Hess's daughter," she said, referring to her mother, who had been teaching third grade in the local elementary school for about twenty years. This familiarity did not discourage her from taking her job seriously. Although little reportable crime occurred in the village, Hess said that people driving while intoxicated was a problem, and that she had no qualms about arresting people for the offense; in fact, she believed she was doing them a favor rather than letting them be killed in an accident. Hess left after two years, becoming an officer with the Department of Natural Resources, where she was not the chief but the pay was considerably higher. She was replaced as chief by a man who had worked in the department during her tenure.

One of the two Minnesota chiefs, Rose Gagnon, was even younger than Hess when she was named chief of the Benson, Minnesota, Police Department in 1986. Only twenty-four, she was the sole woman among the sworn staff of five, although the department secretary was a woman. Although Gagnon and Kathleen Beise, Biwabik's chief, were the only women chiefs in Minnesota at the time, they were at opposite ends of the state and rarely saw one another. Beise and Gagnon voiced similar concerns over the small number of women and the absence of role models and mentors for women, but their careers had taken, and would continue to take, different twists and turns. Beise joined her department in 1980, and spent three years on patrol before being named acting chief, and then chief in 1983. A young widow with two small children, she attended the local community college and earned an associate's degree in law enforcement before she could start her policing career. She remained chief of the department of five full-time and four part-time police officers until 1998, when she and her second husband, a state trooper, retired from their respective departments.

Gagnon's career was shorter; about a year after she was profiled in the *Minnesota Police Chief,* she married, resigned, moved away, and opened a catering business while raising four children, including a daughter from her husband's previous marriage.[16] Gagnon, a native of Benson, and Beise, who had moved to Biwabik from Duluth, were both appointed in the departments in which they had begun their policing careers, as was Linda Waite, who had begun her career as a dispatcher and clerk in Union City, Michigan. A former nurse, she took command of the eleven-member department in 1984.

Christine A. Higgins, who in 1986 was appointed director of fire and police services in Hinsdale, Illinois, was the only one of the women who had moved from a larger agency. Higgins, a fifteen-year veteran special agent with the federal Drug Enforcement Administration (DEA), had served in a number of assignments around the country and in the Far East, including Hong Kong and Japan. In Hinsdale, the chiefs of the police and fire departments reported directly to her. When the position was eliminated a few years later, she returned to the DEA.

Most of the women chiefs of the 1980s spent most of their careers without ever seeing another woman chief, but two of the four women in Texas were neighbors, both leading small departments in Brazoria County in 1985. The two women, Faye (Patricia) Mackwardt in Clute and Theresa Guidry in Brazoria, like Beise and Gagnon in Minnesota, followed different career paths. Mackwardt, who was chief until 1988, began and ended her law enforcement career in the Brazoria County Sheriff's Office. After working as an investigator, she joined the Clute Police Department and reached the rank of patrol lieutenant before being promoted to chief. She resigned in 1988 and returned to the sheriff's office, specializing in investigating cases involving juveniles. Guidry did not remain in policing.

Interviewed by the IAWP, both women attributed their promotions to hard work rather than to their sex, but agreed that women had a harder time proving themselves. "Women have to be just a little quicker, a little sharper, more understanding, a little better at what they do to be 'equal' to a male officer," Mackwardt said. Guidry agreed, stating that although "education is very important," a female chief has to prove herself more than a male would have to do. Chief Mark Wicker, who had worked with Mackwardt in the sheriff's office and as her second in command in Clute, and who replaced her as chief, remembered both women and recalled that "no one thought much about it. They were just two women in law enforcement down here."[17]

Surprisingly, the two women in Brazoria County local law enforcement constituted only half the total number of women chiefs in Texas. The others, Mary Voswinkle, who retired in 1999, and Barbara Childress, who after twenty-three years as chief in Richland Hills is one of the longest-serving chiefs in the nation, each made history of a different sort.

How unusual was it for one state to have four women police chiefs in the 1980s? Although Texas has more law enforcement agencies than any other state in the nation—more than 1,000—in the year 2000 a survey that omitted sheriffs received responses from only eight women out of a total of 183 chiefs who responded to the survey. While this figure may not have accounted for all the women chiefs in the state, it is an indication of just how remarkable it was to have had half that number serving more than two decades earlier. Although Texas is big, its police departments are small—the mean department size was just over twenty-six officers.[18]

Mary Voswinkle (later Bard), another of the early Texas women chiefs, retired from the Rice University Police Department at the end of 1999. Her position had been created specifically for her. Like many university police departments, the Rice Police Department had started as a security department, originally employing a small number of officers who lacked arrest authority. In 1970, one year after the Texas legislature granted private universities the authority to create police departments and to employ licensed police officers, Rice decided to upgrade to a full-service police department. By 1978, when Voswinkle was assistant director, the department had grown to sixteen police officers and a small administrative staff. She oversaw an assessment that resulted in continued growth; the department ultimately employed twenty-five officers and an additional dozen civilian staff members who were responsible for policing the 300-acre campus. In recognition of the work she had done, the title of chief of police was created for her when her predecessor, whose title had been the more civilian-sounding "director," retired.[19]

Voswinkle, who died almost a year to the day after she retired, lived to see campus policing grow into a major employment area for women police officers and for women chiefs. Campus policing dates its existence to 1894, when Yale University, in New Haven, Connecticut, hired two officers to patrol the campus. For many years most campus departments lacked police authority, but in the 1960s and 1970s many, like Rice University, received permission from state legislatures to become fully accredited police departments. This required officers to undergo the same background checks and to attend the same state-mandated training academies as municipal police officers. By the mid-1990s, nine of every ten public institutions and about half of all private institutions employed state-commissioned police officers. Unique to the United States, university policing is one of the fastest-growing segments of law enforcement; by 2003 about 30,000 police officers were employed on campuses throughout the country.[20]

In small communities where a college or university may be the largest single employer or may have more staff and students working or living on campus than in the community itself, the campus police department may be larger, better trained, and better equipped than the town police. In 1994, University of California at Berkeley Police Chief Victoria Harrison oversaw creation of one of the first university SWAT teams in the nation. "My hope," she said at the time, "is that we will never have to use these officers in this capacity," but she also noted that campuses were not enclaves that were automatically immune from situations that might require a specially trained response unit that was heavily armed and skilled at rescuing hostages or capturing barricaded gunmen. The eighty-officer department, which preferred to call the specialized unit a high risk entry team, had only one of a number of similar units at public universities at that time, including the University of Illinois at Urbana–Champaign, the University of California at Davis, and Ohio State University.[21]

Recognizing the growing importance of campus policing, the International Association of Chiefs of Police (IACP) created a University and College Police Section, which has resulted in higher visibility in the organization for a number of women chiefs, including University of Wisconsin at Madison Chief Susan Riseling. Riseling, who has received a number of policing awards and holds many firsts for women, chose a career in campus policing specifically because she felt it would be more "female-friendly." In 2002, the forty-four-year-old International Association of Campus Law Enforcement Administrators (IACLEA) elected its first female president, Dolores Stafford, chief of the George Washington University Police Department, who had joined the department in 1992 after eighteen years in other areas of policing.

Campus policing has also contributed to the increase in the number of women law enforcement CEOs. In 2001, forty of the ninety-six women surveyed (42 percent) for *Breaking the Brass Ceiling* were chiefs of campus police departments. Since these campus chiefs tended to have more years in law enforcement than municipal chiefs, there is some indication that many are moving into these positions after careers in other areas of law enforcement. If so, this presented a career path for women that allowed them to move from middle or top management in local police departments to chief in another agency without having to consider relocation, which tends to present greater problems for career women than for men at comparable ages and stages of their careers.

University policing opened up career movement for a number of women chiefs. One former university chief, Alana M. Ennis, began her policing career with the Dallas (Texas) County Sheriff's Department. A North Carolina native, she returned home to join the Durham Police Department, rising through the ranks to become a captain. She then served two campuses as police chief—the University of North Carolina at Chapel Hill, from 1992 to 1995, and then Duke University until 1998—before returning to municipal policing as chief of the Burlington, Vermont, Police Department, from which she retired in 2003. At Chapel Hill she closely followed Voswinkle's role by expanding her agency into a full-service police department. She is one of the few campus police chiefs—male or female—who was able to move between the two forms of policing quite so smoothly.

A small number of the modern women chiefs have seen their careers last well beyond their own expectations. Two retired in 2003, and two others were still leading their departments in 2004. Despite what has been written about the short tenures of police chiefs, lengthy tenures are more closely associated with small police departments, one way in which the women's careers were similar to those of their male counterparts. Among these pioneers was Glassboro, New Jersey, Chief Patricia Kunchynski, who was the first woman hired by her department and its only woman when she was named chief in 1986. One of only five women officers in Gloucester County, at the time she was also the first woman chief in the state. After ten years on patrol, Kunchynski was named deputy chief after none of the supervisory officers in the forty-five-officer department passed the promotion exam for chief. After a series of tests and interviews, she was offered the job on a permanent basis. She recalled that she was prepared for the process because she had actually been the retiring chief's "handpicked successor." Although promoted from the rank patrol officer, she had been a lieutenant in command of a Military Police unit during her two years in the Army that was almost identical in size to the Glassboro Police Department.

Cathy Stoddard, another veteran chief, who retired in 2003 after thirty-three years, also spent her entire career with one department. She had been chief in the village of Lakewood, Illinois, since 1985. Although Stoddard was regularly described as the first female chief in the state, she was actually the second—after Buckner's Lydia Overturf—but she was the first woman president of her county's (McHenry) police chiefs association. Stoddard, who began her policing career as a dispatcher and matron in 1970, had a family connection to her department. She had been married to the prior chief and had run the department's communications section from their home before deciding to apply for a position as a police officer in the ten-member department.

She recalled "being called names that would make most men blush," but said this was more likely to be by other women than by men. She liked policing, though, and decided to stay with the department. In 1984, when the chief, from whom she was now divorced, retired early, she was named acting chief and then, within the year, permanent chief. Stoddard, who was forty at the time she was selected chief, was the mother of three children, and was married for the third time. Although she chose not to publicize it, she had been the victim of domestic violence earlier in her life. She said that throughout her career, she had found that some women and many younger men had trouble accepting women in policing, but that she had had very few problems with older chiefs, many of whom she found "gracious" and less likely than younger men to be threatened by the presence of a woman.[22]

Stoddard's tenure overlapped that of Karla Osantowski, who was chief in nearby Chicago Heights from 1994 to 1996, and who also had been a victim of domestic violence. Despite their common experiences with domestic violence, and their overlapping careers at a time when there were only four women chiefs in Illinois, Osantowski recalled that she did not know Stoddard well and saw her infrequently at law enforcement meetings. Thirty-seven years old at the time she was named Chicago Heights's chief, Osantowski, the first female police chief in populous Cook County, was also the only modern woman chief with no prior experience in policing. A Cook County assistant state's attorney for five years when she was offered the chief's position, she had worked with the department in prosecuting felony cases but had also, while in the public integrity unit, worked on corruption cases that had involved members of the department. Chicago Heights, a southern suburb of Chicago with about 35,000 residents, had a reputation for government and police corruption that predated Prohibition, and a number of officials had been convicted of charges ranging from taking bribes to protecting drug dealers.

Osantowski admitted that almost none of the department's eighty officers, all of whom were men, were eager to have a chief who not only was a woman, but had never been a police officer, and had been hired specifically to reform the department. She did win some acceptance from the officers, but when her contract ended in 1996, she remained with the department for another year as police superintendent, a position created by a new mayor who wanted to promote her former deputy to chief of police. Osantowski left the department and, in 1998, married one of the officers who had worked for her, which, she believed, would have made it difficult for her to continue as superintendent.

She saw her career in Chicago Heights as just one more of the obstacles she had been overcoming for most of her life. At twenty-two a high school dropout and the mother of two young daughters, she had moved out of her home, gone to live in a housing project, and applied for public assistance to escape an abusive marriage. Overcoming the embarrassment of family members, none of whom had ever been on public assistance or in similar circumstances, she decided that education was her key to a better life. After working her way through Loyola University, she graduated in 1984 with a degree in criminal justice and became the first in her family to have graduated from college. She was on the civil service list for the Chicago Police Department, and while waiting to be hired, she worked her way through Kent College of Law, after which she joined the state attorney's office. In 2002, using her married name, Karla Fiaoni, she ran for, but did not win, a seat on the Cook County Board, after which she resumed practicing law as a criminal defense attorney.

Two early women chiefs were still leading their departments in 2004—Richmond Hills, Texas's, Barbara Childress, who had begun her career in policing as a dispatcher, and Gaithersburg, Maryland's, Mary Ann Viverette. Each had been the first woman chief in her state, and each had exceeded her own expectations and had achieved recognition through a variety of organizations, Childress within the state of Texas and Viverette through the IACP.

Childress began her career in 1970 as a dispatcher in Richmond Hills after talking to officers who stopped by the convenience store in which she worked and listening to the chatter coming over the radios they carried. Even after she became the department's chief in 1983, she never imagined that she would become the first woman president of the Texas

Police Chiefs Association, a chairwoman of the Texas Commission on Law Enforcement Officer Standards and Education, and one of the longest serving chiefs in the nation.

Viverette has been a chief for almost as long as Childress. After about a year as a Montgomery County (Maryland) sheriff's deputy, Viverette joined the Gaithersburg, Maryland, Police Department in 1979 and was named its chief (while still Mary Ann Troutner) in 1986. She has received worldwide attention as the first female member of the IACP board and, if she remains a chief, will become its first female president in 2006.

CHAPTER 4

Twists and Turns on the Road to the Top: Decisions and Detours along the Way

The men in my class were all thinking about becoming chiefs. That got my mind working.

—Chief Jeanne Miller
Reynoldsburg, Ohio, Police Department

I don't think I would have gotten the offer if a woman hadn't been the decision maker.

—Chief Alicia Powers
Hercules, California, Police Department

It's hard for anyone—woman or man—to become a chief. I hope my presence will encourage more women to aim for the top.

—Chief Mary Ann Viverette
Gaithersburg, Maryland, Police Department

I had reached an impenetrable glass ceiling in my first agency. It was time for a change.

—Chief Doris Conley
Lincoln City, Oregon, Police Department

I wanted new challenges.

—Chief Patricia Medina
Rio Dell, California, Police Department

I had spent my entire career in an urban police department.
This job was an opportunity to run my own department.

—Chief Donna Green
Oakland, Oregon, Police Department

Jeanne Miller has never forgotten the day in 1973 she was sworn in as a Detroit police officer. She leaned forward as Commissioner Philip G. Tannian was administering the oath of office and told the woman standing in front of her that someday she'd have Tannian's job. At the end of 2003, a woman, Ella Bully-Cummings, did get Tannian's old job, but by then Miller was just a few months short of a decade as a police chief.

Miller, chief of the sixty-eight-person Reynoldsburg, Ohio, Police Department, retired early from the Detroit Police Department so that she could achieve her dream. She is representative of about two-thirds of the women who were chiefs of police in 2001 and who made one or more moves from their original departments before being named chief. Some women moved on when they felt the brass ceiling weighing them down; some moved because they wanted new challenges or to test their own ideas on how a police department could or should be managed; and some, like Miller, wanted to find a place where her husband, also a retired Detroit cop, and their daughters could improve their quality of life at the same time that she could fulfill her dream.

One of the major ways in which law enforcement differs from most other professions is that very early career decisions can have a long-term and even a permanent effect on opportunities for upward mobility. Not only must a potential chief have virtually always started her career as a police officer, she must also have held one or more middle-management or upper-management positions. Many women who led departments of fewer than 100 officers were captains at the time of their promotion; those who were in lower ranks (police officer, sergeant, or lieutenant) were likely to be found in departments with fewer than twenty-five officers. Women who were chiefs in departments of more than 500 people had all held upper-level management ranks, including major, or assistant or deputy chief. Milwaukee's chief, Nannette Hegerty, held the civil service rank of captain at the time she was named chief, a somewhat low rank for such a large department, but she had taken a leave of absence from the department to accept a political appointment to the position of U.S. marshal, which played a key role in her selection in late 2003.

The requirement of having had police experience is complicated by hiring patterns that often preclude making career moves as a middle manager. In retailing, for instance, a sales associate might begin a career with one store, move up to store manager, and then move to a different company as manager of a larger store or possibly as a district or regional manager. This is less likely to occur in policing. With the exception of California, which permits lateral entry at virtually every rank, a police officer who is on a civil service list for sergeant, the next highest rank, must wait for a position in her department. In Minnesota, a statewide pension system has allowed for some movement among agencies, but lateral transfers are not as prevalent as in California. It is quite rare for a police office to go to an adjoining town's police department without quitting, being hired by the new department, and starting her career as a police officer again.

Due to the localized nature of policing, combined with civil service and union regulations, almost all police departments require higher-ranking officers to have reached at least a certain civil service rank before they can be considered for even higher rank. Thus, police officers who want to become chiefs most often move at either the chief's rank or one or two ranks below it. Some of this is tradition, but career moves are also complicated by pensions that are not portable. Most agencies fund their own pensions, and the time earned in one department is not transferable to another department's pension system. If an officer spends ten years in the Detroit Police Department and decides to move to Reynoldsburg, unless she has retired, she will forfeit the monies paid into the Detroit pension system and will have to start her career and her pension accrual all over again. Although many departments have loosened age requirements to admit older candidates, until the 1990s the option of leaving and starting over at a new department was undercut by age restrictions that limited new employees to those under twenty-nine or thirty-four years of age.

The effect of these policies is that professional decisions must be made at certain points in a career. The policies also create two major career path options, with a third option that is less common. The first is that someone begins her career as a police officer in a department, moves up through the ranks, and is at some point selected chief. The second option is that someone begins her career as a police officer in a department, moves up through the ranks to at least middle management, and applies for a chief's position elsewhere, usually in a smaller department than her home department. The third, and least common, option is to find a department that is hiring middle managers. Outside of California, this occurs primarily when a new police department has been formed in a growing or urbanizing area that was previously patrolled by state police or a sheriff's department, or when an established police department has undergone major reorganization and vacancies have been created in ranks such as captain, major, or assistant chief.

Miller took a chance on the third option, and although her travels involved an extra stop along the way, her sojourn as assistant superintendent (chief) of operations for the Peoria, Illinois, Police Department played a vital role in her move to Reynoldsburg. Miller was also able to defy the conventional wisdom about women being unable to relocate based on a husband's unwillingness to move his career. The ability to retire after twenty or twenty-five years of service from most police departments has created a situation where husbands or other partners, often a few years older than their mates, may comfortably relocate without the need to seek a comparable—or even any—position. For women in policing who want to be CEOs, this has minimized one of the major dilemmas confronting women who must relocate to advance their careers. Generally men are likely to earn higher salaries and to face societal pressure that it is unmanly to leave a good job to become a trailing spouse. But because a number of the women's husbands have retired from their careers, the women chiefs may have greater mobility than women in other professions who are between their mid-forties and mid-fifties, with spouses who cannot consider relocation so late in their own careers.

Dual policing careers are common among women chiefs. Almost half of those who indicated a spouse's or partner's employment said that it had been policing, although fewer than ten of the chiefs had worked in the same agency as their partner. Of the four women selected in 2003 and 2004 to lead large-city police departments, three (Detroit's Ella Bully-Cummings, Boston's Kathleen O'Toole, and Milwaukee's Hegerty) were married to men who had been members of the department they led, and one (San Francisco's Heather Fong) was single. Of the three prior large-city chiefs, two—Portland's Penny Harrington and Houston's Elizabeth (Betsy) Watson—were married to men who had also worked in their agencies. Atlanta's Beverly Harvard was married to a man with no connection to law enforcement.

Trailing spouses and children are a major issue for women in management. In discussing the shattering of possibly the last and the highest glass ceiling—a woman president of the United States—Eleanor Clift and Tom Brazaitis pointed out how conflicts between professional and personal responsibilities weigh more heavily on women than on men.[1] Although they were discussing politics, the same is true for other fields. It takes time to build a career, but women who marry, and particularly those who have children, may never recoup the time they postponed before starting to build their careers. Being married to someone who has completed his own career can minimize the need to defer what could prove to be crucial rungs on the ladder to the top.

A spouse—or a child—who is unwilling to relocate can sidetrack the career of even the most visible working women. When, in 2002, President George W. Bush's director of communications and chief spokeswoman, Karen Hughes, resigned in part because her husband, Jerry, a lawyer in Austin, Texas, did not want to move to Washington, D.C., she went from overseeing the news to becoming the news. Hughes was forty-five; her husband, sixty-three. He did not want to move to Washington, nor did he want to live apart from her for long periods of time. If Hughes and her husband had been in policing, her husband would very likely have been retired. Hughes returned in 2004 to play a role in the Bush re-election campaign, but the identifying lines on her memoir, *Ten Minutes from Normal*, sum up the dilemma: "counselor to the president, wife and mother. The woman who left the White House to put family first, and moved back home to Texas." Hughes also identified the pressure facing a man with a more prominent wife. "When people came up to me in Washington to talk to me, they would by and large talk to me and ignore my husband. In Texas, if I'm in the grocery store and somebody recognizes me, they almost always introduce themselves to my husband, too," she explained.[2]

Hughes's decision that she preferred to spend more time with her husband and teenage son was similar to Miller's desire for a better quality of life for herself, her husband, and their two daughters. While Hughes could not relocate the White House to Austin, Miller could relocate herself and her family to a place more in keeping with her desires. Miller's husband was able to retire with pension benefits. He no longer felt he had to be as well-known as she was, and was willing to subordinate his career to his wife's plans when the family moved first to Peoria and then to Reynoldsburg.

Both women inadvertently raised another issue facing working women—especially those interested in upward mobility—the "mommy track." Felice Schwartz, the founder of Catalyst, an organization dedicated to helping women advance their careers in business, first proposed the mommy track in 1989, as an alternative career path for women who wanted to balance family responsibilities and work demands rather than putting their careers first.[3] She asserted that it cost companies more to employ women than men because women's careers are often interrupted or ended when they have children. She suggested an alternative career track that would permit mothers to balance career and family responsibilities by encouraging companies to create family-friendly polices like flexible hours and day care. She was attacked by detractors who felt that women would not be hired, and certainly would not be promoted, if they made it clear that they placed family concerns above professional advancement.

Despite the interest surrounding career women and child rearing,[4] the chiefs and sheriffs were not asked about children. Because many had been divorced or married more than once, it would have been complicated to determine whether children in the family had actually grown up in their homes or were stepchildren from a partner's previous relationship. Yet conversations with chiefs and sheriffs indicated that many are childless and that the children living in their homes come from the husband's previous marriage. Those with children rarely have more than two.

The prevalence of small families among women police executives is not limited to the United States, nor are the problems surrounding career mobility. In the Royal Canadian Mounted Police (RCMP), where more than half the women are married to men who are also in the RCMP, frequently in higher ranks than their wives, women are often precluded from applying for promotions that involve moving across the country, often to a command where there will not be a post for their spouse.

The RCMP, known as "the Mounties," is unique. There is no comparable agency in the United States, although the transfer policies of the force are similar to those of U.S. investigatory agencies such as the Federal Bureau of Investigation (FBI), the Drug Enforcement Administration (DEA), or the Secret Service. But the RCMP is the only police force that can be described as a national symbol of its country. It is both a uniformed and an investigative agency. Officers may be assigned anywhere in the country (as in U.S. federal agencies), and postings are often in small, rural offices (detachments) rather than in large cities, which generally have their own police forces and do not rely on the RCMP in the same way small cities and rural areas do. This explained the high percentage of in-force marriages, which, added to the small size of many of the offices, means that a transfer for one partner might result in no available assignment for the other. A decision by either spouse to accept a promotion may require living apart for years. These policies have also contributed to a high attrition rate of women from the force. Assistant Commissioner Ghyslaine Clément, the highest-ranking woman in the RCMP and commander of its "A" Division in 2004, has urged women to carefully consider the consequences of putting child care before career (she and her husband are childless).

Gwen M. Boniface, commissioner of the 7,000-member Canadian Ontario Provincial Police (OPP), noted at the end of 2003 that she had moved three times while her only child was in high school, and that in retrospect she wasn't sure she would do that again. The OPP is responsible for an even larger geographical area than a U.S. state police agency, making it almost impossible for an officer to rise through the ranks without having to relocate more than once. Boniface stressed that her husband was not in policing and that he was not only willing—but able—to move to accommodate her career.[5]

The debate over the impact of children on a woman's career has intensified at a time when women seem to be avoiding hitting the glass ceiling by opting out of power positions. Magazines and newspapers have focused on numerous professional women who have left careers to become full-time mothers or to work part-time from home. Although many of the women have referred to these as career breaks, no one knows what the effects of these decisions will be for these women or for others who might follow them. A new genre of what could be called "you really can't have it all" books has focused on the ways marriage and parenthood have detoured—if not derailed—the careers of many American women, but not of American men.[6]

Will companies that are concerned about their investments in personnel find ways to hire or promote fewer women? Will fewer women apply to work in large organizations if they believe this will hamper their family planning? Based on the same notions the chiefs put forth of each indirectly paving the way for the women who followed them, there is the possibility that an increasing number of women opting out of the workplace at midcareer may discourage companies from hiring the next generation of women CEOs.

How did Miller, who achieved her goal of becoming a chief after two moves, the second when her daughters were in the third and fifth grades, avoid both the mommy track and the resentment of a trailing spouse? A key was a husband who was already retired and was as committed to her goal as she was. "Family was always first," she said. "When I interviewed in Reynoldsburg, my family was an asset because I assured the town leaders that I would stay because I knew it would not be good for my daughters if I were to move around to a new place every few years." To her, Reynoldsburg, a 50,000-person town that was home to the distribution centers of both Victoria's Secret and Bath & Body Works, was an idyllic bedroom community. She was so successful in assuring the town leaders of her commitment that not only was she named chief, but she convinced the city council to approve funds for a new Public Safety Building that opened at the end of 2001.

But Miller almost became a mommy tracker. Her dream of being a chief, she recalled, almost slipped away as she learned "the craft of policing, got married, and was busy with two young daughters." In a large police department like Detroit's, it is easy to have interesting assignments that cool the ardor for promotion or to get sidetracked onto glass walls as often as to hit glass ceilings. Linda Wirth, author of *Breaking Through the Glass Ceiling: Women in Management,* has described glass walls as a pyramid beyond which women can't go because they have been moved into feminized areas such as corporate communications, human resources, and training, and away from the core activities of their companies.[7] These positions, according to Wirth, may provide women with impressive titles and large staffs, but do not provide the corporate experiences necessary for top managers. According to this view, only those who have run things—manufacturing plants, divisions within a larger corporation—or have in some way been involved in a company's essential business functions will be considered for the highest levels of management. Some observers of the police have raised similar concerns, namely, that women are often excluded from the highest-profile assignments that are seen as career-enhancing, such as criminal investigations, special weapons and tactics (SWAT) units, or high-level patrol supervisory assignments.

Many of the first women chiefs, particularly in large cities, faced credibility problems with male officers because patrol assignments were often missing from their career résumés. Today this is less likely to be an issue; most women have the required time in uniform or on patrol to quell complaints about their selection. At the same time, the careers of both male and female chiefs are more likely, since the 1990s, to highlight education and management experience over traditional crime-fighting skills.

Miller was able to present each of these skill sets, including sufficient time on patrol and in assignments with a high danger component. In addition to working in patrol and in undercover gang and narcotics assignments, she had developed Detroit's precinct anti–car theft teams (units targeting car thieves), a carjacking squad, and a repeat offender program. She also had worked in internal affairs, which, although often an unpopular assignment, provided the future chief with an understanding of how detrimental to a department's goals corrupt or uncaring officers can be. And she found mentors: two older male officers whom she described as "second fathers." Even in large departments, she said, there are always people looking for a better way to do the job, and a wise move for a young police officer or newly promoted supervisor is to seek them out or respond favorably if they find you.

Training and her competitive spirit, though, are what led to the resurfacing of Miller's goals. In 1989 she was selected to attend command-level training at Northwestern University's Traffic Institute School of Police Staff and Command. She was elected president of her class, was class valedictorian, and received the leadership award. But what rekindled her dream was, she recalled, "the hubris of all my male counterparts, talking about how putting the class on their résumés would help them get this and that chief job. That really got my mind working."

Although she had avoided the glass walls, Miller realized later that she had almost fallen into another trap: that women are often myopic about their long-term career goals; seeing themselves in a job, rather than in a career, as men are more accustomed to doing.[8] Learning from her male colleagues, she decided she, too, would use the training and networking her job provided to return to her first dream; hence the move to Peoria in 1991 with the goal of becoming a chief, if not there, then somewhere else. Miller hedged on whether she had hoped a chief's badge would come in Peoria, but the move was not trouble-free. On March 9, 1994, she had her moment of fame when, on national television, David Letterman, a fellow Midwesterner, listed "the Top Ten Reasons Jeanne Miller Is Leaving Peoria." The tenth was that she was tired of wearing a bullet-proof vest to city council meetings; the first was that her head hurt from bumping the glass ceiling. What more could there be to add?

The comments illustrated what can happen to an outsider unaware of the inner workings of a new city or a new department. Miller admitted that she might have done better research before relocating, and that certainly Reynoldsburg was a better fit for her and her family. She attributed her willingness to keep moving to having moved around quite a bit in her youth before settling down in Michigan, and to her husband's willingness to take an early retirement from his sergeant's position in Detroit so that she, a lieutenant, could follow the career path of many officers in large departments who move to smaller agencies to reach the top. In fact, it was her husband, Bob, who saw the ad for the Reynoldsburg position and convinced her she was ready, and was then able to land a position with the Columbus Airport Authority Police Department. Both her daughters graduated from local schools before heading off to college. Miller enjoyed being recognized in the community and having gained a reputation for sometimes returning to patrol, appearing when her officers made traffic stops or searched suspects.

Police chiefs are often called upon for civic service in small communities, and in 1999 Miller was selected grand marshal of Reynoldsburg's Tomato Festival. After uncharacteristic indecision about what to wear, she nixed the idea of a tomato-red suit and decided on her uniform. Although she does often let down her long black hair, both literally and figuratively, she decided this was not the time. "After all," she said, "they selected me because I was the police chief, and it seemed that I should look like one." As one of only a handful of women chiefs in Ohio, Miller, like many women in nontraditional fields, has been faced with the need to look the part. For this reason, Miller, in her fifties, usually appears in uniform, especially before youth groups, and also because at one state police conference a male colleague failed to recognize her in street clothes.

Miller graduated in 1973 from Marygrove College, a small, Catholic, women's liberal arts college. She began her policing career later that year. "Actually," she recalled, "like many Catholic school girls, I wanted to be a nun, then a teacher, and then a veterinarian before deciding that the best type of service career would be to be a police officer." Her decision was partially influenced by the hip, young cops of *The Mod Squad*, and while she admitted that her image of policing may have been unrealistic, she met her husband in dramatic fashion, while both were working narcotics, although not specifically as partners.

Like almost half the women chiefs, Miller held at least one graduate degree: a master's in public administration from Eastern Michigan University and another in business administration from Capital University in Columbus. In addition to the Traffic Institute, she attended a number of other police executive development courses. Successful networking has always allowed her to fulfill her interest in standards and training by serving; in 1999 she was elected chair of the Ohio Peace Officer Training Commission, a group in which she had been active for the previous four years.

Another chief whose career involved interim moves before she became a chief was Anne Kirkpatrick, who began her policing career with the Memphis, Tennessee, Police Department. A move to Washington led first to the Redmond Police Department and then to a position as director of the criminal justice program at Green River Community College in Auburn, Washington. In an unusual twist, she returned to policing as chief of the Ellensburg Police Department, a department she left in 2000 to become director of public safety in Federal Way. Kirkpatrick, who has a J.D. degree from Seattle University, is one of a growing number of women chiefs with J.D. degrees and one of a smaller number who had left policing and were able to return at the chief level. She was selected as chief in both cities by David Mosely, Federal Way's city manager, who had hired her in Ellenburg when he was city manager there.

Not all the women who have moved as chiefs had been outsiders in their first chief's job. Colleen Moore, who started working for the city of Monroe, Washington, in 1973, answering police phones, became a police officer in 1977; moved through the ranks; and was named chief in 1993. Eleven years later she was named chief at Sumner, Washington.

CALIFORNIA'S UNUSUAL CAREER MOBILITY

When Miller left Detroit for a position below the rank of chief, she was blazing a trail for women in Ohio. In a highly industrialized state where most police departments are unionized and covered by civil service regulations, positions below the rank of chief do not open up very often. When they do, the positions are usually created specifically for someone the incumbent chief wants to bring into the department. But when Susan Manheimer left the San Francisco Police Department to become the chief of the San Mateo Police Department, she was following a line of women who had become chiefs in California by leaving their home department, some far below the rank of chief.

California had seven women police chiefs in 1994. No other state had ever had that many at the same time. The chiefs led a variety of law enforcement agencies, including two municipal, four campus, and one transit police department. By 2002, the number of women chiefs had not increased greatly. When Manheimer was selected in San Mateo that year, she became one of only four women chiefs out of almost 350 municipal police departments in the state.

Although some of the women chiefs had taken advantage of California's greater mobility through its policy that permitted lateral transfers among departments at ranks below chief, Manheimer did not transfer laterally. She followed the more traditional path of leaving a large department at middle rank (she was a captain in San Francisco) to take over the 155-employee San Mateo department as the chief. A native New Yorker, at the time Manheimer was named chief she had an undergraduate degree in business management from Saint Mary's College in Maraga and a master's degree in educational leadership from San Diego State University. Like Miller, she was married, had two children, had attended a number of police management training programs, and wore her uniform frequently because "it is an important symbol of the profession."

Manheimer had career opportunities that eluded the women of an earlier generation. She worked in a high-profile unit to deter robberies, helped create and supervise a tactical investigations unit, and commanded a task force in the high-crime Tenderloin district of San Francisco. Manheimer's assignment as a decoy to attract robbers had an odd twist of its own. Her decision to embark on a policing career at age twenty-seven originated when she and her then two-year-old daughter were robbed near San Francisco's Golden Gate Park.[9]

A number of the California women who preceded Manheimer as chiefs began their careers as policewomen prior to women being assigned to uniformed patrol, and all had worked in agencies much smaller than San Francisco's police department. Each had been faced with having to make twists and turns early in her career to avoid being pigeonholed into traditional women's assignments. Manheimer, who had joined the San Francisco Police Department in the mid-1980s, might have had a hard time relating to the experiences of Hercules Chief Alicia Powers and Los Altos Chief Lucy Carlton, both of whom entered policing before women were considered for patrol assignments.

Powers began her career in 1971 in Long Beach, where it took her more than seventeen years to reach the rank of lieutenant. Recalling that she was "totally ignorant" of what she had gotten into, she was assigned to work in the jail and with juveniles before being transferred to communications only two months later, and then to the intelligence unit, where she spent three years, before becoming the first woman in the department permanently assigned to narcotics. Sometime within the first two years, she finally got to attend a police academy. This was not unusual in the 1970s, when women were often assigned without training because they were not expected to be on patrol or to do much police work that did not involve being assigned with a male officer who, it was thought, would look out for both of them. It took Powers until 1977 to be assigned to patrol, and by the time she was promoted to lieutenant, she knew she wanted to continue to move up the ranks. Because she was quite sure that would not occur in Long Beach, she accepted a position as a captain with the San Clemente Police Department, an option that would have been less unlikely outside California. It took her one more move and a number of interviews where she did not get an offer, but in 1993 she finally became a chief.

Powers had to wait longer than Miller or Manheimer to get her chance at equality. She hadn't even considered becoming a chief until after she became a captain and, she said, it took her a while after she was in charge of her twenty-person department before she realized she was a role model for other women. She was also one of a small number of women chiefs to have been selected for her job by a woman. She did not think she would have gotten the offer if a female city manager not been the decision maker.[10] Powers, who had a bachelor's degree in criminal justice and most work completed for a master's degree in community/clinical psychology, retired in 1996 but remained active in law enforcement. She was a consultant to the California Commission on Peace Officer Standards and Training (POST), which certifies police training for the state, and also worked with the California Law Enforcement Command College, the statewide program for law enforcement executives, of which Manheimer was a graduate.

Los Altos's Lucy Carlton was an accidental cop who became a chief and spent thirty-two years in policing. While a student at San Jose State University, she enrolled in a law enforcement class solely because it was the only one that fit into her schedule. The department chairman assured her that there would be no work for women in policing—possibly explaining why she was one of only three women who signed up for the course. She told him that since she was planning on teaching civics, she thought the course would work for her, and she promised not to take another if he would sign her program. Despite her promise and his prediction, in 1969 she began her career with the Milpitas Police Department as a policewoman.

Notwithstanding a number of sexist bosses, including the chief, in 1972 Carlton was permitted to join the fraud and sexual assault division, and in 1974 she became the first woman on patrol. When she retired, she said she believed that a bet between her chief and another over who would be the first to put a woman on patrol is what got her into uniform and on the street.[11] She had not been allowed to attend a police academy because of her sex, but in 1981 she became one of the first female training officers in California, and in 1985 was promoted to sergeant, teaching male officers how to investigate sexual assault cases.

Although Carlton ranked number one on the captain's test some years later, her promotion met with resistance. In 1991 Los Altos approached her about becoming chief, and she remained there until her retirement in 2001. The department had about thirty officers and a budget of about $4 million. Despite fiscal problems, she left behind a department with a motorcycle unit, a canine team, and laptop computers in its police cars.

Kimberly Plater, who retired in 2002 after a dozen years as campus police chief at Cal Poly–Pomona, began her career as the secretary to the chief of the campus police at Bakersfield while she was still a student. Unlike Carlton, she was certainly not an accidental cop; she was a tomboy who was fulfilling a childhood dream. A child of the Cold War between the United States and the Soviet Union, at the time of her retirement she recalled that she had never played with dolls but had played FBI agent versus Russian spy, her version of cops and robbers.[12] She attended a reserve academy (where part-time police officers took police training, usually on their own time and sometimes at their own expense, rather than being sent by their departments) in 1974 and was hired as a part-time officer, doing secretarial work during the day and patrolling campus residence halls at night. When Plater decided she wanted to do more with her career, both her sex and her stature (or lack of it) stood in her way. At only 5'4", she was too short for most of the departments that still had height requirements. Even if she had been taller, only 40 of the almost 600 law enforcement agencies in the state were hiring women as patrol officers at the time.

Plater became Baldwin Park's first female officer. She recalled, as had Powers and Carlton, experiencing all the tensions that come with the scrutiny of being the first. Each woman recalled feeling strongly that if she did a poor job, it would reflect on all women, and that she would become not only the first woman in her department, but also the last. Despite the pressure, or possibly because she had overcome it to go on to become a chief, Plater kept a newspaper photo of herself in full uniform under a caption describing her as Baldwin Park's first "fully functional" policewoman. The "partially functional" women were those in juvenile and records units, who, unlike Plater, would not be on the street in patrol cars.

Moving once again, in 1979 Plater joined the Covina Police Department and was again the agency's first female officer. By 1986 she had become one of the first female sergeants in the San Gabriel Valley. Three years later, with her college degree in hand, she moved to a lieutenant's position at Cal Poly–Pomona, where the chief was a woman and where she had her first opportunity to work for a woman boss, who became her mentor and recommended her for the chief's position in 1991.

Plater attributed her success not only to a mentor above her in rank, but also to other women police officers. She believed that Baldwin Park hired her only because an adjoining city, El Monte, had seven women officers and a woman sergeant. "Had they not been successful and had they not had excellent reputations, I doubt I would have been hired," she said. She believed that she performed the same function for the other women Baldwin Park hired before she left for Covina.

This is exactly what Rosabeth Moss Kanter had discerned in her observations of women "tokens" in a large corporation. When there are only a small number of women (or minority men) in a particular group or workplace, each stands out, each attracts more attention than members of the majority group, and each comes to be seen as a representative of the entire group. When this occurs, if the token woman performs inadequately, she comes to symbolize the entire group, and all members are seen as inadequate. But Kanter's theory also stated that women who meet or exceed the low expectations of the majority are seen as exceptions and therefore do not change the opinions of the larger group.[13] Luckily for Plater and the women hired after her, this portion of the theory did not seem to hold true.

By the time Plater was named chief, she was working in her fourth police department, and although she was only in her mid-fifties when she retired, she had been in policing for thirty years. Plater was somewhat atypical of many of the other women chiefs in the number of moves she had to make to reach the top, but she was similar to many in that virtually her entire working life had been spent in policing.

MANY PATHS TO THE CHIEF'S CHAIR

Susan Riseling, chief of police for the University of Wisconsin at Madison, had also made a number of strategic moves to foster her career, which had taken her to three university police departments in three states. She began her career at the University of Maryland–College Park in 1982, while still a student there. Moving up the ranks from manager of security for residence life, she relocated to become the second in command at the State University of New York at Stony Brook Police Department, and moved in 1991 to become the chief at Madison. She was one of the youngest chiefs at the time, barely thirty, and the first female chief of a Big Ten university. This was only the first of many firsts she would achieve, including becoming the first woman and first university police chief elected president of the Wisconsin Chiefs of Police Association. She was one of the first women to serve as chair of the College and University Police Section of the International Association of Chiefs of Police (IACP) and one of a handful of women on the IACP's executive committee, and she was a founding member and past president of the National Association of Women Law Enforcement Executives (NAWLEE), which in 2003 honored her as the first recipient of its Woman Law Enforcement Executive of the Year award. In 2004, she was promoted to associate vice chancellor but will remain in command of the police department. Riseling, who is unmarried, was willing to relocate because she "wanted to lead, to be depended on, and to be responsible."

The numbers of agencies in which women chiefs worked ranged from one, representing those who became chiefs in the department in which they began their career, to a high of five. Slightly more than one-third of the women reached the rank of chief in the agency in which they began their careers. Of the two-thirds who moved, just over half reported that the agency they now led was only the second one for which they had worked. Of these, some moved very early in their careers, generally leaving one department as a police officer to start at the beginning in another department: sometimes a larger one, sometimes one they perceived to be more female-friendly, or sometimes a city that was unrelated specifically to their employment. These women actually moved through the entire rank structure in the department they now headed even though it was not their first agency. Others, like Los Altos's Carlton and San Mateo's Manheimer, moved specifically to become chiefs.

When Mary Ann Viverette decided to leave the Montgomery County (Maryland) Sheriff's Department after two years as a deputy sheriff in 1979, she was taking quite a chance, since she was moving to the much smaller Gaithersburg, Maryland, Police Department, which at the time had fewer than ten officers. But Viverette has always been something of a risk taker. At eighteen, already a trained emergency medical technician, she joined the Bethesda Chevy Chase Rescue Squad after a number of men urged her to join so that a woman they didn't like wouldn't be the first woman on the squad. She left after two years to join the county sheriff's department, and then made what turned out to be her major career decision—the move to the Gaithersburg department, where she became the first woman motorcycle officer. Two instructors, unexpectedly, were women, both from the Maryland National Capital Park Police, who had been riding without much publicity for a number of years.

Gaithersburg grew as Viverette did; she was the first woman in every rank she held, and when she became chief in 1986, she also became the state's first female chief. Somewhat later she was joined by Carole A. Merhling, who in 1995 became chief of the Montgomery County Police Department, and by one of her original motorcycle instructors, Betsy Kreiter, who became chief of the Maryland National Capital Park Police.

Viverette attributed the importance of these other women in her career development to her interest in networking and in becoming a joiner. One of the organizations that she joined, the IACP, is the largest organization of police chiefs in the world, and if Viverette remains a chief until 2006, she will, based on the group's accession policy, become the first woman president in its more than 100-year history. Viverette was the first woman in numerous positions with the IACP, all while continuing to fulfill her responsibilities as chief. Like many of the women chiefs whose careers started when they were very young, she returned to school, receiving both bachelor's and master's degrees from the University of Maryland. Her position on the IACP board has required her to be away from Gaithersburg frequently. Childless, she attributed her ability to travel extensively and internationally to an understanding city government and an understanding husband, a retired Montgomery County police officer who spent much of his twenty-seven-year career in traffic and with whom she shared a Harley-Davidson until they decided to purchase a second one rather than having to decide who would ride or who would be primary when they rode two-up.

Almost 30 percent of the women have had multiple career twists and turns. Of these, about 20 percent, including Reynoldsburg's Miller, were chiefs in the third department in which they had worked. A few of the women who were in their third department were actually chief for the second time, having moved from one chief's position to another chief's position, almost always to a larger department. This mirrored the career paths of male chiefs, whose general pattern, if they are chief in multiple jurisdictions, is to move from a small department to a larger one. There are some exceptions to this pattern among men, and one of the pioneer large-city chiefs, Houston's Watson, moved from there to Austin, a smaller department.

In 2001, at least twelve women had been chief in more than one city. The number has increased since that time, although no woman was located who had been a chief in more than two agencies. This may change. Chiefs such as San Mateo's Manheimer have already had their names mentioned in conjunction with departments larger than the ones they are leading, and as more women become chiefs and as departments begin to take for granted that a woman can be the chief as easily as a man can, it is likely that the number of women who are already chiefs and who are offered opportunities in other cities will increase.

About 9 percent of the women had moved more than three times, although none more than five times. The majority of these women, like Cal Poly's Plater, made most of these moves fairly early in their career. They were less likely to be faced with trailing spouse issues if they were single at the time of the earliest moves or if they remained single for much or all of their careers. These multiple career moves, particularly among the older women, were influenced by how receptive their individual agencies were to women generally and to women in leadership positions specifically. In a profession in which entry above the lowest ranks is still rare, many of the women who spent time in more than one agency reported that they had changed jobs after reaching the rank of detective or investigator, sergeant, or lieutenant, and that the job change was not to accept a chief's position but a position in a rank equal to or higher than the one they left.

A number of these women left municipal or county police departments for campus police departments. A fast-growing segment of policing, campus departments, which are sometimes less military in their organizational structure, seem more willing to hire outsiders at the middle-management ranks, as both Plater and Riseling learned in their careers. In some cases, the moves to campus police departments did not require relocation of home and family if the departments were in overlapping or adjoining jurisdictions. Campus policing represents this type of opportunity, since women who are members of municipal police departments can become chiefs without having to move. This might explain why some of the 66 percent of the college/university chiefs who began their careers elsewhere may have accepted a chief's position at a campus located within or close to the area in which they had been working.

Maureen Rush was able to do this in 1996, when, as a lieutenant in the Philadelphia Police Department, she left to join the University of Pennsylvania's Department of Public Safety, located in the heart of Philadelphia. She was promoted twice, moving up to vice president for public safety—all without having to leave her hometown. Did she think she'd ever be a police chief? When she joined the Philadelphia Police Department in 1976, and became one of the first women to attend the police academy, her highest aspiration was to be a rape decoy, hoping to work in street clothes to draw potential rapists for her backup team to capture. The entry of women onto patrol in Philadelphia was fought by both department management and the labor unions. There was much ill will, and Rush didn't realize how accepted she had become until 1992, when her domestic partner had their baby, a girl who died a few hours after birth.

When her sexual orientation became known, she expected hostility, but found strong support from her colleagues.[14]

Janeith Glenn-Davis, a seventeen-year veteran, the highest ranking woman, and the only female commander in the 800-member Oakland, California, Police Department, took early retirement in the fall of 2002 to become public safety director and chief of police at California State University–Hayward, from which she had graduated in 1984. Glenn-Davis is one of a growing number of African-American women chiefs. Her husband was still a captain in the Oakland department, so in addition to returning something to her school, she was able to become a chief without requiring her husband and three children, the youngest of whom was still a toddler in 2004, to relocate.

There appears to be a small number of women committed to reaching the top who are willing and able to move to where opportunities appear. Jane Perlov is an example of this. Perlov, who was named chief of the 540-member Raleigh, North Carolina, Police Department shortly after the September 11, 2001, terrorist attacks on the World Trade Center in New York City and the Pentagon, used her swearing in to focus on security assessments and rapid response plans rather than on her becoming the first female chief of the department. Her focus on terrorism reflected her roots in New York, where many of her family still lived and where she had spent eighteen years with the New York City Police Department, leaving in 1998 as a borough commander with the rank of deputy chief.

Perlov's route to the chief's chair took an unusual twist when she left policing in 1998 to become Massachusetts' secretary of the Office of Public Safety, a cabinet-level umbrella agency with oversight authority of twenty state agencies employing more than 10,000 people. Perlov's detour into managing a civilian agency—even one that is considered the highest-ranking public safety job in Massachusetts—was an unusual one. She replaced another woman in the post, Kathleen O'Toole, who had had a long career in Boston policing, and who in 2004 was named Boston's police commissioner.

How did a cabinet-level political position spawn two women police CEOs? The answer provides insight into the importance of taking career chances where you find them. For O'Toole, who was from Massachusetts and had roots in state politics, the move was a natural one, but for Perlov it meant leaving a department in which she had been considered a star since she entered as a police officer in 1981 and where she had received rave reviews as a precinct commander, as the first woman to lead a borough detective command, and then as a borough commander of uniformed officers. Although it is sometimes easy in a large department to get sidetracked into glass wall assignments, Perlov never had that problem. In fact, she was known as a hard charger who went one from high-profile assignment to another, but a not-quite-chance encounter at a leadership event at Harvard University led to the decision to risk a detour rather than risk reaching a plateau at home.

One of the people Perlov networked with at Harvard was Lieutenant Governor Jane Swift, who played a role in her selection for the Massachusetts position in December 1998. Although Swift was never closely associated with law enforcement issues, she was also responsible for appointment of a woman sheriff for Suffolk County, Andrea Cabral, the first woman and second African-American in that position.

Perlov's career was atypical from the start. She was the daughter of upper-middle-class parents who expected her to be a doctor or a lawyer; they were at first horrified by her choice to become a police officer, and begged her not to tell her grandmother what she did for a living. As she began to rise quickly through the ranks, though, her family became accustomed to the idea of a daughter with a gun and a badge. When Inspector Perlov married in 1996, she was no longer the only one with a gun and a badge; she married a sergeant she had known for many years. Childless, she was able to consider relocating to Massachusetts and then to North Carolina without the concerns over child care and family relocation that had sidetracked the careers of many working women.

Yet, as Miller found out in Peoria before her move to Reynoldsburg, coming to a department as an outsider can be a mixed blessing. Although it presents the opportunity to begin without the baggage of having been known throughout one's career and having subordinates who remember you when they might have been your commanders, it may be impossible to leave behind the culture of the department that formed your attitudes and work habits. In Raleigh, the often blunt, urban style that Perlov brought with her has met with some resistance. The Police Benevolent Association leaders, who have claimed that officers' workloads have doubled since Perlov arrived, may be accurate or may be reflecting unhappiness with an outside chief, particularly a high-profile woman from a much larger police department with a different history and approach to policing.[15] One of Perlov's captains may have summed it up best: "It's culture shock," he said of Perlov's expectation that managers be available at all hours in a department where they had become accustomed to leaving the job behind when they left the office for the day.[16]

CHAPTER 5

One-Agency Chiefs: Local Girls Break Brass at Home

Sex abuse cases can be very rewarding because you are really helping people, but to help yourself move ahead, you must have supervisory experience.

—Chief Christine Ziemba
Cheektowaga, New York, Police Department

When a police [officer] who came to my high school said there was no place for women in policing, I knew he was very, very wrong.

—Chief Carolyn Hutchison
Carrboro, North Carolina, Police Department

I would like people to like me, but that's not my most important goal. I want them to respect me.

—Chief Annetta Nunn
Birmingham, Alabama, Police Department

I'm just flat-out thrilled. Dreams do come true.

—Chief Carla Piluso
Gresham, Oregon, Police Department

Annetta Nunn doesn't really remember the 1963 Birmingham civil rights demonstrations when Police Chief Bull Connor enforced existing segregation laws by turning police dogs and fire hoses on thousands of marchers. At the time she was the four-year-old daughter of a nurse and a coal miner, living in the African-American section of Ensley, Birmingham. Yet as she started to grow up, she had her own negative recollections of the police. She had seen too many officers taking bribes from local "shothouses" in return for not curtailing illegal activities. Although she could not explain why, she could sense there was something wrong in their furtive and angry mannerisms. While still in grade school she began to think about becoming a police officer. "I knew," she said years later, "that there must have been other ways it could be, and that I could get interested in this and make a difference and help people."

In spite of her dream and a bachelor's degree in criminal justice magna cum laude from the University of Alabama, Nunn was able to become a police officer in 1980 primarily because of a consent decree the city had signed with the federal government to assure that women and African-Americans joined the department. Research has shown that both women and minority males have increased their presence in departments with consent decrees faster than in those without them.[1] In fact, many advocates on behalf of women have voiced concern that the expiration of these court-ordered decrees will discourage police departments from continuing to recruit women. They have been fearful that without the decrees the numbers of women in policing will remain stagnant or even begin to decrease. But while consent decrees in the 1970s and 1980s did increase the numbers of women and minorities in policing, many of these officers, including Nunn, faced resentment from their white male co-workers and had to overcome continuing questions surrounding their suitability for policing. Nunn recalled that she would always get comments that she was hired because she was black and female, not because she was qualified and could do the job. She said, though, that she refused to let it bother her, primarily because her mother raised her and her four sisters "to believe we could do anything that anyone else could do."

Nunn proved that her mother's goals were too modest; not only could Nunn do anything anyone else could do, she did something no other woman and only one other African-American had ever done. On March 7, 2003, she was sworn in as the chief of the Birmingham, Alabama, Police Department, one of the sixty largest police departments in the country, the largest in the state, and one of the largest municipal police departments in the South. In taking over the 850-person department with a $72.3 million budget, Nunn received more attention because of her race than her sex.

Two other African-American women have held top law enforcement positions in the South: Beverly Harvard as Atlanta's police chief from 1994 to 2002 and Sheriff Jackie Barrett of Fulton County (Georgia), but Nunn was the first African-American woman selected as CEO of a major police department in the heart of the original Confederacy. Although Nunn's department was smaller than Harvard's (about 850 officers vs. 1,700, with a $72.3 million budget vs. $100 million), there are parallels between their careers. Like many men and women in policing, each joined her department while young and at a time when departments were actively trying to recruit women, and each came up through the ranks. Each was also the first black woman to hold high rank in her department. A third minority woman chief, Detroit's Ella Bully-Cummings, who was appointed in Detroit less than a year after Nunn was named in Birmingham, fought similar battles and resentment over colleagues' beliefs that she had been hired only to fulfill a quota, or to help the department avoid imposition of one.

In selecting Nunn, forty-four at the time, Mayor Bernard Kincaid minimized references to her sex, stating that his first consideration was qualifications, and that, based on her education, her experience, and the level of respect she commanded within the department, Nunn was the natural choice to replace Chief Mike Coppage. Coppage, also a veteran Birmingham officer, had been chief since 1998 and had recently been named director of the state's Department of Public Safety. Admitting that he was mindful of the diversity that Nunn brought, Kincaid termed it "secondary" to the other factors that went into her selection.

What did concern him, he said, was being able to select a candidate from within, because he believed it was important for morale and to show that anyone who started out as a beat officer had the chance to rise to the highest level of the department.[2] This was certainly the case with Nunn. She started as an intern in the city jail, a position below that of police officer and the equivalent, in the civilian workplace, of a mailroom or clerical employee who ascends to the CEO's office. Nunn is truly the local girl who caught the brass ring while remaining in her birthplace. She attended local schools, was the valedictorian of her high school class, and completed the police academy the same year that she graduated from college.

Even the 1988 movie *Working Girl*, which portrayed a secretary's rise into the professional ranks, did not capture the breadth of Nunn's success. The movie's working girl eventually achieved a windowed office and a secretary of her own, but she did not take over the firm. A romantic comedy with Cinderella aspects, the movie, which starred Melanie Griffith as the big-haired secretary who made good after a haircut, better clothing, deception, and sex, tapped into the notion that with the right combination of grit and good luck, anyone could make it to the top, a notion that is less true than many want to believe.

Such climbs to the top are actually more common in policing than in other businesses. Internal selections are generally favored by the community and by officers in the department, who often interpret selection of an outsider as a slap in the face not only of ranking officers but of all ranks.

Why the strong desire for an inside chief? The old political adage that all politics is local is particularly true in policing. Most police departments, even those without residency requirements, are made up primarily of police officers who grew up or now live in or near the community they patrol.

Despite this, only slightly more than one-third of the women police chiefs had spent their entire career in the department in which they were chief. Additional women were accurately described as internal candidates because they were members of the department at the time they were promoted, but they were "twisters and turners"—women who had made strategic moves on the way to the top, sometimes well before they actually broke brass. Thus, not all internally selected candidates have spent their entire career in one agency.

Research into why a department selects a particular candidate as its chief is sparse, but in 1986, Jack Enter found, based on an examination of the career paths of 117 male police chiefs, that insiders were more prevalent than outsiders.[3] He also found that insider chiefs had longer career paths (by which he meant it took them more years to reach chief), lower educational levels, and fewer important staff assignments. But as police chiefs have become better educated and more mobile, these findings may no longer be true. They certainly are not an accurate description of the single-agency women chiefs. Generally those women were well-educated. Except in the smallest departments of fewer than ten officers, the chief had a bachelor's degree, and most had a master's degree. Although many had an undergraduate degree before becoming a police officer, virtually all had continued their education and earned a graduate degree during their policing career.

While the women chiefs did not support Enter's study, they did closely match more recent research that identified the ten criteria that were considered important in the police chief selection process. The two top criteria were police management experience and extensive education and training.[4] Another study, of midsize police departments in California, which were defined as those with 25 to 199 total staff (60 percent of those in the state), was unable to determine any single factor more important for the selection of a police chief than the ill-defined "fit" between the individual chief and the various sectors of the community involved in the search.[5]

A study in Texas, where there are more than 1,000 police departments, found that moving up through the ranks was the most common means of attaining the chief's position.[6] In that study, where only eight of the respondents were women, more than half the chiefs were already employed by the department in which they became chief, although it was unclear whether all had spent their entire career there or had moved to that department prior to becoming the chief, as many of the women had done. About 38 percent of the Texas chiefs were employed in a different police department at the time they were named chief.

This study did not ask whether the chief had been in a lower-ranking position in the previous department and left to become chief elsewhere, or had retired from the previous department, or had moved from one chief's position to another in a different department. Less than 10 percent had not been employed in law enforcement at the time of their selection, but again, there was no indication if these might have been retirees who had left recently, or who had worked in a number of police departments but were currently not employed in one. This was the path taken by Boston's Police Commissioner Kathleen O'Toole, who was not in policing at the time she was selected, but had worked in a number of police departments, including Boston's.

Despite the somewhat idyllic portrait of the local boy—or now the local girl—making good by staying at home, only about one-third of the women chiefs were able to break the brass ceiling in the agency where they started their career. Some were truly "local girls" who were born or grew up in the cities they now served, such as Birmingham's Nunn; Cheektowaga, New York's Christine Ziemba; Springfield, Massachusetts' Paula Meara; and a number of the big-city women chiefs.

The others, such as Palo Alto, California's Lynne Johnson, regardless of their birthplaces, were viewed as "hometown" girls because they had spent their entire career in the department where they became chief. Of the women chiefs who had spent their entire career in one department, Ziemba and Altoona, Pennsylvania's Janice Freehling were also their department's first woman officer. Meara, who started her career in the early 1970s, had been told that even with a college degree, she could be hired only as a "provisional policewoman," although men with only a high school diploma or equivalency certificate received permanent, civil service appointments as patrolmen.

It is difficult to generalize about the departments that select locally for a police chief. Cheektowaga is an old, ethnic community in western New York State located near Buffalo; Altoona is also an old, industrial city whose development was influenced by the presence of railroads and railroad repair facilities. Carrboro, North Carolina, and Palo Alto are located near universities, and are home primarily to well-educated, white-collar professionals, although their populations have become more mixed in recent years. The only thing the cities—and their police departments—had in common was an available woman candidate who wanted the job.

Ironically, although Nunn was the epitome of the local girl rising to the top, her ambition originally went beyond a career in Birmingham. Like many local police officers with a college education, she thought she would use the local department as a stepping-stone to becoming an FBI special agent. Since most police departments, particularly until the 1990s, rarely required more than a high school diploma for entry as a police officer, it was—and still is—common for many officers with a college education to aspire to federal law enforcement positions, where entry requirements are higher and which are seen as more prestigious or more exciting. Federal law enforcement, though, requires attending training away from home for up to six months, followed by an assignment away from home and frequent transfer nationally or even internationally. When Nunn married Robert Nunn, Sr., in 1983, she decided it would make more sense to remain in her hometown department. Her husband, like many of the men married to chiefs, was also in law enforcement; he was former Federal Bureau of Prisons corrections officer. Their two sons were sixteen and twelve at the time of her promotion to chief.

For Nunn, avoiding the stresses of relocation and family dislocation aided rather than hampered her career. Once she became a police officer in 1980, she moved quickly through the ranks. In 1983, she was promoted to sergeant, and then to lieutenant in 1991, and to captain in 1995. Her initial promotion came much more quickly than for many of the other women chiefs, who averaged about ten years as a police officer before becoming a sergeant. In some cases, this was due to having to fight for promotional opportunities; for some it was the realization that they had achieved all they could in that rank, and needed to begin more strategic career planning; and for some it was the vagaries of when civil service promotional exams were scheduled.

Nunn had been considered for the chief's position in 1997, although at under the age of forty, she would have been very young to lead a department of Birmingham's size. Although she did not get the top job, in 2000 she became the first black woman appointed a deputy chief and she was placed in command of the department's patrol force, an assignment that enhances any manager's—but particularly a woman manager's—credibility with lower-ranking officers. By 2003, she was the media favorite for the position and was Coppage's heir apparent who had been groomed for the position of chief, including attendance at the FBI's National Academy in 1997.[7] This perception was reinforced when her appointment was announced on February 11, 2003, only a day after Coppage's new position was announced. It was greeted enthusiastically by the police union, whose president, Sergeant Allen Treadaway, said his members would have nothing but good things to say about her.[8] She was also honored soon after her selection by the 23rd Street Baptist Church in Ensley, where she worshiped, taught Sunday school, and sang in the choir.

When she was named, Nunn made no reference to her sex, but stressed instead that in each of her assignments, her primary concern had been not to be liked, but to be respected. "Sure," she said, "I would like people to like me, but that's not my most important goal; I want them to respect me." Part of Nunn's concern with being respected harked back to the consent decree, but also to her philosophy of "Christian-based" policing. When she took over as captain of Birmingham's North Precinct in 1995, she insisted that churches could and should play a crucial role in helping reduce crime, particularly domestic violence, gang activity, and drug use. North Precinct was also where she began to draw the attention that would lead to her subsequent promotions and to her selection as chief. While stressing the importance of church-based counseling, she also took a hard line on crime that involved intensive incident tracking and zero-tolerance policies in high-crime areas. She reduced crime in her precinct by 16 percent and was the only precinct commander to meet former Mayor Richard Arrington's challenge to cut crime by at least 15 percent.

Nunn, like many of the women chiefs in cities with high crime rates, was able to combine a community-based philosophy of policing with a stricter, crime-control orientation, often by focusing on gangs or youth violence. While this approach is not inherently female and has also been taken by male chiefs in cities where street crime and gangs are closely related, women have been successful at presenting themselves as simultaneously soft and stern in approaching their city's problems. In this way they seem to embody what political analysts say the first female president of the United States will have to be: a "sister mister," someone in the body of a woman with the character traits of a man, who will come from the moderate-to-conservative segment of the ideological spectrum.[9]

Since becoming chief, Nunn has also addressed a problem that has arisen for many chiefs throughout the South and the Midwest: that the community has become more racially and ethnically diverse. Many such cities previously were divided solely by race, but today many also have large Hispanic and Asian populations. It was, coincidentally, such changing demographics that led another chief, Carrboro's Hutchison, to be hired because she spoke Spanish. Nunn, who did not speak Spanish, supported efforts by the city, the police department, and Latino advocacy groups to form Alabama's first Spanish-language Neighborhood Watch group because she was concerned that many Spanish-speaking immigrants had little trust in the police, which meant they would be victims of crime out of fear of contacting police.

Nunn saw this effort as part of her philosophy of relying on the community while also upgrading the department both philosophically and technologically. She issued a new mission statement, "Serving with Dignity and Respect," that outlined her expectations for all staff, "starting with me," and also hoped to find funds for computers and video cameras in police cars. Another of her priorities was to improve training throughout the department, particularly in areas that resulted in lawsuits and poor community relations, such as excessive force and police chase policies. She was familiar with these issues, having been called upon to represent the department in a number of lawsuits. In fact, on the same day that she was sworn in, she spent the afternoon in federal court as the department's representative in a civil suit that claimed two officers had used excessive force to detain a man with a knife. She had been criticized in the past for defending the department in a number of shooting situations, a common difficulty faced by chiefs who came from the ranks of the department and who must satisfy the often conflicting constituencies of members of the department and members of the community.

CAROLYN HUTCHISON: CREATING
HER OWN DIVERSITY

Carolyn Hutchison is an unlikely local girl, a self-described Army brat who has lived more places than she can list quickly and who spent much of her youth on military bases until her father retired at the rank of colonel. While she was attending high school in Fayetteville, North Carolina, a police officer visited her class. When she asked him how he felt about women in law enforcement, he didn't hesitate. "There's no place for them," he replied. Although Hutchison set out to prove him wrong, he was almost right.

Armed with an honors degree from Duke University with majors in both sociology and Spanish, she discovered in 1981 that few police departments were eager to hire her. She joined the Carrboro Police Department in 1984 only because the Durham Police Department turned her down three times. She couldn't say for sure it was because she was a woman, since the official reason was that the department feared she would leave to go to law school. But she enjoyed the irony that in 1998, when she was promoted to chief of her thirty-three-member department, she became the fifth woman chief in the state and that one of those chiefs was Durham's Theresa Chambers.

Carrboro was only slightly more interested in Hutchison than Durham had been. Chief A. Sid Herje, who would eventually become Hutchison's major booster and mentor, spent most of the interview trying to talk her out of the job, saying she'd soon be bored with small-town policing. He certainly did not see her as someone who would ever be labeled either a one-agency woman or a hometown girl, although he did at some point see her as a potential chief. Hutchison had actually been ready to give up her search in North Carolina when the Carrboro job was offered to her, probably because the community had a large Spanish-speaking population and few officers with whom they could communicate. "Actually," she recalled, "like most nonnative speakers of any language, I could understand more than I could say, but the fact that I tried and apologized for my mistakes showed I was trying to help and that I had respect for the people I was talking to." One man was so thrilled that he asked her to marry him.

Like many of the women who attended smaller, regional police academies rather than those run by large, municipal departments, Hutchison was quickly made aware of her token status. There were only three other female recruits in a class of twenty-six, but since she was neither the first woman nor the first college-educated officer in her own department, she thought that her feelings of being different would pass. She turned out to be correct, at least in the short run. Her career within the department was relatively smooth. Although she was the first woman captain, there had been one woman supervisor, a sergeant, before her. Carrboro, located in the Research Triangle area that includes Durham and Chapel Hill, is a university community with a well-educated citizenry and well-educated police officers. Although a degree is not a requirement for the job, it was not particularly unusual for an officer to have a degree.

Hutchison was initially overprotected and put "where I couldn't do much damage." Being overprotected may be more pleasant than being ignored or resented, as Springfield's Meara and Palo Alto's Johnson were, but it can be equally damaging for a police officer's career. Police officers, particularly women, must establish credibility with their male colleagues. Since they are perceived by their colleagues to be physically weaker than male officers and less likely to engage in physical altercations with suspects, they must establish that credibility by showing a willingness to be aggressive. It is impossible to do this if you are not assigned to street patrol or are assigned only to parades or fairs, as initially happened to Hutchison. She was able to establish that she was willing and able to work on an equal basis with others in the department, and, once accepted, she received steady promotions, reaching the rank of captain in 1991.

Throughout her career Hutchison has taken advantage of training, gaining certification in a vast array of skills from crime prevention to child abuse and neglect to fingerprinting and tactical crime analysis. In 1988 she earned a master's degree in public administration from the University of North Carolina at Chapel Hill. She served as interim chief for about four months after the prior chief retired. Selected as one of the six finalists, whittled down from fifty applicants for the position, she was thirtynine and a fourteen-year veteran of the department when her selection was announced on November 10, 1998. She was sworn in a week later.

Yet it was not as clear sailing as it first appeared. Hutchinson overcame a vocal cord disorder called spasmodic dysphonia that has left her with a voice that others have described as "weak, quivery, soft, etc." "Whatever you would call it," she said, "it's not the sort of voice that you'd call 'commanding,' and it's not the sort of voice the public expects from a police officer, much less the police chief. People can't help but notice it."

Although she professes to be self-conscious about her voice, Hutchison is not particularly concerned about being noticed. If she were, she most likely would not have become pregnant prior to becoming the chief. Pregnant police officers are no longer a novelty, but Hutchison was living with a female partner. Although her sexual orientation had never been discussed with Chief Ben Callahan, who by then had replaced her mentor, she remembered him telling her she was "stupid." "As you might imagine," she said, "he wasn't too supportive," although he ultimately warmed to her daughter and wished her well when she replaced him as chief.

Hutchison's family arrangements became an issue two years into her tenure as chief when she battled to retain domestic benefits for her partner and their children. Hutchinson and her partner had been together for ten years when Jack Daly, a candidate for state auditor in 2000, challenged Chapel Hill's and Carrboro's 1994 decision to allow unmarried employees to extend health coverage to their dependents. The costs to Carrboro were small; in fact, Hutchison was the only one who registered. But the benefits to her family were huge, because they made it possible for her partner to be a stay-at-home mom to their two children.

Hutchison went more public about her private life than she had ever intended to do. She, her partner, and their two children, a son who is her partner's biological child and a daughter who is Hutchison's biological child, were featured in local newspapers. She attacked Daly's campaign, and argued that her partner and their children were as dependant on her as any other parent and children were on their family's primary wage earner. Community leaders and residents supported Hutchison not only in her appointment as chief but also in her battle to keep her benefits.

The oldest of five children and the only girl in her family, Hutchison would have preferred to remain out of the limelight, but she realized that as one of very few openly gay police chiefs, it was important for her voice to be heard. In 2003 Chief Ron Forsythe of Suison City, California, a bedroom community between Sacramento and the San Francisco Bay area, announced his sexual orientation, stating that he and his partner no longer wished to leave the county when they wanted to go out together. He indicated that his community, where he has been chief for nine years, has been "quietly tolerant."[10]

Carrboro, though, has been more than quietly tolerant. It has been featured on Websites as one of the gay-friendliest communities in the country. Hutchison's sexual orientation was not an issue in her selection as chief, in part because when the town's mayor ran for re-election, he was unopposed and there was virtually no mention that he was a gay man. Residents are equally unconcerned about her sexual orientation, she said, preferring to focus on her accessibility, her management and people skills, and her outreach to the community—especially Hispanics—during her years with the department.

Hutchison attributed part of her community orientation to her own negative experiences with police. First, there was the Fayetteville police officer mentioned earlier, but there was also a Fort Bragg Military Police (MP) officer who gave her and a friend a difficult time because they looked like hippies. She recalled: "I lived on the base; my friend had come by bus to visit me. We both had long hair, and he wore a backpack and was lugging a sleeping bag. This MP demanded that I get into his car, but I refused and told him he could follow me home and talk to my father, the base commander. He did follow me home, but he never had the confidence to meet my father. When he saw me go inside, he drove away. That's not the kind of person who should be a police officer."

These memories led Hutchison to place more emphasis on personnel than on equipment or facilities. Within four months of being named chief, she had hired three officers. She also relied on an outside assessor, unusual in a small department like Carrboro, to measure the skills of two candidates to replace her as a captain. Her other priorities were community outreach, crime prevention programs, and Spanish-language training for the department's officers. Almost twenty years after she was hired largely because she knew Spanish, she was still seeking Spanish-speaking officers. The need for this training was reinforced when she hired a Spanish-surnamed officer who did not speak Spanish, leading her to realize that it might be easier to teach language skills than to wait for someone like herself to come knocking on the door.

Hutchison knew what it felt like to almost have that same door slammed in her face. Despite that, she felt it was "pretty terrific to become chief of the only department you've ever worked in, for a community where you live and are well known." Indicating her enthusiasm at her selection, she had invited the whole department to attend her installation and had retained her involvement with Dream Makers, a program that matched Carrboro police officers with elementary school students, most of whom came from single-parent homes, and allowed the officers to act as mentors and to provide another adult influence for the students.

CARLA PILUSO: THE FIRST HOMEGROWN CHIEF

Hutchison was not the only stay-at-home chief who rose to the top of a department that wasn't her first career choice. When Gresham, Oregon, selected Captain Carla Piluso as the first chief in its twenty-six-year history to come up through the ranks, few knew that she had planned to start her career in the Portland Police Bureau. She had recently graduated from Willamette University with a degree in political science and speech, but a hiring freeze in Portland pointed her elsewhere, and in 1979 she became Gresham's second woman patrol officer. Although Piluso seemed a natural selection, she, like Hutchison, was one of a number of applicants for the position. There were originally thirty-six would-be chiefs, and when the city's human resources director told her she had made the cut to the final twelve, she thought that was his polite way of telling her she would not get the job, rather than his deciding that the most qualified applicant was the one waiting at home.

"This is my community, this is my home, this is where I've decided to raise my daughter," she said when she was selected in October 2002, referring to her nine-year-old, who attended a local school and who, she said, she would take out of classes that day after telling the principal that "the police chief wants to take her to lunch." This is exactly the type of scenario that makes up-from-the-ranks chiefs so popular with politicians and civic leaders. By selecting a local candidate, the town was also able to short-circuit what would otherwise have been a period of interim leadership. Piluso's predecessor, Bernie Giusto, had been elected Multnomah County Sheriff but would have remained until shortly before he was to take office on January 1, 2003, a situation that became unnecessary when Piluso was selected more than a month ahead of the original timetable for a new chief to be appointed. When she took over the 160-person department, more than 110 of whom were sworn officers, she became the third woman chief in the state.[11]

After ten years as a police officer, Piluso moved through the ranks of sergeant, lieutenant, and captain, and served in a number of uniform, plainclothes, and administrative assignments. Like Hutchison, she stressed the importance of having a broad range of policing experiences. She had been a field training officer, a crime scene investigator, a hostage negotiator, a domestic violence unit commander, and coordinator of the major crimes team. And like Nunn, her position immediately before being named chief was commander of field operations—the patrol force.

Piluso had a number of plans for the department, but within the first year of her appointment she was forced to draw on her popularity within the community and within the department when budgetary problems in Gresham forced her to cut positions and to reassign school safety officers to patrol duties. In total, she had to cut $1.28 million from the department's $18.6 million budget, primarily by eliminating eight positions. Because the major cost in police departments is personnel, budget shortfalls usually mean staff cuts, which can easily erode a chief's popularity. She had, though, relied on her reputation to maintain the department's credibility in the community despite having to cut a number of services.

CHRISTINE ZIEMBA: MANY FIRSTS ON THE WAY UP

Christine Ziemba wasn't actually born in Cheektowaga, and no longer lived there at the time she decided to compete for the chief's position, but residents could be excused for overlooking this technicality. She grew up in the community, a suburb of Buffalo, attended local schools, and in 1976, a month after receiving a degree from Buffalo State College, became the department's first woman officer and the first woman officer in suburban Erie County. She had worked as a police officer at the university while attending school, and she had also been an intern in Cheektowaga before becoming a sworn officer.

By the time Ziemba was named the first woman chief in western New York State and one of only a handful throughout the state, residents had gotten used to seeing her name mentioned in conjunction with "the first." Although Ziemba's predecessor, Bruce Chamberlin, had long before made her his "go-to person when things got dicey," and she was considered to be his handpicked successor, and endorsed by the local newspaper, had placed number one on the civil service list for chief, she still faced competition for the promotion.[12] Most states' civil service regulations, including New York's, follow the so-called one-in-three rule, which means that three candidates who place consecutively on a civil service list can be considered for a vacant position. In Cheektowaga, where all sworn positions are covered by civil service regulations, Ziemba was one of three inside candidates for the position of chief. One, a brother of Chief Chamberlin, asked not to be considered, leaving her and another lieutenant as the only applicants.

Despite what would seem to have been one of the easiest routes to the chief's office by a woman, Ziemba said it wasn't until she placed number one on the civil service list and Chamberlin said he was going to retire that she actually began to think seriously about vying for the position. "Even though I took every promotion test, and gave every assignment 100 percent, and kept climbing the ladder, and knew that the chief kept putting me on the front lines of many controversial and hot-topic situations, I can't say that I fully realized what was happening," she explained. Reinforcing observations by those who have studied women in business, Ziemba did not begin her career with a plan to reach the top. "In fact," she said, "I'm amazed that as chief, I interview new candidates for the department who indicate they want my job someday, and I can honestly say those thoughts were far from my mind when I was hired in 1976."

Ziemba's career has been typical of many of the women chiefs who rise through the ranks of one department, including the large amount of local publicity that has followed her since that first day in 1976, such as the obligatory comparisons to television's *Policewoman* that described her as young, slim, pretty, blue-eyed, blonde, and so on. Despite these stereotypical comments, Ziemba recalled having no problems at the Erie County Police Academy, or early in her career, once the close scrutiny ended. When she was promoted to lieutenant in 1985, she again became the focus of newspaper articles and her fellow officers, but she said that she had not anticipated any major problems and none had occurred. Since the department did not use the rank of sergeant, she was actually the first woman to hold any supervisory position. She believed that the promotion aided her career in an important way by taking her out of the detective division and back into uniform. As a midnight tour supervisor, she was able to handle a number of situations that enhanced her credibility with citizens and with officers she supervised.

Ziemba, like the other women chiefs, avoided the glass walls that often trap women in feminized areas outside the core activities of either private companies or police departments.[13] Although she found investigative work particularly rewarding and also enjoyed some of the high-visibility tasks that her predecessor assigned to her, she knew that without patrol experience, the core function of any police department, she would have a harder time moving up in rank.

Single and childless throughout her career, she was able to return to patrol and shift work. She was also able to risk the financial considerations of selling her house and moving back to Cheektowaga when she decided to campaign for the chief's position without any guarantee she would be successful. These are the types of risks that often hamper married women or those with children from moving up in rank. She realized that her ability to do this, as well as earlier to have changed assignments and hours, could have been a bigger problem for a woman with a family.

Ziemba may have been compared with Angie Dickinson of *Police-woman* early in her career, but only Lynne Johnson, another "almost local girl," who was named chief in Palo Alto in February 2003, had once been dubbed the "Goddess with a Gun." Johnson was born in Colorado Springs, Colorado, but moved to Los Altos at age five and grew up there except for the years she attended school before returning to the area to attend San Jose State University, from which she graduated with a degree in psychology. Johnson is the second alumna of San Jose State to become a police chief; the first was her hometown chief Lucy Carlton, Los Altos's chief of police from 1991 until her retirement in 2001.

Johnson's connection to Carlton is not the only way in which her career echoes some of the aspects of the California women who undertook a larger number of twists and turns to become chiefs. Each of the California women who began her career in the mid-1970s was faced with finding a department that would hire her. At about the same time that Kimberly Plater, who would become chief at Cal Poly–Pomona found her first job in Baldwin Park, Johnson was hired in 1975 as Palo Alto's eighth female officer. As chief, she led a department that was about 25 percent female, but it wasn't always that way. In 1979 she became the department's second woman sergeant; in 1982 she became the first woman lieutenant; and in 1985 its first woman captain. In 1988 she was named assistant chief.[14]

Through the early years of her career, Johnson found prejudice against women among her colleagues despite the chief's willingness to hire them. But, she said, her experiences were not as bad as those of the first woman officer, who would walk down the hall without anyone acknowledging her presence. Even in this environment, she was able to eventually prove herself and develop mentors. Some assignments, though, were women's work. The "goddess" actually was assigned to portray a masseuse for a series of massage parlor raids in 1978 when she and other women were used in undercover roles so that male customers, as well as the prostitutes working in the parlors, could be arrested.

ANNE BEERS: "LOCAL" CAN MEAN MANY THINGS

To most people, "local" means their city, town, or village. Depending on where they live, they might know almost everyone or only those on their block or in their building. For one of the women who rose to the top of her department, "local" meant the entire state. Only two women have directed state police agencies; one, Colonel Anne Beers, who was named in 1997 as chief of the Minnesota State Patrol, and was still its leader in mid-2004, had spent her entire career in the department. She began as a cadet in 1975, was one of its first three women officers, and was the first woman to hold the ranks of lieutenant, captain, major, deputy chief, and chief. Chief Annette Sandberg, who in November 2000 announced that she would retire in January 2001 after six years as chief of the Washington State Patrol, was the only other woman to head a state police department. Sandberg spent about six months with a municipal police department before becoming a trooper in 1983.

State police agencies tend to adhere more closely to the military model than local or campus police departments do. Police academy training usually takes place in a live-in setting for approximately six months; rookie officers are often not permitted to return home for the first weeks of training, and then only on weekends. Physical requirements for entry and throughout training tend to be more rigorous than those of other police agencies. Troopers (as most state police departments call their entry-level officers) are generally assigned to work alone, often doing traffic work on the interstate highway system, and they may be assigned anywhere in the state. All of these factors tend to lessen the presence of women in state police departments. Of the approximately 56,000 sworn officers employed by the forty-nine state police departments in the nation (Hawaii has no state police) in 2000, fewer than 5 percent were women.

In 1997, Anne Beers, a twenty-one-year veteran of the Minnesota State Patrol who had been its first female trooper, was named the department's chief. Reflecting the military trappings of state police departments, her official rank is colonel. Beers, who has a bachelor's degree in education, had considered becoming a physical education teacher, but when the pre-academy cadet program opened up to women, she decided to try it because she felt she would have the same opportunity to serve her community, but far greater independence, as a trooper than as a teacher. She spent about eight years on patrol, and recalled that as a twenty-four-year-old rookie trooper she had resented CBers referring to her as "Honey Bear," and had bristled when women she stopped referred to her as "dearie." Yet she loved being on the road, and said later that she took the promotion exam primarily because it didn't seem wise to be a fifty-five-year-old trooper still running up and down the freeways.

Once she left the freeways, Beers moved into a variety of assignments, including two years managing a federal project, five years as a lieutenant in charge of planning, and another two years in administrative services, the assignment she held when she was selected to run the State Patrol. By 1984 she was a lieutenant, and in 1993 she became the first woman in the more-than-500-person agency to head a district office. In 1997, when Beers was named colonel, there were only thirty-seven women in the department and only 400 women police officers of the more than 8,000 in the state. She said that diversifying the patrol force would not be easy, noting that even during the time she had been in charge of selection and training, she had been unable to promote much change.[15]

Although Beers said that no one specific person helped her throughout her career, she believed that the opportunities she'd been given to manage special assignments prepared her to lead the patrol. Beers's selection by Governor Arne Carlson met with approval within the agency, and when the administration changed, Governor Jesse Ventura's new public safety commissioner announced in early February 1999: "We're keeping Beers, that's a done deal."[16] In addition to her responsibilities running the patrol, in 2000 Beers chaired a statewide task force on racial profiling and the collection of racial data related to police decisions to question, detain, or arrest suspects. In December 2003, she publicized a campaign for safe holiday driving by returning for the first time in ten years to the roadways that had paved her way to the top.

Despite the different culture of her department from those the other women led, particularly those in charge of small, service-oriented departments in well-educated and affluent communities, Beers reinforced a point made by all of them. A career in one agency does not mean a career in one assignment. Each of the women found different ways to avoid being sidetracked into assignments that didn't lead to credibility with male peers and supervisors or into assignments that did not permit career growth. This can be a problem for women, particularly those with family or child care responsibilities that make a 9 A.M. to 5 P.M. assignment particularly appealing.

FINDING WOMEN TO PROMOTE

A 1998 survey of chiefs by the International Association of Chiefs of Police (IACP) indicated that they believed women actively sought promotions and that it wasn't difficult for women to win promotions. The chiefs, overwhelmingly men in charge of departments of fewer than 100 sworn officers, stated that their biggest problem involving the promotion of women was that there were no women to promote. Fewer than 10 percent indicated that they believed there was bias against women, while another 5 percent indicated that something in their union contracts—they were not asked to specify what—might have a negative effect on promotions of female officers.[17] The chiefs' comments about the lack of women to promote stemmed from three factors. The first was the absence of women, since 38 percent of the departments of fewer than twenty sworn officers and 10 percent of those between twenty-one and fifty sworn officers had no women officers at all. The second factor was retention. Many of the smaller departments said it was difficult to retain women because they typically left at the patrol level after about five years, primarily for better job opportunities (often with larger police departments) or due to family obligations.

Family obligations are the direct link to the third factor; what Arlie Hochschild and Anne Machung have called the "second shift"—the family, household, and child care responsibilities that may deter women from concentrating as fully on their careers as men are able to do. According to Hochschild and Machung, women work the equivalent of an extra month a year fulfilling their child-rearing and homemaking duties.[18] This represents a staggering amount of extra work, since, according to the authors, two-thirds of mothers, whether married or single, worked in 2000, and more than 70 percent of mothers with children between the ages of three and five were in the workforce. The initial interviews, conducted in the 1980s, coincided with the period in which many of the women chiefs and sheriffs were making their initial career moves toward assignments or promotions that would be vital to their success in breaking through the brass ceiling.

Studies of job characteristics that attract applicants have found differences based on sex. Women have shown greater interest in job enrichment factors such as development of knowledge and skills, rewards for good performance, and opportunities for advancement, many of which are sorely lacking in very small police departments. They also rate a supportive work climate and comfortable working conditions more highly than men. Most important, though, they have been significantly more interested than men in factors that relate to the relationship between work and home, including family-friendly scheduling and maternity leave.[19]

While little specific attention has been paid to these issues in policing, research conducted at an unnamed Midwestern police department with more than 650 police officers found that women's rates of promotions lagged behind their male colleagues and that constraints from outside the police department—overwhelmingly family concerns—contributed to the lack of parity. Although male and female officers listed current assignment or shift as the major reason they declined to participate in the promotion process, a substantially higher percentage of women (70 percent) than of men (51 percent) indicated this as their primary reason to forgo upward mobility. More telling, both male and female officers selected child care and family relations as the second reason, but the percentages were farther apart; 40 percent of the women and only 19 percent of the men indicated this was an important consideration. Although a larger percentage of women than men reported that they did not participate in the promotion process due to a perception of bias, the percentages were less far apart (21 percent vs. 16 percent). Interestingly, the women believed the administration favored men in the promotion process, and the men, particularly white men, complained of bias in favor of women or minority men.[20]

Although relocation issues have seemed to have a disproportionately negative effect on women's careers, even women who remain with the same agency for their entire career may face professional constraints based on society assigning to them a larger responsibility for child care and household tasks. Such constraints are reinforced by the large number of chiefs who have no children or small families, rarely more than two children.

CHAPTER 6

Family Power Brings Political Power: From Sheriff's Wife to Sheriff

If I ever see John Dillinger, I'll shoot him dead with my own gun.
—Lillian Holley
Lake County (Indiana) Sheriff (1933–1934)

I don't want to go up those steps.
—Florence Thompson
Daviess County (Kentucky) Sheriff (1934–1938)

Today women are becoming police officers for themselves, but I was
a stay-at-home mom who ran just to keep my husband in office.
—Gloria Bridenhagen
Door County (Wisconsin) Sheriff (1967–1969)

It was sixteen guys and me running for office.
—Norma Jean Santore
Fayette County (Pennsylvania) Sheriff (1982–1999)

When Sylvia Boma joined the La Crosse County (Wisconsin) Sheriff's
Department in 1961, the only job she was considered qualified for was
in the women's jail. Twenty years later, she ran for sheriff because, she
said, "the department needed upgrading and I figured I could do the
job as well as anybody." The voters agreed; in 1981 she became the first
woman sheriff in Wisconsin who was not the wife of the previous
incumbent.

Boma was not the first female sheriff; far from it. Almost 200 women
held the title before her, but she was one of the first women to be elected
who was not the widow or wife of the man who held the office just before

her. Boma had no idea her run was unique; after all, Wisconsin had been electing women sheriffs since 1924, and a number of states had appointed women to the position even earlier.

Well before women began to enter U.S. police departments during the late nineteenth century and the first officially titled "policewoman" was appointed in Los Angeles in 1910, a number of women were already working in sheriffs' departments, primarily as jailers (women jailers have traditionally been called matrons) or as clerical assistants (office deputies) for their sheriff husbands. By the second decade of the twentieth century, a few women achieved the position of sheriff. These women were almost always widows or wives; a few were daughters. The widows were replacing husbands who had died in office; the daughters were replacing fathers; and the wives were running as stand-ins for husbands who were barred from running due to term-limit laws. Even earlier, a handful of women had been de facto sheriffs when their husbands seemingly did not like the job and were rumored to have turned over many of their responsibilities to their wives.

Sheriff James Latty of Des Moines County (Iowa) reportedly turned management of the county jail in Burlington over to his wife soon after his 1870 election. Although she took the job seriously and her activities were reported on frequently in the local press, she was always referred to, in the style of the era, simply as "Mrs. Latty." She was praised for never having lost a prisoner despite the local practice of keeping the cells un- locked during the day. Similarly, Kate Weakley, although pregnant with their fifth child when her husband, Jim, was elected on November 2, 1875, packed up their household goods for the move to Russell City, county seat of Russell County (Kansas) and then, through the years, played hostess to visiting sheriffs and their deputies, jurors who lived a distance from the courthouse, and an assortment of thieves lodged in the county jail. Farther west and somewhat later, in 1893, in Yuma County (Arizona Territory), Sheriff Mel Greenleaf may have been the first sher- iff to actually deputize his wife so that she could take charge of women inmates. Also in Arizona Territory, Apache County Sheriff James Scott was reputed to have disliked the job so much that he permitted his wife, Linda, to fulfill his responsibilities until he resigned in 1896, before the completion of his term.[1]

Today television and movies are where fact and fiction overlap, but the same has also been true in literature. By the beginning of the twentieth century, Susan Glaspell, an early feminist author, based a fictional char- acter on a sheriff's wife whom Glaspell had observed during her career in journalism. She wrote "A Jury of Her Peers," based on Margaret

Hossack, a farmer's wife accused in 1901 of murdering her fifty-nine-year-old husband, John, near Indianola, Iowa. When Hossack was arrested at John's gravesite immediately after his funeral, the sheriff's wife rode with Hossack to the county jail, visited her in her cell, and sat by her side in the courtroom throughout the weeklong trial. After Hossack was found guilty and sentenced, it was the sheriff and his wife who drove her to prison. This received wide newspaper coverage, and, like Mrs. Latty, the sheriff's wife was always identified by her married name or simply as "the sheriff's wife."[2]

The "sheriff's wife" continued to be an unpaid, but well-defined, role even after some women were elected sheriffs on their own. A 1979 a study of rural sheriffs found that wives throughout South Dakota still functioned as unpaid jail matrons. Indicating how the family nature of jail administration could cross generations, in 1980 a West Virginia sheriff's mother served as his jail administrator, and a Missouri sheriff swore in his daughter as a special deputy to handle female prisoners.[3]

The image of Mrs. Sheriff also persisted for many of the women who were the actual sheriff. Most of the early women sheriffs were well-known in their communities primarily as widows or wives, and most continued to portray themselves in those terms. Few cast images as law enforcers, and those who did were most often associated with campaigns to eradicate gambling, illegal liquor, or similar morality-related offenses. The support the women received from county politicians had nothing to do with women's rights or women's liberation. It had everything to do with keeping the sheriff's position under either Democratic or Republican control. Although some of the women were figureheads, others were actively involved in running the office, and a few—either eagerly or reluctantly—became involved with the policing aspects of their titles.

Whatever their image, these early women sheriffs provided some historical basis on which modern women who were not widows or wives could capitalize when they began to run for office in the 1980s. The first modern women sheriffs were also aided by the varied duties assigned to the sheriff. In some states, sheriffs' deputies patrol and provide virtually all police services, but in many others, they do little direct policing, primarily providing courtroom security, enforcing judgments of the county courts, and managing county correctional facilities. This provided an opportunity for women candidates—some of whom were not career deputies or who had little or no policing experience—to appeal to the voters' sense that the sheriff, whether male or female, was as much an administrator as the county's "top cop."

FAMILY TIES HAVE LONG COATTAILS

The selection or election of women sheriffs based on their husbands' careers followed a well-beaten path to political office by generations of American women officeholders. It was, and continues to be, common for women to succeed in elective politics on the coattails of husbands or other male relatives.

One of the earliest spouse campaigns was waged in Texas, the state that has appointed more widows as sheriffs than all others combined. In 1924, Miriam Amanda "Ma" Ferguson ran for governor after her husband, Jim, who had been impeached during his second term as governor, was unable to get his name on the ballot. Using the slogan "Two Governors for the Price of One," Ferguson, a Democrat, won by making it clear that she was running in her husband's place and that he would make most, if not all, the decisions. That same year, women in Wisconsin began to run for sheriff in place of their husbands, a practice that continued until the state's term-limit laws were overturned in 1967. Ferguson won despite the opposition of newly enfranchised women, but she was defeated in her attempt at renomination in 1926; she ran again in 1932 and was governor from 1933 to 1935.

In Wyoming, there was another woman running for governor in 1924 to succeed her husband. Nellie Tayloe Ross, a Wyoming Democrat, succeeded her husband, William, who had died in office. Ross was the first woman governor in the United States by virtue of having been inaugurated sixteen days before Ferguson.[4] Like Ferguson, she served only one term, but continued to be active in Democratic Party politics and was later appointed director of the U.S. Mint by President Franklin D. Roosevelt.

In 1966, Lurleen Wallace ran to succeed her husband, George, as governor of Alabama, but she died of cancer after serving only sixteen months of a four-year term. No woman served as governor in the years between Ferguson's second term and Wallace's election. The first woman elected governor in her own right was Connecticut Democrat Ella Grasso, who was inaugurated in January 1975 after defeating her opponent by about 200,000 votes. The first Republican woman governor was Kay Orr, of Nebraska, who served one term, from 1987 to 1991. She was also the first woman to defeat another woman in a race for governor.

Women's paths to both the House of Representatives and the Senate were similar.

Throughout the 1920s, ten of the eleven women in the House were relatives of male politicians. The sole exception was Jeanette Rankin, who was elected in 1916 after promoting women's suffrage in her home state of Montana and in Washington, New York, California, and Ohio. She campaigned on a platform calling for national women's suffrage, an eight-hour day for working women, and prohibition of alcohol. She is remembered primarily for having been the only member of Congress to vote against American entry into both World War I and World War II, the first vote coming only four days after she entered Congress. Rankin served one term, 1917 to 1919, and in 1940 was re-elected to Congress, where she cast the sole dissenting vote in the declaration of war against Japan after the bombing of Pearl Harbor.

Also in 1940, Margaret Chase Smith succeeded her husband, Clyde, who had been elected to the House of Representatives in 1936 and who died in 1940. Smith, who had been her husband's secretary, was a former Republican state committeewoman from Maine's Somerset County, and she had been president of the statewide Federation of Business and Professional Women's Clubs before her marriage. After four terms in the House, she was elected to the Senate in 1948, becoming the first woman elected to both houses of Congress. In 1960 she became half of the first all-female Senate contest when former schoolteacher Lucy Cormier was her Democratic opponent. Smith won then and again in 1966, but was defeated in 1972.

The first woman to enter the Senate who wasn't "a wife," was "a daughter." Nancy Kassebaum, a Kansas Republican elected in 1978, followed her father, Alf Landon, who had been the Republican presidential candidate in 1936. The second woman senator, Maurine Neuberger (D., Oregon), filled the seat left vacant by the death of her husband, Richard. Like many current two-career families and like some of the Wisconsin women sheriffs, she and her husband had always been something of a team; they were the first married couple in the nation to serve together in a legislature when, in 1951, he was elected to the Oregon State Senate and she to the Oregon State House. The first woman to enter the Senate without officeholding family connections was Barbara Mikulski (D., Maryland), a former social worker, city councilwoman, and member of the House, in 1986. Like Margaret Chase Smith in 1960, Mikulski ran against another woman, defeating Republican Linda Chavez.

Family ties have continued to play a large role for women in elective politics. In 1998, Mary Bono won a special election to fill the seat of her late husband, songwriter and entertainer Sonny Bono. The California Republican was re-elected in 2000, and remarried in November 2001. In 2000, Jean Carnahan (D., Missouri) became a senator in place of her husband, Mel, who was killed in a plane crash on October 12. His name remained on the ballot, and when voters elected the dead man, Governor Roger W. Wilson, who had been appointed governor when Mel Carnahan vacated the office to run for the Senate, named Carnahan's widow to fill the Senate seat. Running as the incumbent in 2000, she defeated John Ashcroft, but lost her bid for election in 2002. In 2003, when Senator Frank Murkowski (R., Alaska) resigned after winning the election for governor, he appointed his daughter Lisa to fill the position. Lisa had never held statewide office, but she was a member of the Alaska House of Representatives when her father appointed her. To prevent similar, long-term appointments, a law passed in Alaska in 2003 requires that a special election be held within 60 to 90 days after a Senate vacancy occurs. The bill became law without Governor Murkowski's signature. Although neither Senator Hillary R. Clinton (D., New York) nor Senator Elizabeth Dole (R., North Carolina) succeeded her husband directly, each was preceded in elective politics by her spouse.

THE COUNTY'S EXECUTIVE OFFICER

Thomas Jefferson called the county sheriff "the most important of all executive offices of the county." Sheriffs are also the nation's oldest law enforcers and civil administrators. They are descended from the "shire reeve," the British crown's chief law enforcement officer in a "shire," an area similar to a county. Shires had been created prior to the reign of Alfred the Great, but when he ascended to the throne in 871 he enhanced their importance as military and administrative entities, thereby also enhancing the powers of the reeves, who served as the king's administrators. Their functions were similar to today's American sheriffs, including collecting taxes, preserving the peace, and holding and feeding the king's prisoners of war. During the reign of King Edgar (959–975) the reeves continued to gain in importance, and by 970 they were described in ways similar to modern sheriffs even though the actual title sheriff does not seem to have been in use until 1055.[5] The responsibilities and even the title were not unique to Britain's Anglo-Saxon kings; the Danes had an official known as a reeve, and an office similar to sheriff also existed in Holland. Within a year of their 1624 arrival in Beverwijck (now Albany, New York), Dutch settlers were policed by a *schout*. When the Dutch government organized a court system in New Amsterdam (now New York City) in 1653, the *schout* was designated to prosecute cases (as a county attorney does today) and to execute the court's orders and judgments. In 1665, less than a year after the Dutch surrendered to him, British Governor Richard Nicolls replaced the Dutch magistrates but retained the office of *schout*, now designated the "sheriff." In Albany, too, the Dutch *schout* was replaced with an English sheriff.

Even before the office of sheriff had traveled across the Atlantic Ocean to the New World, two women held the office in England. In 1216, King

John appointed Dame Nicolla de la Haye. Although she was sixty-six, she is said to have defended Lincoln Castle from the king's enemies, including French invaders. Approximately 400 years later, Lady Ann Clifford, one of the wealthiest women in England, was appointed sheriff of Westmorland. Despite her reputed talents with a crossbow, she was the last woman sheriff for the next 300 years.[6]

The first two sheriffs in North America were appointed by King Charles I in 1634: William Stone in Accomac County (Virginia) and Lord William Baldridge in Saint Mary's County (Maryland). Although colonial citizens relied on what they were familiar with to set up their institutions, they made changes to fit their own image. English sheriffs held their positions for as long as they pleased the king, but in the United States, the sheriff became an elected official, serving not at the monarch's, but at the voters', pleasure. Maryland began to elect sheriffs as early as 1776, and has done so continuously except for the years between 1812 and 1867. In 1925, the initial two-year terms were changed to four years.[7] In some states, sheriffs were limited to one-year terms. These short terms in office were to prevent individual sheriffs from becoming too powerful.

Another way that states limited the power of sheriffs was by limiting the number of consecutive terms they were allowed to serve. Wisconsin had a law limiting sheriffs to only one term (they could run again as long as someone served between their terms) until 1929, when it was replaced with a law permitting two consecutive terms until 1966, when it was changed again to allow an unlimited number of terms. This law led to the election of almost fifty women sheriffs between 1924 and 1966; all of them were wives who ran as stand-ins for their husbands. The last group of wives, who were elected in 1966, served from 1967 to 1969; no other women were elected until La Crosse County's Boma in 1981.

A major reason that voters limited the length and number of terms of the sheriff was their fear of the power the incumbent could amass. This power accrued to the office because the sheriff, like the British "shire reeve," was also the tax collector and, often, the county assessor. As the official who often set the assessed value of property and then collected the county's tax revenues, the sheriff was a powerful politician who controlled vast amounts of the county's income.

Most people associate the sheriff with the American West and think immediately of Wyatt Earp and Bat Masterson, real law enforcers who served as sheriffs. This image was falsely reinforced by *Gunsmoke*, which was televised from 1955 to 1975, in which Matt Dillon, the character portrayed by James Arness, was not a sheriff but was the local marshal of Dodge City, Kansas, in 1873. Even a real-life sheriff became confused. Jackson County (Kansas) Sheriff Daina Durham reminded voters who in

2000 questioned the wisdom of electing a woman sheriff that "We're not running the Matt Dillon type of sheriff's office anymore."[8]

Despite the blending of fact and fiction, even in the Western boomtowns of Tombstone, Arizona (in Cochise County), and Dodge City (county seat of Ford County), the sheriff spent more time serving summonses, warrants, and subpoenas for local courts; issuing licenses; collecting fees and fines; and maintaining security in the courtroom during hearings and trials than fighting crime in the streets. He was more county clerk than crime fighter. Another very important job was running the county jail, usually a small, informal place that often adjoined or was located within the home of the sheriff and his family.

These roles as tax collector and jailer—rather than as law enforcer—paved the way for the appointments and elections of sheriffs' widows and wives. Since it was common for sheriffs' wives to work unofficially in the jails and as office deputies, some sheriffs formalized their wives' positions, often so they could be paid a small salary or expenses for their labors. A few sheriffs even designated their wives as the undersheriff, the position immediately subordinate to the sheriff, generally because it paid a bit more or, infrequently, because they didn't trust anyone else. This affable, family-oriented view of the rural county sheriff was memorialized on television in *The Andy Griffith Show*, which ran from 1960 to 1968, in which Andy played the good-natured sheriff in the small town of Mayberry. Although Aunt Bee didn't run the jail, the presence of her and of Andy's young son, Opie, and their involvement in the office's activities were more representative of some rural sheriffs' wives' duties than most viewers realized.

Sheriffs were also able to appoint their wives because, as elected officials, they had an exceptionally free hand in running their offices. They could appoint friends, relatives—or spouses—as deputies. Some counties appointed the sheriff's wife to fill his position even when she had held no official position beyond "Mrs. Sheriff," particularly if the sheriff had died in office. Although Mrs. Sheriff became sheriff primarily to complete her husband's term or to serve as his stand-in, sometimes she went on to win the office in her own name.

If voters were unhappy with the selection, they could vote the sheriff—or his widow or wife—out of office at the next election, sometimes only months away and never more than two or four years away. Generally, though, voters approved of these arrangements because they understood that the position of sheriff in the early-to-mid-twentieth century, particularly in rural counties, could be compared to a family business. The sheriff received only a small salary. In some parts of the country, his income was derived solely from the fees he collected. One benefit of the job was that it often came with a residence; the downside was that the residence served as the sheriff's office and was often attached to the jail or only a few feet away from it. If the sheriff's wife worked unofficially, the county got the benefit of her labors. If her husband named her to an official position, she received a small salary that most citizens seemed to feel was her due.

These wives were not doing anything as nontraditional as it might appear. They were helping their husbands, providing housekeeping services for the jail, and keeping track of the paperwork—all jobs that broke few gender barriers. Some of the women held the title of sheriff for as little as two months; others served for years; and in the case of the Wisconsin women sheriffs, some were elected twice and one was elected three times. Although many of the Texas women sheriffs have not been positively identified, Texas appointed or elected more women sheriffs than any other state. At least seventy were appointed prior to the 1980s, and a few of the 254 counties continued to appoint widows until well into the 1980s. The pattern of rewarding widows with their husbands' position was so entrenched in Texas that it continued after some women were elected on their own records and reputations.

Texas and Wisconsin were far from the only states to have appointed or elected widows and wives, but no other states relied on this method either to assist widows or to maintain male sheriffs in office to the degree that these two states did. Wisconsin, a much smaller state than Texas with far fewer counties, has elected almost fifty women sheriffs since 1924. Primarily because of the large number of women sheriffs from Texas and Wisconsin, more than 200 women have served as sheriffs since the first documented appointment in 1916. Although little information exists about many of these women, it seems they were more likely to be offered the position if their husbands had died violently at the hands of a criminal. Other factors included the regard in which the widow was held in the community, the level of concern for her emotional or material wellbeing, the knowledge that she had been her husband's unofficial deputy, and local partisan concerns over maintaining control of the office. There is no way of knowing how many women might have been offered the position and turned it down, nor is there any way of knowing whether any fought for the job and were denied it.

Regardless of the reasons, the strength of family power as a route to the sheriff's position remained strong even after women began to be elected in their own right. More states had women sheriffs before the 1980s than since, reinforcing that it has been easier for women to follow in their husbands' paths than to establish their own reputations and records in such a male-oriented field.

FROM MRS. SHERIFF TO *THE* SHERIFF

The first woman in the United States confirmed to have moved from being Mrs. Sheriff to *the* sheriff was Daisy Dickinson, who was appointed in 1916 in Lamb County (Texas) to complete her husband's term after he died of influenza. Little is known about Dickinson, except that it didn't take long for another woman to be named sheriff. Emma Susan Daugherty Bannister, the second Texas woman sheriff, was appointed in August 1918. She had been a teacher before her marriage on September 25, 1894, to John R. Bannister, a career police officer, and she had given up her career to become his office deputy, purchasing supplies and preparing meals for the prisoners. The family was probably larger than the number of prisoners; John brought four children from a previous marriage into the family, and Emma bore an additional five children. When John died on August 1, 1918, the county commissioners appointed Emma to fill his term, and although she was offered the opportunity to run for the position that November, she declined. By the time she died in 1956, a large number of women had followed her career path.[9]

Despite the importance of the vote in women's quest for legal power, many of the women sheriffs were elected before they had gained the right to vote. In 1919, male voters elected Minnie Mae Weedin Talbott the sheriff of Lafayette County (Missouri) after her husband was killed while transporting prisoners. Talbott had a number of things in common with Bannister. She, too, was a native of her state, and she also bore five children, the oldest twelve and the youngest only two when she assumed her husband's job. Like Sheriff Bannister, Sheriff Joseph Talbott had been popular, and his death had been violent, two factors that influenced the decision of the Republicans to select his widow as their candidate. Talbott was the first woman *elected* sheriff; but her sex—and partisan politics—played a role in the campaign.

Before it became politically incorrect to comment on a candidate's sex, race, or other distinguishing factors, the *Lexington* (Missouri) *Intelligencer*, the Democratic paper that opposed Talbott, tried to convince voters that they would be "delegating and imposing responsibilities on her beyond the ability of her sex." With support from the United Mine Workers, Talbott won by more than 700 votes and served the remainder of her husband's term. She and her children lived in the jail complex, which she ran on a budget of $80 a month. She, too, cooked for the prisoners as well as for her family. Ill health prevented her from running again; she moved to Colorado to escape the symptoms of consumption, and remarried there. She died in Texas in 1962.[10]

State historians have disputed the career of Clara Dunham Crowell, sheriff of Lander County (Nevada) from 1919 to 1921. Clara, the youngest of five daughters, married George Crowell and by 1911 was the mother of two small children. George was active in Lander County politics but was defeated in two runs for sheriff until he was elected in 1916 and re-elected in 1918. He died of bronchitis shortly after taking office in January 1919. After assuring citizens that being a woman would not "in any way interfere with the performance of duty," Clara was appointed to the position and may—or may not—have been the first crime-fighting woman sheriff. She was described by one commentator as "a woman of action," who "collared some crooks by working undercover" and undertook a number of dangerous assignments, but her exploits were dismissed by another as "unsubstantiated claims" about a woman who was largely unknown and whose appointment was resented by men in the community. Whether her efforts were fact or fiction, Crowell did not run again even though women in Nevada had by then won the vote. She remained in the county until 1940, working in more "feminine" professions, first as a nurse and then as an administrator at the county hospital.[11]

By the 1920s women sheriffs were not the oddity they had been only a few years earlier. Ruth Lane Garfield was appointed by the Golden Valley County (Montana) commissioners in December 1920 to complete the two-year term that her husband, Jesse, had been due to begin on January 1, 1921. When the county was created on June 24, 1920, Jesse was elected its first sheriff, and when the county held a second election that November, Jesse was re-elected to what would have been a full two-year term. On December 6, while investigating a dispute between two neighbors, he was shot by one of the disputants, and died on December 18. Ruth, who had wed Jesse in 1912 and borne his son, Ford, in 1913, served her husband's full two-year term. In an early sign of equality, she received the same salary he would have ($166 a month), although she admitted in an interview with the *Billings Gazette* in 1966 that she had never carried a gun because she felt that if she had, "some man would have taken it away from me." That might have been Ruth's reason for not carrying a gun, but a number of the women sheriffs as late as the 1960s indicated that although they did not carry a gun, neither had their husbands. Regardless of her concerns over being disarmed, Ruth served her full term and her successor, Dick Carr, appointed her his undersheriff and probation officer, positions she retained for the duration of his two-year term. After four years in law enforcement, her career ended as suddenly as it had begun.[12]

SHERIFF ROACH TESTIFIED AGAINST HER HUSBAND'S KILLER

Not all the women sheriffs were mere objects of pity waiting for jobs to be offered to them so that they could keep a roof over their family's heads. Women like Lois Cole Roach fought to win the job by either appointment or election, and some fought even harder to retain it at the next election. Political considerations also played a part; many were selected by party leaders as a way to retain the position until at least the next election, rather than see it go to a member of the other political party.

Despite local political support, Roach fought tenaciously for her husband's job and then testified against her husband's killer while fighting to retain her job. Sworn in on March 11, 1922, as sheriff of Graves County (Kentucky), Roach was in office and oversaw court security during the murder trials of her husband's accused killer, who had been one of his deputies at the time he died. Lois and John T. Roach had met while they were studying at the Western Kentucky Normal School in Bowling Green. They were married in 1917, and returned to Mayfield, Kentucky, where Lois taught school before assuming her husband's job after his death. Although she had never worked in the sheriff's office, when John was shot and killed by a deputy in a dispute over salary on March 6, 1922, residents petitioned for his widow to fill the vacancy. In addition to concern for her financial well-being, politics and her own actions to win the job played a role in her selection. John Roach, who had grown up near Mayfield, was a well-known and popular local politician. He had previously served in the sheriff's office, and when he ran in 1917 to represent the county in the Kentucky General Assembly, he won all thirty-four precincts. Lois, twenty-six, the daughter of a prominent Barren County (Kentucky) farmer, and a mother and a teacher, was also popular, and it was likely that local citizens envisioned them playing a role in countywide or statewide politics for years to come.

By the time John Roach decided to run for sheriff in 1921, women had won the right to vote, and he and other Republicans believed this might help them hold onto the office. Roach had been only the second Republican sheriff in the county, and when he was killed, his backers were concerned that their efforts to wrest the position from Democrats "would be buried with their dead sheriff" if they did not find a way to prevent an immediate election.[13]

Ironically, Roach's victory in November 1921 set in motion the dispute that led to his death. By the time he took office on January 1, 1922, there were misunderstandings among his deputies as to who would work full-time and who would work part-time, and to which part of the county each would be assigned. Not only prestige, but also money, played a role. When Sam Galloway shot the sheriff three times on March 6, Galloway was disgruntled because he believed he had been promised the job of chief deputy at $1,500 a year, but was downgraded first to a regular deputy at $70 per month, and then to a part-time deputy earning only $50 a month. The shooting occurred in the sheriff's office, and Galloway was immediately taken into custody by other deputies.

Roach was buried within twenty-four hours of the shooting, the same day on which the grand jury returned an indictment charging Galloway with murder. The next day, within only forty-eight hours of the shooting, politicking surrounding who would be the next sheriff had begun. The coroner, who upon the death of the sheriff became the chief officer of the county, supported Roach's chief deputy, Norman Carr, who was also the son-in law of the county judge whose task it was to name a sheriff until the next general election. When Carr withdrew from consideration, the judge offered the position to the county tax commissioner, Perry Roscoe Brown, if he would agree to give Lois two-thirds of the proceeds of the office while he served as sheriff. Brown had been elected by an overwhelming majority of voters, so this seemed a logical compromise.

But Lois Roach had other ideas. Although her husband had been dead only three days, Lois let it be known that she wanted to be appointed sheriff and also to hold the job of revenue collector that came with it. Despite the groundswell of support for her, the judge believed the position of sheriff was "a man's job." He soon learned, though, that Lois had other allies, including the company that bonded the sheriff. In states where sheriffs collect fees, they must post a surety bond before they are permitted to assume office. The firm that had insured John threw its support to his widow, as did the local newspaper and the 3,000 people who signed petitions demanding that she be appointed.

To support her efforts, Lois devised the compromise that was ultimately agreed to—rather than Brown becoming sheriff and providing for her, she would become sheriff and would accept Brown as her chief deputy. Continuing the whirlwind pace at which this drama was unfolding, she was sworn in on Friday, March 11, only five days after her husband's death. She immediately announced that the sheriff's office would be open for business on Monday, March 13, and she appeared that morning to begin her term.

All, though, was not as calm as it seemed. On April 4, she appeared at court for what was to have been the start of the trial of her husband's killer, only to learn that the trial had been postponed due to defense claims that public sentiment, including the petitions to have her named sheriff, were an indication that Sam Galloway could not get a fair trial during the current court term. The trial was put off until June, but by then Lois was fighting another battle. Democrats were trying to get her out of office by forcing an interim election, a move that ultimately failed. She was still the sheriff in June 1922, when she testified at Galloway's trial before a standing-room-only courtroom crowd. Galloway pleaded self-defense; claiming that he believed Roach was about to shoot him. A hung jury resulted in a new trial, and the death of one of the jurors forced a third trial. On August 4, 1922, the third jury convicted Galloway of voluntary manslaughter and sentenced him to seven years at Eddyville Penitentiary. Lois declined the opportunity to escort Galloway to prison; instead, her deputies rode the train with him.

Meanwhile, Lois had learned in July that there was no need for a special election in November 1922, and that she would be able to serve as sheriff until the election in November 1923, when she defeated two opponents, including Norman Carr. With strong support from women voters, she won by a majority of 1,248 votes and used this support to undertake a campaign to rid the county of moonshiners. Lois did not run again in 1925; she was succeeded by Perry Roscoe Brown, the tax collector she had accepted as her chief deputy. Lois neither returned to teaching nor retired from politics. Despite the backing she had received from the Republicans, she changed parties and in 1926 led the women's campaign committee to elect Alben Barkley as Kentucky's governor (he would later become Harry S Truman's vice president). She died on May 19, 1979.

WELL-KNOWN INMATES BRING UNWANTED FAME

Neither of the two women sheriffs who achieved celebrity sought it, and neither remained in the limelight after her fleeting fame. Both were widowed mothers whose jail inmates catapulted them into controversy.

Sheriff Lillian Holley was completing the term of her husband, Roy, in Lake County (Indiana) when famed gunman and gangster John Dillinger, who was awaiting trial on a charge of having murdered an East Chicago, Indiana, policeman, escaped from her jail on March 3, 1934. Dillinger walked out of the "escapeproof" jail after intimidating guards with a wooden pistol he had whittled and darkened with shoe polish. The escape made page 1 of newspapers around the nation. To make matters worse, Dillinger fled in Holley's new black sedan equipped with a police shortwave radio, and the media made her the butt of numerous jokes. Incensed, she told reporters, "If I ever see John Dillinger, I'll shoot him dead [or through the head, as others quoted her] with my own gun." No one doubted her; the *New York Times* described her as a "crack shot" who carried an automatic pistol and who practiced on the firing range with her deputies.

Holley, the mother of eighteen-year-old twin daughters, had been appointed after Roy was shot dead on the seventeenth day of his second term as sheriff. She survived attempts by Indiana politicians to make her the scapegoat for Dillinger's escape even though it was Lewis Baker, the jail's warden, and at least five male jailers who were locked in cells by Dillinger. The manhunt ended four month later when Dillinger was killed in a gun battle in Chicago with Federal Bureau of Investigation (FBI) agents. Holley, described as "gutsy, tenacious and as fireproof as asbestos," completed her term but did not run for election. She had been photographed with Dillinger prior to his escape, and when she died in 1993, at the age of 103, the photo often accompanied her obituary. Other photos depicted her standing in front of a cell, dressed in a midcalf-length long-sleeved dress and lace-up high-heeled boots, her five-pointed star pinned on her chest.[14]

Florence Thompson, the only other woman sheriff who gained international attention, was sheriff of Daviess County (Kentucky) at the time of the hanging of Rainey Bethea on August 14, 1936, for rape and murder. Media coverage came from as close as Paris, Kentucky, and as far away as Paris, France. Most wondered whether the hanging would be done by the "lady sheriff." It became such a media spectacle over speculation as to whether the hangman would be a hangwoman that it ended up being the last official public execution in the country.[15]

Thompson, a quiet mother of four, was appointed sheriff when her husband, Joseph Everett, died of pneumonia. She unwittingly contributed to the circus atmosphere by refusing to indicate in advance whether she would pull the lever to release the trapdoor that would bring death to Bethea. Widowed on Good Friday, April 10, 1936, Thompson became sheriff only three days later. In a detailed account of the case, Perry T. Ryan, a Kentucky prosecutor, found that although Thompson was known to have sometimes pinned her badge to her dress, she functioned primarily as an administrator and left most of the police duties to her deputies. But she was also known to have made arrests when none of the deputies were available. Finding it difficult to fulfill her dual roles as a mother and as the sheriff, she sent her three sons to boarding school soon after she was appointed; her daughter remained at home with her.

Bethea's crime, committed within two months of Florence's appointment, was an emotional one. Bethea, a twenty-two-year-old African-American, raped and then killed Lischia Edwards, a prominent white, seventy-year-old widow, after he entered her second-floor apartment, apparently intending to steal her jewelry. Bethea, intoxicated at the time, woke Mrs. Edwards. Within a month he was caught by members of the Owensboro Police Department, tried, convicted, and on June 25 sentenced to death.

Florence had been in office for only four months when she was faced with overseeing the hanging. Journalists had a field day wondering if she would perform the execution. She did not; it was a task she turned over to A.L. Hash, a former Louisville police officer who was drunk and nearly botched the job. A crowd of more than 20,000 people witnessed the hanging, and although many newspapers criticized Thompson and even ridiculed her, she also received letters from men who wanted to date her. Voters approved of her decision; when she was forced to run for election in November 1936, she received 9,811 votes, and her two opponents received a total of three votes between them. After leaving office in 1938, she was appointed a deputy by her successor. She remarried, but despite attempts to get on with her life, she was never able to put the hanging behind her. Her daughter later said that Sheriff Thompson had nightmares during which she screamed, "I don't want to go up those steps."[16]

WISCONSIN'S UNUSUAL PATTERN OF "TWO FOR ONE"

Western states—whether because women won the vote there sooner or because smaller populations required that they use talent where they found it—were more likely to appoint or elect women to nontraditional positions than other parts of the country. Southern and border states often appointed sheriffs' widows as part of larger political battles due to the importance of the sheriff's office in countywide politics and its revenue-collecting functions. The northeastern portion of the country, where large populations made talent readily available and where large cities' governmental functions negated much of the power of sheriffs, appointed the fewest widows.

Patterns are most difficult to discern in the Midwest, where each state acted individually. Wisconsin had the largest number of women sheriffs, almost fifty (second only to Texas); Michigan had fifteen between 1921 and 1992; and Illinois, Ohio, and Minnesota had only a handful. Only two of the Michigan women were elected. The first Michigan woman sheriff, Estella S. Gates, held office in Benzie County from 1921 to 1922;

and the last, Brenda Garrard Skyles, held office in Lake County from 1990 to 1992. Ileea H. Henkel, a Montcalm County Republican, was the first elected female sheriff in Michigan. She was nominated to take her husband's place, and won on the fifth caucus ballot, after he had been slain in an altercation with two moonshiners. A teacher, she held office from September 1926 until the end of 1928.[17] In 1939, Ida Bergh was appointed when her husband died within hours of beginning his second term in Keweenaw County. Her son, William Howard, quit his job in Detroit to serve as her deputy. She was re-elected three times, and was said to have reduced crime and applied a philosophy of "kindness and cleanliness to the courthouse and jail." Later she and her son opened a group of cottages in Copper Harbor, a resort area in the Upper Peninsula.[18]

Bergh was not the first woman to appoint her son. Helena Dolder, DeKalb County (Illinois) sheriff after the death of her husband in 1928, appointed her son Fritz as chief deputy. The jail was known as "the lace curtain jail" after Dolder placed curtains on the windows of the room in which her son slept. Despite this feminine touch, which was also a feature of police departments' women's bureaus and juvenile courts, Dolder told prisoners that they could "eat or go hungry" when they complained about her food. She ran and won in 1930, and like many of the other women sheriffs who undertook crime-fighting roles, she gained popularity through her efforts to curtail gambling and to undercut liquor distribution in her county.[19]

In Ohio, "Sheriff Maude," the widow of Fletcher Collins, in 1925 became the first woman to complete her husband's term. When she ran in the Democratic primary that August, she won decisively (957 votes to 232 for her opponent), and in the general election she received 3,182 votes, almost twice the number her opponent received and the largest vote total in Vinton County. Collins had her been husband's jail matron, and, like Roach, she testified against her husband's killer, a local man he had been trying to arrest when he was shot dead. While serving her own term, she solved a double homicide by proving that the suspect was not male, based on the depth of footprints in the soil. When she put the boots on her own feet and saw how shallow the impressions were, she hypothesized that the killer was a woman, and she was correct. At the end of her term as sheriff, Collins was elected clerk of the courts and later worked as a matron at the Columbus State School. She died in 1972, at the age of seventy-eight.[20]

With the exception of these few women, the history of women sheriffs in the Midwest is primarily a history of Wisconsin's long and unusual history of electing women, beginning in 1924, when Hannah Saunders replaced the outgoing sheriff, her husband, Charles. Many of Wisconsin's women sheriffs were elected more than once, and one, Katherine Moore, was Polk County sheriff three times.[21] More than one-third of Wisconsin's seventy-two counties have elected women, some as many as four times. What was most unusual about Wisconsin was that the women were elected not because they were widows, but because their husbands were alive and unable to run for office due to term limits. Until 1966, the last election before the law was changed, these women ran as stand-ins to maintain their husbands' hold on the office.

Few other states in any part of the country followed this pattern, and then only rarely. One that did was Moore County (Tennessee), whose county seat is the tiny town of Lynchburg, the home of Jack Daniel's whiskey. Of the county's two women sheriffs, one, Pearly Ervin Hobbs, was appointed in 1932. The other, Margaret Wiseman, was elected in 1950, after her husband had reached the term limit and was unable to run again. As in Wisconsin, her husband, Thomas, served as her chief deputy; then, beginning in 1952, he was elected to five additional terms. According to local lore, neither Sheriff Wiseman carried a firearm.[22] Gloria Bridenhagen, sheriff of Wisconsin's Door County, said that was still true for her and her husband in the 1960s.

Many of the Wisconsin wives had been active in their husbands' work before their elections. Since the majority of the sheriffs and their families lived in the jail, it would have been almost impossible for the wives to avoid some involvement in their husbands' work. Even if they did nothing else, they were expected to cook meals for the prisoners, and often to supervise any visitors to the jail. One of the most active law enforcers was also one of the first women sheriffs. Mary Jacobson (Barron County) had been her husband's deputy prior to taking office in 1926, and had arrested a visitor to the jail who was in possession of moonshine. The local newspaper commended her on a job well done and congratulated the voters for having elected her. The man she arrested was, no doubt, less pleased; he was found guilty, fined $200 and court costs, and sentenced to three months in the very jail he had visited under the supervision of the woman who had locked him up and who was now the sheriff.[23]

The practice of electing wives became so widespread that in 1950, six women, all Republicans, were elected to succeed their husbands. Although they ran to skirt the law, the six still hold the distinction of being the largest number of women sheriffs to serve at the same time in the same state. In 2000, Kansas, with half that number of women sheriffs (three), had the largest number serving at the same time since 1950. Katherine Moore, elected in 1950, held office three times (1945–1946, 1951–1952, and 1957–1958), earning her the nickname "First Lady of the Law" and a congratulatory letter from J. Edgar Hoover, then director of the FBI. Indicative of the women's reconciling of their roles as wives and sheriffs, Moore served as the first female board member of the Wisconsin Sheriffs and Deputy Sheriffs Association at the same time that she served as president of the association's women's auxiliary. Residents also accepted the Moores' overlapping roles. They were routinely treated as a team; when James retired for the last time at the end of 1970, the local newspaper reported, "Moores Retire After 40 Years."

By the time a large number of women were elected again—1966, when five women, again all Republicans—Wisconsin's legislators were ready to change the term-restrictions law to permit sheriffs to succeed themselves for an unlimited number of terms. Each of the five women who won in 1966 was similar to those who had run before her. None sought the position for any reason other than as a stand-in for her husband. One, Delores Lein (Sawyer County), recalled that she had specifically run on a platform promising two for the price of one, which voters understood meant that her husband, Ernie, would continue acting as sheriff as her unpaid deputy. Whether, in an age of blossoming women's liberation, this seemed too much of an anachronism, or whether some politicians feared that women would soon run on their own, it appeared that changes in society contributed to the decision to endorse unlimited terms for sheriffs. The change resulted in the disappearance of women sheriffs in Wisconsin until 1981, when Sylvia Boma, the La Crosse County Republican, was elected to a term that began on January 1, 1982.

Boma was a career employee of the sheriff's department. She had worked as a jail matron and then a deputy, but she, too, had a family connection to the position. Her father-in-law had been the sheriff in the 1950s and 1960s. Boma's ties to the office were complicated; both she and her husband, Bill, had worked for her father-in-law, but her husband had become a Wisconsin state trooper. She tried to talk him into running, and when he didn't, she did. She served two terms before being defeated in the 1986 primary.

Boma's decision to run as her own woman reflected not only family changes, but changes in law enforcement as well. By then, matrons had won a number of lawsuits requiring that they receive equal pay and equal opportunities with male deputies. The most important of these was *County of Washington v. Gunther*, in which the Supreme Court ruled in 1981 that under Title VII of the 1972 amendments to the 1964 Civil Rights Act, it was unlawful to pay matrons less than male personnel working in men's jails.[24] Boma recalled that she benefited from a similar pay discrimination lawsuit brought by Dorothy Lord, who became the first woman jail employee in the state to advance to the rank of sergeant after her own lawsuit for equal pay for women. Lord continued to work in the sheriff's department throughout Boma's tenure and after her defeat. Lord retired in 1988 after seventeen years with the department, and died in March 2003, at the age of seventy-nine.[25]

Other women began to run on their own records at the same time Boma made her decision. One was Fayette County (Pennsylvania) Sheriff Norma Jean Santore, who had been in law enforcement for twenty-five years when she became sheriff in 1982. A widow with two grown children, she ran when the incumbent decided against another race and encouraged her to run. This is similar to many of the current women sheriffs, who also were encouraged to run by the men they succeeded. Despite support from her sheriff, Santore had considerable opposition; she remembers that in her first campaign it was "sixteen guys and me." She won, and after beating her opponent in her second campaign, ran unopposed for her third and fourth terms. In 1996, her ten full- and part-time deputies were responsible for court security and prisoner transport, served court papers, and oversaw the sales of tax delinquent properties, but they were not certified police officers and did not provide patrol services to the county.[26]

Santore was not as successful as some of the earlier women sheriffs in appointing family members to assist her. In 1995 she was criticized for appointing her son Mark, who had no prior law enforcement experience, as a deputy and then promoting him to chief deputy. Although she claimed he met the requirements for the job, in 2000, after she had announced in 1999 that she would not run again, she was fined $4,000 by the State Ethics Commission for attempting to obtain salary increases for her son. Although he ran to replace her, Mark was defeated by Gary Brownfield, a retired state trooper.[27] Santore claimed that politics influenced the judgment against her, but her unsuccessful attempt to ensure a continuing connection with the sheriff's position for a family member is an ironic reversal of the history of women being appointed or elected sheriff for just such family reasons.

CHAPTER 7

Modern Women Sheriffs: Getting Elected on Their Own

My opponents all wanted to be the toughest guys in the valley; I explained I'd be the CEO.

—Sheriff Carolyn "Bunny" Welsh
Chester County (Pennsylvania)

I wouldn't have lobbied for the job or run if the sheriff hadn't suggested it.

—Sheriff Beth Arthur
Arlington County (Virginia)

I get along very well with most of the Texas sheriffs. They may be good ole boys, but I'm from Texas, too, and I'm a good ole girl.

—Sheriff Margo Frasier
Travis County (Texas)

One more glass ceiling has been shattered, and I'm delighted it happened here in the South.

—Sheriff Jackie Barrett
Fulton County (Georgia)

"If you mess up, 'fess up," is how Chester County (Pennsylvania) Sheriff Carolyn "Bunny" Welsh described her management style. Being an elected official has affected her life in many ways, and not the least is her language. Before becoming one of the few women to succeed in being elected sheriff, she was one of the few to succeed as a building industry executive. She admitted that in her prior CEO life, she was just as likely to replace "mess" with a five-letter word starting with "s" that, in addition to its slang meaning, is also the description of a common item employed in the building trades.

If Welsh really followed her own advice, she would be advising the county's Republican organization that it, too, almost messed up when it reluctantly supported her for sheriff. The response to her interest in running in 1999 was somewhere between incredulity and disdain. She couldn't even get a straight answer as to who might be her primary opponents. Not too surprisingly, they were all men; all had more law enforcement experience than she had; and all tried to prove to the Republican county officials who would select the candidate that they were tough. In fact, as each tried to convince the delegates that he was the toughest cop in the valley, Welsh displayed an organization chart with the sheriff on the top, the chief deputy underneath, and then the four lieutenants who each supervised one of the divisions of the sheriff's department. "That would be me, on top here," she explained, "and I've been a CEO, I've supervised men in a male industry, and I can handle this multimillion-dollar budget with its sixty employees because I've done more than that; I've handled businesses a lot larger."

It took her until the second vote to win, but how did she ever think she could? "This is an upscale, well-educated community. The delegates are doctors, lawyers, merchants, people like that, but none of them really knew what the sheriff did. I explained that it wasn't *High Noon*; Gary Cooper wasn't going to march through downtown West Chester (the county seat) looking for a shoot-out and then throw down his badge and ride off into the sunset. The sheriff is the chief executive; supervising people who don't do road patrol, but who transport criminals, oversee firearms registration, sell real estate to satisfy tax liens, and similar kinds of things," she explained. The department also administered a number of community programs, including the D.A.R.E. drug resistance program in the schools, the TRIAD Program that helps senior citizens protect themselves against fraudulent vendors, and a junior deputy program aimed at youths. Although the deputies had limited patrol jurisdiction, they provided support to other departments' officers in emergencies, and they were authorized to stop and detain someone if they observed a flagrant violation of the law, but they did not provide routine patrol service within the county.

Although Welsh did things her way, including keeping her nickname "Bunny" despite advice that it would make her seem too fluffy and feminine to get elected, she didn't just decide one day to run for sheriff. She knew that she needed to have at least some police experience to be taken seriously as a candidate. Years earlier, she had become a state constable so that she could attend police training, which, she said, "I absolutely loved, including the part where I had to do defensive tactics with a partner who was a lot bigger than me, but at least close to my age. We were both over forty. I wanted to prove something, but I didn't think I needed to throw any twenty-year-old ex-Marines on the ground to make my point." The training and her work in the constable's office were sufficient for her to win the support of the Chester County Police Chiefs Association. That, combined with her party's endorsement in a county that is overwhelmingly Republican, virtually assured Welsh, fifty-six at the time she ran, the job. Even after one of her convention opponents switched to the Democratic Party to run against her, she won with about 60 percent of the vote in the 2000 general election.

Although Welsh maintained that she never considered her sex an issue, she has seemed to go out of her way to remind people that they have a woman sheriff. When she and her almost totally new command-level staff were sworn in on January 2, 2001, she announced that she would bring PMS to her new position. She was referring, she quickly added, to "patience, mutual respect, and a sense of humor." Welsh has learned, though, that public sector and private industry humor can be very different. When she selected as her new chief deputy a man who had previously held the Mr. World bodybuilding title and glibly said that she thought all women should be surrounded by beautiful men, she was quickly chastened by politicians who were more experienced. Welsh said she was razzed, got some ugly letters, and came to realize that the remark would have been inappropriate if made by a man, and therefore also was not right for her, although the chief deputy, his wife, and the rest of her staff took it in the vein she had intended. She also was sued by the former chief deputy, one of her rivals for the sheriff's position, but the agency is not civil service and it was within her power to select a chief deputy of her choice.

As if that weren't enough, Welsh risked comments about women having a penchant for redecorating by doing just that to her predecessor's office, although she said it was because he hadn't let her into the office until he vacated it. She also approved a redesign of the deputies' uniforms and patches immediately upon taking office. "I was afraid it would be seen as typical female, but the staff wanted it," she said, a view confirmed by a local newspaper article.[1] Although she carries a firearm, Welsh tried to steer constituents away from thinking of her as the legendary, gun-toting, sharpshooting Annie Oakley. She tackled head-on the issue of her wearing a uniform, something she said she did not feel comfortable with because it appeared "too much a costume after so many years as a civilian

CEO." She wasn't sure how to respond to requests from her deputies that she, too, get one of the new uniforms, although she was leaning toward getting one and wearing it primarily for ceremonial events.

One ceremonial event Welsh had attended in street clothes was the funeral for a sheriff she had befriended in October 2000 at the National Sheriffs' Institute Executive Program, a two-week training program run by the National Sheriffs' Association for newly elected sheriffs. She recalled how amazed she had been that twenty-four strangers could become friends in such a short time and how proud she, the only woman in the class, was to have been elected class president. One of the sheriffs she looked forward to relying on for advice was DeKalb County (Georgia) Sheriff Derwin Brown, who was also a sheriff-elect just like her, but had extensive law enforcement experience. Brown was shot and killed in December 2000, in the driveway of his home. Welsh recalled later that Brown had told her he had received threats from the man ultimately convicted of masterminding the crime: Sidney Dorsey, the former sheriff, who had lost the election to Brown and who, according to prosecutors, had hoped to win the job back in a special election that would become necessary with Brown's death.[2]

The Georgia case stemmed from what was believed to have been years of corruption in the department, which Welsh attributed in part to the absence of new blood that existed in many sheriffs' departments. That was, she said, part of her own reason for running. "I felt that if I hadn't run when the prior sheriff decided not to, his deputy would have run, and they could have just kept switching the job back and forth indefinitely." Although she was not aware of it, Welsh had described exactly what had led to Wisconsin's experience with women sheriffs, who until 1966 had switched back and forth with their husbands as a way to retain the position despite a term-limit law.

Welsh, who described her department as the law enforcement arm of the Chester County Court of Common Pleas, also ran because she wanted to enhance the department's role and image. After eighteen pipe bombs were discovered in the county between March 2000 and June 2001, she enhanced court security and added to the "staff" a bloodhound to work with a deputy partner to help track lost children and Alzheimer's patients. She said it was somewhat coincidental that both the dog and her handler were female. She also instituted free firearms safety courses for those who renew firearms licenses.

In Louisiana's Calcasieu Parish (County), Sheriff Beth Lundy instituted firearms safety courses at the Southwest Louisiana Regional Training Academy, including some that were women-only. Although the program was motivated partially by an increase in crimes against women, the aim was to provide women with greater familiarity in gun use, to review legal issues surrounding gun ownership, to teach home safety, and to permit women to get on a range and practice loading, firing, and unloading their weapons under the supervision of a sheriff's department certified firearms instructor.

Welsh, the divorced mother of four children and grandmother of two at the time she took office, was an only child from a political family in nearby Delaware County. Her father, John R. Welsh, whom she described as her mentor and her inspiration, was an Upper Darby councilman for whom a branch of the municipal library was named. She said she had been known as "Bunny" at least since she was a teenager, and that since her move to Chester County, friends and colleagues had come to know her by the nickname. She attended local schools and the University of Pennsylvania's Wharton School of Finance and Commerce.

Partially because one of her daughters lived in Chester County's Nottingham Township, Welsh jokingly refers to herself as the sheriff of Nottingham, drawing on the Robin Hood legend to humanize the sheriff's department. She was unaware that there was a sheriff of Nottingham, England, who was also a woman—Joan Casson, who had taken a long career break to raise her family before being elected to the Nottingham city council in 1995 and then being named to serve from 2001 to 2002 as Nottingham's sheriff. Unlike Welsh, Casson had no need to be concerned about a uniform; her position came with a white and yellow 18-karat gold chain with enamel and pearls, and a blue silk robe trimmed in black velvet that is worn with white gloves, a lace jabot and cuffs, and a silk cockade hat decorated with ostrich feathers.[3]

Sheriff Casson was not the only woman sheriff in Great Britain. Although American sheriffs are descended from the British crown's "shire reeve," the offices have evolved very differently. American sheriffs are elected and are viewed in many parts of the country as their county's chief law enforcement officer. British sheriffs, known as "high sheriffs," a title still in use in parts of the United States, perform primarily ceremonial duties and still receive their annual appointments from the crown. Although many in Great Britain believed there were too few women sheriffs, the numbers and percentages are much higher than in the United States, where only about 1 percent of the 3,000 sheriffs are women. In 2003 there were seven women sheriffs in England and Wales out of a total of fifty-four, or about 13 percent. Scotland, which is part of the United Kingdom but whose justice system differs considerably from England and Wales, in 1999 had seventeen women sheriffs out of a total number of 108, almost 16 percent.[4] The appointment process obviously has resulted in more women in Great Britain serving as sheriffs, but the position is unpaid and primarily ceremonial, which allows for greater manipulation of the selection process.

In the United States the selection process centers on the ability to get elected. Despite the political component of sheriffs' departments, only two of the women sheriffs in 2001 had held prior elective office. Welsh had been a Republican state committeewoman, and the other, who did not want to be identified, had been a Democratic city council member. Belying the image of law and order as a Republican issue, of twenty-one sheriffs, eighteen had run with party endorsement, but only three were Republicans. The other two Republicans were significantly different from Welsh. Anita Parkin, sheriff of Mineral County (Montana), was a nineteen-year veteran of her department who started her career as a dispatcher and had become its first female deputy when the sheriff offered her the job. By her seventeenth year she was the undersheriff (second in command), and she decided to run when the incumbent chose to retire. The other Republican was also from Montana. McCone County Sheriff Paula Dunham had been a deputy for eight years in another sheriff's department before deciding to run for sheriff of the small department, which had only three sworn officers, after she returned home to live in the Circle, Montana, area. Also unlike Welsh, neither had any significant jobs before beginning her policing career. Despite her history of political activity, Welsh declared that she had no further political ambitions.

Since sheriffs usually run with party affiliation, the strength of the party in a particular county will affect the outcome of the election. But the women sheriffs run counter to the analysis that women political office-holders are likely to be associated with social welfare, education, health, and environmental issues. Women legislators have not traditionally been active in pushing law-and-order issues even though women constituents are more likely to fear crime than men are. The women sheriffs reinforced research that women politicians, particularly at the local level, are more likely to be elected as Democrats than as Republicans and that they are more ideologically liberal than their male counterparts.[5] Further studies of women in elective office, mostly state legislators, have found that women are more likely to prioritize, sponsor, and vote for women's-issue bills than their male colleagues.[6] Women in state legislatures who describe themselves as feminists—a label few of the women police chiefs but more of the sheriffs were eager to adopt—also are more likely to be Democrats than nonfeminists are.[7] None of these studies of women politicians have included sheriffs in their analyses.

The women sheriffs' party affiliations opened areas of speculation. Generally, those who win county offices have run with the label of the stronger party in the particular jurisdiction. But as more women run for sheriff, will they be attracted to the party that seems to support more liberal issues, even if this hurts them in establishing credibility as crime fighters, or will their decisions be based on party strength to gauge their chances of winning an election? Suffolk County (Massachusetts) Sheriff Andrea Cabral's successful strategy of switching from the Republican to the Democratic Party in order to have a better chance to win the office in 2004 may indicate that support by the party in power is more important than ideology.

BETH ARTHUR: BRINGING FEMINISM INTO THE JAIL

Because they are elected officials, sheriffs come to their positions from a wider variety of backgrounds than police chiefs. Although their counties are in some ways similar, both populated primarily by well-educated professionals, Welsh and Arlington County (Virginia) Sheriff Beth Arthur personify these differences. Arthur, who was a member of her department for more than fourteen years, was appointed before she ran for office in 2000 as the handpicked successor to the sheriff she replaced; had strong party support; was a vocal feminist; and was almost young enough to be Welsh's daughter. If they shared anything in their backgrounds, it was that both had been steeped in politics for as long as they could remember. Welsh was a traditional, suburban Republican, while Arthur described herself as a "yellow dog" Democrat, a party loyalist who will vote Democratic no matter what.

Welsh's political activism came from her father, but Arthur's came from a long line of women. While her mother, her grandmother, or a number of aunts had ever held office, they had worked for numerous candidates, which is how Arthur began working as a campaign volunteer even before she had reached her teens. It was also how she got her start in politics and then in law enforcement. When Sheriff Tom Faust told her he was stepping down and suggested her as his interim replacement, she said her first thought was that she had always been happy "being the kingmaker and not the king, being behind the scenes, doing the hands-on stuff, but then I got to thinking, why should I help someone else again? I can do this."

Arthur came to the sheriff's department through her political contacts, and although she was always a sworn officer, her experiences in the department were all administrative, something her two male opponents dwelled on throughout her 2000 campaign. She had worked as a volunteer for Charles Robb in two of his three Senate campaigns, and through him she met one of her earliest mentors, Sheriff James Gondles, who, when he found out she was interested in relocating from Richmond to northern Virginia, hired her, a self-described "mouthy twenty-five- or twenty-six-year-old who didn't mind asking or saying whatever," as his director of administration. In 1990, Gondles left to become executive director of the American Correctional Association and, in a preview of how Arthur would later replace her predecessor, the Circuit Court judges appointed his chief deputy, Thomas Faust, as his successor. Faust reappointed Arthur to director of administration, the position she had held for more than a dozen years the day he called her into his office, told her he was resigning to become executive director of the National Sheriffs' Association, and, in answer to her question "Who will be the sheriff," replied, "You."

By the time she was appointed to fill Faust's office on July 8, 2000, by the Circuit Court, just as Faust had been appointed to fill the vacancy created by Sheriff Gondles, Arthur was responsible for the day-to-day administration of an office with a budget of more than $20 million and almost 300 employees, most of whom worked in the new detention facility (jail) and courthouse. She had been involved with the transition from the old to the new facilities and had worked closely with accrediting agencies to ensure that the jail, which housed more than 500 detainees, met the highest professional standards.

Although it seemed easy, it wasn't. Arthur was the wife of a man who was younger and quieter than she, and who she wasn't sure would take to the idea of his wife having to run for office and open the family to public scrutiny. She was the mother of two sons, three and almost six, and she would no doubt be opposed by candidates with stronger police backgrounds. Although getting the position by appointment made it seem easier, it actually resulted in her having to run twice in four years: later in 2000 to fill out Faust's term and then in 2003 for her own full four-year term. She won both elections, but the first one was the more difficult.

In strong parallels with Welsh's race to head a much smaller department, Arthur's opponents vied for the mantle of the toughest cop. Arthur sounded eerily like Welsh, also dropping her voice to a baritone to imitate the tones of voice of the men who ran against her. Although neither of her opponents specifically raised the issue that she was a woman, one, Elmer Lowe, a retired deputy who had left the department just before Arthur was appointed sheriff, stressed that he had been to the police academy and had worked his way to middle management, something that Arthur could not claim to have done even though she had always been a sworn officer.

The other, John Baber, was a former Arlington County police officer who had run before and had almost defeated Sheriff Gondles. He assured voters that their sheriff would be out in the middle of the night, patrolling along with his deputies. Like Welsh, Arthur countered this by saying that the sheriff's job was to be a manager, not a deputy, and that she had managed a budget, hired staff, and worked with outside agencies. "The sheriff's job," she told voters, "is not to serve court papers or work in a courtroom, but to manage those who do." And she reminded them that although deputies had police status in the state, none were assigned to patrol and they were not riding around at midnight, so there would certainly be no reason for the sheriff to be doing so.

But Baber, running as an independent with Republican support and the endorsement of the Northern Virginia Fraternal Order of Police, persisted by asking voters if they wanted a sheriff who knew how to purchase office supplies. Arthur admitted that this annoyed her, since he had demoted her from director of administration to the sheriff's administrative assistant. She refused to describe the appeal as overtly sexist, preferring to attribute it to his age (over sixty) and his years in law enforcement before women were active partners on the job. She got her chance to get even, though, at a candidates' forum where he was asked how he would be able to work with the judges he had insulted by implying that they had selected an unqualified candidate when they appointed Arthur to replace Faust. He replied that he would meet with the judges and would explain the situation to them "man to man," providing Arthur with the opportunity to remind the voters that four of the nine judges were women.

Despite these experiences, she said she was not surprised that a number of the women sheriffs had not been street police officers before running for office, although she did not think any could get elected without some relationship to law enforcement, most likely as administrators, as she and Fulton County (Georgia) Sheriff Jackie Barrett had been. Arthur, who was forty-one when she ran in 2000 and had earned a bachelor's degree in mass communications from Virginia Commonwealth University, won her first election with about 58 percent of the vote. It was easier in November 2003, when she ran unopposed in both the primary and the general election to earn a full four-year term.

Although her job is nontraditional for a woman, Arthur embodied findings that women in public office are often more willing or able than men to tackle public policy problems that are seen as women's issues. Many of the policies she has supported or implemented might be described as "soft" or "compassionate," two words rarely associated with a sheriff. Since she also gained her experience in the department handling large building projects and budgets, she has been able to transcend survey data that have revealed voters perceive that men are better at maintaining law and order and formulating fiscal policy, while women are better at handling issues of social welfare (especially on behalf of children or the "needy"), education, health, and the environment.[8]

These elements are embodied in programs that Arthur began for incarcerated mothers. One, Read Me a Story, allowed the women to tape-record books for their children. The other program opened the women's detention area for visits by their children. The contact visit program allowed inmates who had been charged with or convicted of nonviolent crimes to have visits from their children, and led to Arthur's selection as one of three "persons of vision" by the Arlington Commission on the Status of Women for 2002. Nationwide, in 2003, about 75 percent of women in jail were mothers, and two-thirds of them had children under age eighteen. Although the number of women inmates in the Arlington County Detention Facility is smaller than the number of male inmates (typical of jails and prisons around the nation), in December 2003, fourteen women had the chance to receive visits from their children.[9] Arthur tried to implement a similar program for men, but there has been less interest among the substantially larger male inmate population.

"Am I a softy because I'm doing something like that?" she asked, then answered her own question in the negative. "No, I think we need to recognize that these kids need to maintain contact with their parents, and hopefully that contact will help them not to end up where their parents are. And does it help these parents, when they're sober, when they're locked up in jail, to recognize how their actions are affecting their children? But maybe I do care about that because I'm a mother and a woman, but I'd like to think that there are a lot of men out there who care about those issues as well." She has also broadened the Addiction, Corrections and Treatment (ACT) program for jailed substance abusers by increasing the number of cells set aside for the program, which aims to create a therapeutic community behind bars for those who volunteer to participate in drug and alcohol treatment programs.

To protect all inmates, but primarily women, Arthur also instituted a six-hour training program for new deputies and annual refresher training for staff on sexual misconduct. She recalled that several years before she became sheriff, a spate of sexual misconduct allegations led to the termination of five employees, the resignation of one, and other disciplinary action being taken against two others. Arthur worked with the advocacy group Stop Prisoner Rape and instituted a zero-tolerance policy of sexual contact between staff and inmates, reminding staff members that it is not only inappropriate but also illegal.[10]

Arthur also worked to raise the department's profile in the larger community by increasing its efforts surrounding a number of programs to aid children and senior citizens, including Operation Identi-Child, which provided fingerprinting of children for parents to retain in the event the child goes missing; and Safety for Our Seniors Plus (SOS Plus), which distributed crime prevention information geared to seniors and also permitted senior citizens who are living alone or are disabled to register to receive phone calls and in-person visits from deputies and volunteers to help ensure that they are not mistreated or isolated from their community. But since politicians—who include sheriffs—are never immune from criticism, Arthur recalled that when she provided literature on all these programs at the department's booth at the county fair, some wondered where the money had come from and whether the flyers were little more than campaign literature.

Arthur felt that her management style reflected that she had grown up in a woman's world. She and her four sisters were raised primarily by Arthur's mother and grandmother, both of whom were strong influences on Arthur. And then there were the two very political aunts. She said she believed her style was more hands-on than a man's might be, although she did admit that she could be easily irritated by those who were unwilling to make the time commitment to their jobs that she had done. As if reading from a management text, she observed that women, whether they were chiefs, sheriffs or CEOs of corporations, had difficulties establishing a style. "If we are soft, that's no good because we are seen as weak. If we are aggressive, we get called the 'b' word," she said in summary.

Arthur even admitted to having baked cookies for those who worked in the jail, particularly around holiday times. The last time she did that, though, her co-baker was a male captain. "He said if I wanted to do it, he'd come over and help. We both drove my husband crazy, but the staff appreciated that and the prepared food we ordered for them so they would have something of the holiday," she recalled.

MARGO FRASIER: THE GOOD OLE GIRL FROM TEXAS

One sheriff who seemed to have spent little time worrying about style was Margo Frasier, who frequently describes herself as "just a good ole girl from Texas," and who wears the hand-tooled cowboy boots that go with the image. For those with long political memories, she is an echo of Senator Sam J. Ervin, Jr., the North Carolina Democrat and self-described "old country lawyer" who managed in 1974 to get the best of every one of the Watergate conspirators who had the misfortune to appear before the Senate Select Committee to Investigate Campaign Practices, known as the Ervin Committee or the Watergate Committee.

Frasier's description was equally misleading but equally indicative of her view that she is who is and that people have to accept her that way.

Frasier joined the Travis County Sheriff's Department as a corrections officer in 1975. She had worked briefly for the Texas Department of Corrections and had earned a bachelor's degree in criminology and corrections, with honors, from Sam Houston State University, and was doing graduate work in criminal justice. Although Frasier said she never faced the rites of passage that many women in policing faced in the 1970s, she recalled that other deputies found it amusing when she was forced to fend off a psychotic sexual predator they had released from a cell. Despite this message that she—or any other woman—wasn't really welcome, she decided to make her presence felt.

Working nights and somewhat bored, Frasier spent time drafting policies and sending them to the sheriff. Although she did not get much response, she was aggressive enough, when a captain's position became available, to suggest herself as a candidate. She didn't get that job, but she did get the next supervisory position. "No one told me for sure," Frasier said, "but it seemed there was discussion about appointing the brightest person with the most potential, and it was like, 'Ugh, what are we saying?' when my name came up. But I guess I can't complain too much, because I got the position." This led to one of her many firsts; she was the first female lieutenant in what until then had been a man's job.

But Frasier was still restless. In 1984 she earned a J.D. degree from Florida State University Law School, which led to clerking for a federal judge and ten years in private practice in Texas, much of it representing police and sheriffs' departments being sued over civil rights and employment law matters. In 1996, again restless and having discovered that she missed being in a leadership position, she decided to run to become Travis County's first woman—and first openly gay—sheriff. More was made of her sex than her sexual orientation. She faced six opponents in the Democratic primary, first as a novelty and then as the front-runner, defeating the candidate who had originally had the most support.

The actual election was also spirited. Unlike either Chester County or Arlington County, Travis County elections are rarely one-party affairs, and Frasier's predecessor, a man she believed was heavy-handed and too political, was a Republican. She received 52 percent of the vote, defeating her predecessor's handpicked successor, his chief deputy—who, Frasier believed, would have allowed the former sheriff to maintain influence in the office, similar to what Welsh believed her predecessor had been planning. Frasier, who knew of the Texas tradition of appointing widows to fill their husbands' unexpired terms and was interested to learn about

Wisconsin voters electing wives so their husbands could avoid term-limit laws, believed that many sheriffs maintained a similar practice without the added fillip of sex by having sheriffs and their undersheriffs take turns running for office, particularly in rural or one-party areas.

Frasier's officers perform a full range of police services. Even though she was the incumbent in the race in 2000, opponents complained that she had never made an arrest, since her career in the department had been spent in corrections. She preferred not to dwell on whether this was a veiled reference to her sex and, like Welsh and Arthur, explained to voters that they didn't need a sheriff who would brag about having strapped on a gun belt every day for however many years; what they needed was an administrator and a leader who could run a $60-million-plus operation. They agreed.

Frasier was responsible for substantially increasing the size and budget of her department. When she took over in 1996, the budget was about $52 million; when she unexpectedly announced in late 2003 that she would serve out her term until the end of 2005 but would not run again, the budget had grown to $87 million, the largest of any agency in the county. Although the department had grown to more than about 1,300 people, some of the increases reflected higher salaries for the deputies, which Frasier fought for as a way to stanch the flow of sheriff's deputies leaving for the better-paying Austin Police Department.

Armstrong County (Texas) Sheriff Carmella Jones had faced a similar problem when she was elected in 1994. A career member of her department whose opponent's strategy of telling voters they needed a sheriff with balls backfired, she set as one of her first priorities raising the pay in her small, seven-person department because she was constantly losing deputies to bigger departments. Sheriff Mary Choate, of Bowie County (Texas), whose career overlapped Jones's and had been a Texarkana police officer and then a health care professional before running for sheriff, did not have this problem. Bowie County is located in a rural area with no large police departments, and the 135 employees in the sheriff's department, including the thirty-five deputies, considered it one of the best agencies in the area for which to work.[11]

Frasier also expanded the network of substations throughout the county. This made deputies more accessible to the rural residents who relied on them for general police work. She implemented a separate 911 emergency network for the more than 126,000 residents who lived in the more than 700 square miles of unincorporated Travis County. She was also able to convince legislators and voters to pass a $13.7 million bond plan for jail construction and improvement. Despite years of litigation and millions of dollars to hire additional deputies, pay overtime, and send some inmates to other counties to prevent illegal overcrowding, by 2002 the state Commission on Jail Standards found the county jails in compliance for the first time in a decade.

Frasier established herself as one of the more visible women at annual meetings of the National Sheriffs' Association (NSA). Often dressed in slacks, sometimes wearing a department polo shirt that identified her as Sheriff M. Frasier, and sporting star-shaped silver earrings and the ever-present cowboy boots, she was not a national officer the way Gaithersburg, Maryland, Chief Mary Ann Viverette is in the International Association of Chiefs of Police (IACP), but she was president in 2004 of the group's Major City Association. She has been a featured speaker at numerous police and women's events, and since the late 1990s has become more visible at gay and lesbian events, a number of which had been fund-raisers for her or occasions at which she was honored. It had been known in the county since at least 1997, when Frasier was featured in the *Dallas Morning News*, that she and her partner, a member of the Austin Police Department who was the first African-American woman to be promoted to lieutenant, are the parents of an adopted, biracial daughter.[12] She frequently refers to her daughter and says that she may have developed a more nurturing management style due to her role as a mother. She said she has never chosen to run on the basis of her sexual orientation because she hasn't seen heterosexuals base their campaigns on a like issue.

Yet Frasier has been mindful of her role as a model and mentor for other women. She believes that sheriffs' departments are unfairly given a "bad rap" as places that are not female-friendly. She says, rather, that because the departments have women's jails, there will always be a need for women employees. "Part of getting ahead is just being there; everyone in my agency is extremely aware that they have a woman sheriff. My guys, as I call them, don't think I'm less a sheriff because I'm a woman, and I think they would challenge anyone who did think so," she adds. She has also worked to increase the number of women in her command staff, and toward the end of 2002 promoted three women to captain and one to major.

Why did Frasier, Texas's lone woman sheriff in 2004 in all its 254 counties, announce so far in advance that she would not run again? Part of it was the privilege of being a sheriff, who, unlike a police chief, is frequently able to set her own career agenda. Some thought that after having been elected at only forty-three, she was once again displaying her restless side, particularly when she was vague about whether she would practice law or perhaps would run for office—the state legislature and Congress have been mentioned. Since President George W. Bush's Crawford ranch is located in her county, maybe she had an opportunity to talk to Karen Hughes, the president's adviser who left Washington to return home to Texas to please her husband and teenage son. Frasier said only that she wanted the time to dine at restaurants with her domestic partner and ten-year-old daughter without being interrupted to talk about law enforcement.[13] At one point after her notice that she would not run, eight candidates had announced for her position, although it was expected that some would drop out. Frasier endorsed a former member of her department who had become the chief of enforcement for the Texas Alcoholic Beverage Commission.

JACKIE BARRETT: THE COSTS OF A POLITICAL CAREER

When Fulton County (Georgia) Sheriff Jackie Barrett announced in the spring of 2004 that, like Frasier, she would not run again, it signaled the loss of another veteran woman sheriff. Barrett had shattered a number of glass ceilings when she was elected in November 1992, becoming the first female African-American sheriff in the nation, but her decision, unlike Frasier's, was not personal preference but the result of a number of growing scandals involving management of the county jail and the loss of $2 million in public money through bad investments.

Although Barrett had never been a working police officer, she defeated a former deputy by a margin of almost two to one in a bitterly fought race that had included a primary and a runoff before the general election. Like Welsh and Arthur, she overcame her lack of street policing experience by explaining to voters that the almost 800 deputies in the department were jail and courthouse officers who served warrants in a busy jurisdiction that included Atlanta but did not patrol the streets or provide police services within the county.

But Barrett, like Arthur, also stressed that she was a certified sworn officer. "I was running against someone who was 6'5", very macho, very masculine, who wore a cowboy hat, so I don't think the pure 'it's a CEO's job' would have worked for me," she recalled. "I reminded voters that, yes, I was a police officer, although few people asked for many details beyond that. But I couldn't back away from the fact that it was a cop's job," she added. At the time, she was the director of the Fulton County Public Safety Training Center. Prior to that, Barrett had been the administrative officer for Fulton County Sheriff Richard Lankford, whose election in 1985 made him the first black sheriff in Georgia. Earlier, she had been a member of the Georgia Peace Officer Standards and Training Council, the state oversight board for licensing and training officers throughout the state, all of which totaled about sixteen years of experience in police training and administration. In addition to earning a bachelor's degree from Beaver College in Pennsylvania and a master's degree in sociology from Atlanta University in Georgia, she had been a civilian planner in a number of police departments in the state.

Barrett, forty-four at the time of her first election, was one of the few women sheriffs who defeated an incumbent, although he was technically an interim sheriff who had been appointed to complete the term of a sheriff who had been indicted while in office. In the Democratic primary she defeated Sheriff Robert McMichael, and then she defeated Morris Chappell, a former deputy sheriff who owned a private investigation company, in the general election. She was re-elected in 1996 and in 2000, in both cases with greater support from within the party than during her first race. In 2000, Barrett received about 60 percent of the vote.

Barrett believed she was able to defeat McMichael because, since he hadn't been the elected sheriff, the position was really "open" and the deputies were sufficiently demoralized by previous events that someone like herself could make a case to the voters that real change was required. Although others, including her opponents, believed her lack of street police experience was a serious handicap, she did not. Race was not an issue; McMichael was also African-American, contributing to Barrett's belief that her sex was more important in the campaign than her race.

She said part of her success was based on her being well known to officers throughout the county who had been in her classes. They understood that she would put into practice what she had taught. Generally, she thought that men and women have become too focused on patrol experience as the only way to reach higher ranks. "Maybe it is still different in policing, but there is no reason to confine yourself and say you've got to come up through the ranks. I'd say there is value to carving out a niche—administration, computer literacy, education, and training—particularly for a sheriff, because you are appealing not only to the deputies, but to voters who want to know what you will bring to the department, what they will be getting for their money," she explained. This reinforced the views of virtually all the sheriffs that there were substantial differences between what was expected of them and what was expected of police chiefs. Although police chiefs must also have public faces, they are not elected officials. This limits the number of constituencies to which they must appeal. And, of course, they need not have roots in the community.

Like Frasier, Barrett promoted a greater number of women into middle-management ranks. Even in departments that are covered by civil service, as Barrett's was, there is often more flexibility in sheriffs' departments at middle ranks than in many large police departments and less dependence on objective testing for filling positions. In a department that by 2001 was 30 percent female, Barrett had been able to appoint a woman chief jailer and a number of women captains. Although she said women needed to become more aggressive in managing their own careers, she also believed that sheriffs sent fewer officers to advanced training than police managers, and that because the numbers were low, women were often overlooked.

Another major difference between police and sheriffs' departments is the need for sheriffs to expend not only time but also money to win their jobs. Because Barrett had already been through three elections, she had experienced the toll these twin concerns take on a candidate and her family. The mother of adult children, she recalled their discomfort at hearing her attacked on a regular basis during her campaigns. The election cycle took up about nine months of each four-year term. Despite the benefits of incumbency, each of her campaigns cost more than the one before it; starting with between $50,000 and $60,000 for the first, about $80,000 for the second, and more than $120,000 for the third. Barrett attributed the doubling of expenses to the need for more and more sophisticated marketing to voters, including fancier mailings and a Web site. In addition, there were more than 30,000 new inhabitants of the county, particularly young people who had moved into Atlanta, who were unfamiliar with her or her record.

Part of the problem this presented for women, she noted, was women's unwillingness to contribute large sums to political campaigns even when they supported female candidates. Barrett is far from alone in this observation. Women candidates have trouble raising funds because they are often not seen as serious candidates by men and because women are less involved in the campaign funding process. Historically, women have worked on behalf of candidates as volunteers, contributors of their time rather than of their money. Both Democratic and Republican woman have sought to counter this. Emily's List, which is an acronym for Early Money Is Like Yeast, was established in 1985 to undertake fund-raising for pro-choice Democratic women candidates. A similar fund, the WISH List, was established by Republican women in 1992, also to support pro-choice women candidates. Other groups have also sought to encourage women to become more politically active in financial ways.

Barrett believed that the successful campaign of Shirley Franklin in 2001 to become the first African-American female mayor of Atlanta would depend on her ability to raise more money than any woman in Georgia had previously been able to do. Franklin's success in winning substantiated Barrett's prediction, but one of Barrett's hopes—that she, Atlanta's

Police Chief Beverly Harvard, and Mayor Franklin would be "a triumvirate of qualified women in Fulton County"—was not borne out. Shortly after her election, Franklin did not consider Harvard for re-appointment as police chief, and then, two years later, Barrett announced that she would not run for re-election and, when that failed to abate the controversy surrounding her, was forced on July 16, 2004, to announce that she would take a leave of absence beginning on August 1 that would continue through the end of the year, when her term in office officially ended.

Although Barrett had previously spoken of retiring due to pressures of mounting a fourth campaign, her choice not to run again reinforced the vagaries of politics, the problems that money can bring in an agency with millions of dollars in county funds to invest, and the pitfalls of assuming CEO status. All this was evident in the two controversies in which Barrett became embroiled in early 2004. One involved a class action suit on behalf of jail inmates and another surrounded the investment of more than $7 million in funds controlled by the sheriff's department due to its role selling property to satisfy tax debts through what are known as "sheriff's auctions." The jail suit raised management issues based on claims that overcrowding was due to bureaucratic delays in handling inmates who were incarcerated for days or weeks beyond their release dates and were subjected to illegal searches.[14] While not a positive development for any sheriff, an unproven lawsuit would not normally result in a decision to forgo seeking re-election. Since the mid-1980s, the number of county jails that have been under federal judicial supervision due to overcrowding, unclean conditions, and various other inmate complaints is too great to document. But few of those lawsuits resulted in management of the jail being removed from the sheriff, as it did in Fulton County when Barrett in early July 2004 agreed to the appointment of an outsider to manage the facility, which at the time held 3,000 inmates, more than three times the number it was intended for, and that had been found to be unsanitary, with broken laundry facilities, poor ventilation, and sewage seeping into living areas.[15]

Barrett's questionable investments of the more than $7 million in the sheriff's auction, and in other funds that made up part of the $30 million the department controlled in addition to its $80 million budget, had earlier led to calls for her resignation from the *Atlanta Journal–Constitution*.[16] About $5.2 million of the money had been invested in the MetLife insurance company and had been returned when it was established that the funds could not be loaned out of state other than for investment in federal securities. The other $2 million had been invested with a Florida company that made high-risk loans to private firms and whose principals said the money was not available to be returned when the state determined that the investments were improper. Amid allegations that Barrett had received campaign contributions from the Florida company, she announced on April 20, 2004, a day after the editorial calling for her resignation, that she would not resign but neither would she seek re-election to a fourth term. But after the jail was turned over to an outside administrator and the controversy surrounding the money continued, on July 16, Barrett announced that on August 1 she would go on leave for the remaining five months of her term.[17]

It was an unlikely end for someone who had been endorsed by the *Atlanta Inquirer* in 1996 because she had changed the culture of the department so that voters no longer needed to "hold their breath every morning before reading the paper in anticipation that their chief law enforcement officer is likely to be indicted for some corruptive act."[18] Many had believed that like Frasier, Barrett would someday seek a statewide office.

How a history-making sheriff who had wanted to change the stereotype of the Southern sheriff as an entrenched politician of questionable ethics ended up having her own ethics questioned may be instructive for sheriffs and police chiefs—women and men—who come into CEO jobs as outsiders and as reformers. Some might be overly optimistic about the changes that can be made in a department's culture within a short time and in a situation where most of the personnel do not change along with the top administrators.

CHAPTER 8

Big-City Pioneers:
The Women Who Broke the
Bulletproof Barriers

Controversy and confrontation were my constant companions.
—Chief Penny Harrington
Portland, Oregon, Police Bureau (1985–1986)

Very often I would take a very hard stand on things that I believe
in. Whereas in a man that might be called strength and determina-
tion, in me it was called arrogance and stubbornness.
—Chief Elizabeth Watson
Houston Police Department (1990–1992)
Austin Police Department (1992–1997)

I believe my appointment will probably open up new opportunities
for women to serve in ranking positions around the country.
—Chief Beverly Harvard
Atlanta Police Department (1994–2002)

More than 400 women police officers sat on the edges of their chairs in
Anchorage, Alaska, on a mild September day in 1985 as Chief Penny
Harrington was introduced at the International Association of Women
Police (IAWP) meeting. Although there was a smattering of women sergeants in the room, and even a few lieutenants and captains, most of the
women were in the entry-level rank of police officer. Like some of their
male colleagues, as rookies a few of the young women had been asked
by the media or family and friends where they thought they would be in
twenty-five years. Many had, somewhat flippantly, replied, "the chief."
Yet although there had been a handful of women chiefs by 1985, it
was likely that no more than five of the women in the auditorium had

ever met a woman chief of police. Probably some didn't even know that women chiefs really existed, but now they eagerly awaited Chief Harrington, the first woman to lead a big-city police department. Harrington did not disappoint her audience. In fact, she shocked most of them when she announced boldly that she had sued her department forty-two times in her climb to chief. When the next day's *Alaska Daily News* described how Harrington had "sued her way to the top," the women were divided over whether to be thrilled or horrified. What did this say about women chiefs? What did it say about policing? What did it say about their futures? Would they, too, be forced to litigate their way to higher rank, or had times truly changed?

Some saw Harrington as a heroine, battling for what she believed in; others saw her as a pariah, too strident and unwilling to be the type of team player usually rewarded in police organizations, where being different has never been the way to fit in. It had always been that way for Penny Harrington. She shattered the obscurity in which women chiefs worked when she was named in 1985 to lead the Portland, Oregon, Police Bureau—becoming the first woman to lead a big-city police department.

Mayor Bud Clark, a tavern owner who was a political novice and something of a media sensation, said when he selected her to run the 940-person department that it was because of her "commitment to community policing and her record as an administrator."[1] Appointing Harrington was Clark's second most controversial act; the first was appearing to be standing, fly open, flashing a statue in an "Expose Yourself to Art" poster that became a collector's item in Portland. There were many controversies—too many—during Harrington's seventeen-month tenure as chief, and sexist rhetoric even surrounded her resignation. Years later, she would refer to Clark having consoled her during her final controversy with the comment "tits up." Women's groups encouraged her to add this to her final lawsuit, which was not resolved until 1991, but this time she decided to walk away and to leave Portland behind.[2]

Although Harrington was certainly the first woman to lead a big-city police department, the definition of big-city policing is inexact. Like the Fortune 50 list of the largest companies in America, the U.S. Department of Justice (DOJ) annually lists the fifty largest police departments. While *Fortune* bases its listing on a company's revenues, DOJ bases its determination on the number of full-time sworn officers in the department. Police administrators talk in terms of the number of personnel they command rather than the size of their budget. Since personnel costs are the major item in police budgets, it is fairly standard that the larger the force, the higher the budget, although higher salaries for officers may result in a higher budget for slightly fewer officers than in a city that pays lower salaries. Generally, though, size and budget are closely related, and chiefs focus on the number of people in their departments rather than on budgets or bottom lines—particularly when determining the importance or influence of a particular police department.

Sizes of the largest police departments range from New York City, which is always the largest, to departments of under 1,000. In 2000, forty-seven of the fifty largest departments employed more than 1,000 officers; the smallest, Buffalo, New York, had just over 925 officers. An additional thirty-seven departments had between 500 and 999 officers. Although some of the numbers and the positions of individual departments change annually, the fluctuations in the top twenty usually represent a few departments switching places.

In 2000, only 87 city or county police departments out of the total of about 18,000 police agencies in the nation employed more than 500 officers. Indicative of population shifts in the nation, a number of the largest departments were not in cities, but were county police agencies responsible for policing a large city and its surrounding suburban and rural areas. In recent years departments in the South and the West have grown, while those in the Northeast and Midwest have stayed stable or even fallen a few places in the rankings. Thus, a city like Buffalo, which will not see growth in its police department, is likely to fall out of the fifty largest departments by 2005.

Fewer than ten women had led top-fifty departments, but by January 2004, women were at the helm of four of them. The most obvious sign of women's progress in policing may have been the relative lack of attention each woman received outside her home city. Neither Ella Bully-Cummings, named to lead the Detroit Police Department on November 4, 2003, nor Nannette Hegerty, who was announced as chief of the Milwaukee Police Department in late October and officially took office on November 18, 2003, made the mandatory—but by now cliché—remarks about being the best person for the job regardless of sex. Both, rather, stressed their roots in their city and their need for community support in reducing crime and enhancing their department's image. When Kathleen O'Toole was named Boston's police commissioner in February 2004, she, too, chose not to dwell on her sex; and when Heather Fong was named acting chief in San Francisco in January 2004, and then chief in April 2004, more attention was paid to her Asian heritage than to her sex and to the fact that the city also had a female fire chief, a far more rare event. Although Bully-Cummings, who is generally referred to as African-American, is the daughter of an African-American father and an Asian mother, Fong is the first Asian-surnamed woman to lead a police department and one of only a few Asians ever to have served as the chief of police in an American city.

The convergence of four women leading major police departments in the nation in 2004 is a milestone. Each of these chiefs has, to some degree, risen on the shoulders of those who came before her, and has brought renewed attention to the big-city pioneering chiefs: Penny Harrington in Portland, Elizabeth (Betsy) Watson in Houston and Austin, and Beverly Harvard in Atlanta.

PENNY HARRINGTON: BEING THE FIRST IS NEVER EASY

Of the women heading large police departments, Harrington's selection was the most surprising and her career the least typical. Her tenure, from January 25, 1985, to June 2, 1986, was shorter than average for large-city chiefs, and she recalled in later years that "controversy and confrontation" were her "constant companions" not only during her time as chief, but throughout her career.[3]

Harrington is the only woman to become chief of a large department who entered policing at a time when women's careers followed a more limited path than men's. Her interest in policing was piqued by a high school visit to the Lansing, Michigan, Police Department during a career day. She was the only woman to sign up to tour the police department, primarily because, she said later, it was a day to get out of her regular classes. She was assigned to the department's policewoman, who explained that police officers helped people, especially children. Armed with this knowledge, Harrington took a job after high school as a legal secretary and enrolled at Michigan State University to study police administration.

Despite the small number of women in the university's program—fewer than a dozen out of several hundred students—Harrington was unfazed by the limited careers in policing for women. Married while still in college, she graduated at age twenty-two, and she and her husband, a fellow law enforcement student, moved to Portland, Oregon, after a former professor offered them jobs in the Multnomah County Sheriff's Office. When they arrived, they learned that the county would not hire a married couple. Her husband took the job, and Harrington returned to working as a legal secretary until a position opened up in the Portland Police Bureau (Department) in 1964. She was assigned to the women's protective division, the only division in which policewomen were allowed to work. Despite their more advanced education (women were required to have a college degree, and men needed only a high school diploma or general education diploma), the policewomen were paid less than policemen and had limited promotional opportunities. They were not issued uniforms, but were expected to dress in business attire, including tailored suits, silk blouses, pumps, hats, and gloves—traditional dress in women's bureaus. Portland was not unique; its rules were virtually identical to departments throughout the country.

The work was also traditional. The policewomen were present whenever a woman or child was questioned about a sex offense, and they were assigned to cases involving young children. The women's division and the roles of women in the department had changed very little since 1905, when Portland had hired Lola Baldwin, a social worker, and given her police authority to protect the moral safety of women and young girls during the Lewis and Clark Exposition. Baldwin and her small force of women were considered so successful that in 1908 they were reorganized into the Department of Public Safety for the Protection of Young Girls and Women. Baldwin wielded considerable political power in Portland. She worked through the incumbency of six chiefs of police and five mayors, retiring with the rank of captain. She so opposed policewomen being associated with policing that she had her officers called operatives. Her influence over the assignment of Portland's policewomen continued until 1973; Harrington was one of the first women to question Baldwin's legacy.

Harrington was not initially bothered by her and the other women's segregation within the department. She considered her work "interesting, challenging, exciting and a far cry from traditional careers for women," but she became burned out working cases involving abused children. Also, by 1967 she was a mother, and by 1968 she had become a feminist. When a civil service test for detective made it plain that policewomen need not apply, Harrington applied anyway. Her application was rejected, but in 1969, when one of the three policewomen sergeants retired, she took that test. Despite what she later described as resistance from her husband, who refused to help care for their young son, she passed the exam and ranked number one on the promotion list. Whether it was because she had tried to take the detective exam or to support an "old girl" network, Harrington was bypassed for promotion. It went, instead, to a woman who had scored lower on the exam but had been there longer. Ironically, it was the policewoman captain—not a man—who brought her face-to-face with this professional disappointment, compounded when she learned than she was the first person in the history of the department who had been passed over on a promotion list.

Other events also began to change her outlook. Harrington worked with the police union, only to learn again that women were not considered the equals of male officers. When her marriage broke up, she became involved with the officer with whom she worked on union affairs. These events dovetailed into her leaving the women's division, although only after the intervention of her boss, the man with whom she had become romantically involved. Even he was unable to ensure her an assignment that could have been filled by a man. She actually went downtown to ask the mayor to ensure her transfer, something he denied he had the power to do, only to learn when she returned to headquarters that her transfer had been approved. "The chief was angry," she said, "but it brought the whole house of cards down—because once he transferred me, he had no excuse not to transfer other women."[4]

By 1971, Portland, like many cities, eliminated the titles of police-woman and policeman (or patrolman) for the unisex title of police officer, and opened entry-level and promotion exams to both men and women. This time Harrington was eligible for the detective exam; of the four women who applied, she scored the highest, and in February 1972 finally won her promotion.

Although Harrington had been in the Portland department for eight years, the other women who would become chiefs were barely beginning their careers. None faced the same battles to achieve promotion that Harrington did, which may explain why she has remained the most militant of the past chiefs. Other promotions followed, but not without their own frustrations. Her promotion to sergeant, in mid-1972, landed Harrington back in the women's division, where she was not permitted to work in uniform and where she supervised only one person—her sister Roberta, who had followed her into the department as a policewoman a few years earlier. The first women police officers (distinct from policewomen) were not hired until the end of 1973.

After a leave of absence, Harrington returned in July 1975 and learned that she would become the first female sergeant supervising male officers on patrol. She had taken the promotion exam for lieutenant in November 1974, but was promoted only after a series of lawsuits and a class action suit in which the American Civil Liberties Union asked her and Roberta to participate. After being passed over for a number of lieutenant's assignments, Harrington was finally promoted in early 1977, and promoted again to captain in 1980. She was the first woman captain since the men's and women's divisions had been merged eight years earlier, just as she had been the first woman detective, the first woman sergeant (other than those who had supervised only policewomen), and the first woman lieutenant who supervised male and female officers. Even though she had sued for every step she had taken out of the women's bureau, she was still, at thirty-eight, the youngest person ever appointed a captain. By 1982 Harrington got her chance to command a precinct. As the first and only woman captain, she saw herself as an advocate for women in the department, although she realized that not all of them agreed with her history of bucking the system.

As a precinct commander, Harrington became embroiled in a conflict with her chief, Ron Still, over his order to arrest prostitutes but not their customers. Bud Clark defeated the incumbent mayor in May 1984 and was due to take over in January 1985. Harrington assumed that Still would remain the chief, but he retired in September 1984. A month later there were fourteen applicants for the position, which Clark's panel whittled down to four finalists—three men and Harrington. Clark selected her.

When she was named chief, Harrington's department was composed of about 800 police officers and 400 civilians and had a budget of about $57 million. Her second husband, Gary, a police officer whom she had married in 1982; her sister; and her brother-in-law were members of the department, all in ranks below hers. Harrington claimed to have been as shocked as anyone at her selection, although she had brought a new suit, had flown her parents in from Michigan, and had told her son to stay home from school just in case. She was unable to plan fully because Clark had decided to make his selection known only hours before it would be announced to the press. Harrington found out via a morning call from the mayor to "Chief Harrington." The press conference was less than three hours later. This is not unusual. When O'Toole was named Boston's police commissioner, she, too, was the only woman of four finalists and also found out only hours before Mayor Thomas Menino's press conference announcing her selection.

Harrington recalled that after the phone call she began to scream, "I'm the chief, I got it, I got it, I'm the chief!" She had expected press coverage because she was the first woman named to lead such a large department, but did not expect the approximately fifty television, radio, and print media representatives who jammed the event. And it didn't stop. She appeared on numerous television news programs and was interviewed by *People*, *USA Today*, *The New York Times*, *Ladies' Home Journal*, *Time*, *Ms.* magazine, and countless other publications. A local paper, the *Downtowner*, published a Penny Harrington paper doll, complete with such outfits as a street uniform with trousers; a dress uniform with a skirt; a dress-for-success business suit much like what she had worn in the women's division; a number of plainclothes outfits (one with a number of hidden revolvers); and an evening gown. Nonclothing supplies included a file cabinet, a marked police car, and a replica of police headquarters. The Penny doll was stylishly dressed in pumps, a slip, and a ballistic T-shirt.[5]

It took at least a month for Harrington to get down to police administration; she had given nearly 200 interviews, including one to the *Today Show*'s Jane Pauley, who insultingly had asked Harrington if Clark had appointed her as a "stunt" despite her twenty-one-year career in policing. The first woman chief of a major city would not attract similar attention again until her resignation seventeen months later.

What happened in that short time? How did the *Downtowner*'s Penny Harrington paper doll become *Time*'s "tarnished Penny"?[6] During her tenure, drug arrests increased by almost one-third and citizens' complaints against the police dropped by almost the same percentage. But three black citizens died because of police misconduct, and she was forced to lay off sixteen police officers and leave sixty positions unfilled during her first months in office.

Mayor Clark wanted greater input into department priorities than Harrington had anticipated. His priority to cut the city's high burglary rate forced her to consolidate the vice and drug divisions, which caused further deterioration of Harrington's relationship with the union representing police officers. In a union poll, 91 percent of the officers called Harrington's performance "poor" or "below average." She described union president Stan Peters as going for her throat because she had not stood up to the city council.[7]

The ill will over the layoffs was fueled by two situations on the extremes of labor-management relationships. In the simpler of the two, Harrington banned smoking on the job, allowing only one office and one squad car in each precinct where smoking would be permitted. More volatile was the controversy that ensued when officers killed an African-American security guard by using a grip known as the "sleeper hold," in which officers subdue an individual by applying force to the carotid artery in the neck to make the individual go limp. After Harrington banned use of the controversial grip, two officers responded by selling T-shirts inscribed "Don't choke 'em. Smoke 'em," with a picture of a smoking gun. The community responded with outrage, and although Harrington had the officers fired, they were reinstated by an arbitrator at their appeal hearings.

There was also criticism of her family members working in the department, leading to claims that she ran it like a family business. The final controversy centered on allegations that Harrington's husband had improperly associated with, and given information to, a man under investigation for narcotics violations, an allegation that Harrington claimed was made solely to discredit her and to assure that "the heat would never let up." The allegations led Mayor Clark to set up a special investigative commission chaired by a former United States attorney who selected a state circuit judge and a commander of the Oregon State Police to serve with him. After a number of public hearings, at which Harrington and her husband, as well as many other members of the department testified, the commission characterized her administration as a failure, stating that she had not consulted with her commanders and that her management style was unyielding, despite her own claims that her goal had been to move from a "militaristic, rule-driven organization to one that operates in a value-based, participatory style."[8]

This assessment was particularly hurtful to Harrington, who was an early supporter of community policing and has continued to espouse it as a less authoritarian and more participative model of policing that is consistent with women's leadership styles. Although popular with chiefs, community policing is less popular with lower-ranking officers, who view it as moving away from fighting crime to focusing on social problems, and as inviting more community input into police activity than they believe is required.

Harrington has remained the most controversial and the most vocal of all the female chiefs. From 1995 until 2002, she was the director of the National Center for Women & Policing (NCWP), a division of the Feminist Majority Foundation, which lobbies to increase the numbers of women at all ranks of policing. Although a few chiefs and sheriffs are members, many have shied away because they do not support the Feminist Majority's positions on other issues.

ELIZABETH (BETSY) WATSON: TEXAS'S PISTOL-PACKIN' MAMA

In 1990, Elizabeth (Betsy) Watson, then an eighteen-year-veteran of the Houston Police Department, became the first woman to head a force in a city of over 1 million people. Her appointment was likened to the selection of the first woman CEO of a Fortune 500 company. Two years later, a new mayor selected a new chief, but within the same year, Watson became chief in Austin, a position she held until 1997.

Watson did not work in a women's bureau, as Harrington had, but when she joined the Houston Police Department, she had been handed a dress pattern and told to sew her own uniform. This was a year after Title VII amended the Civil Rights of Act of 1964 to prohibit public agencies, including police departments, from discriminating on the basis of sex, and many departments had given no thought to what women would wear on patrol. It is difficult today to envision the fuss over dressing women police officers. Considerable energy was expended redesigning the women's military uniforms that had existed since World War II and that some police departments had been issuing to policewomen since the 1950s. Many departments actually sent women on patrol looking like an early generation of flight attendants, dressed in short skirts and pumps, white shirts with little Navy-style ties, and leather shoulder pocketbooks in which to carry their guns, handcuffs, summons books, and lipstick and compact.

Within a short time, though, the women changed into uniforms that were virtually identical to those men wore, although this, too, caused problems, because many of the women's smaller waists left little room for all the equipment that officers carry on their belts. Like so many problems that seemed insurmountable, this eventually became part of the routine of policing. Current ads for women's uniforms, including body armor with darts to accommodate a woman's upper body, can be found in any police publication.

Although Harrington had been legally barred from many assignments early in her career, Watson had a different problem. She was eligible for all assignments, but she later lamented that she had been shielded from many types of hazardous duty. She recalled especially that although she had briefly been assigned to a Special Weapons and Tactics (SWAT) unit, male supervisors had limited her to working in communications. She declined to speculate whether this was chivalry or concern on the part of her male colleagues that she would be inadequate for the tasks, although it was more likely the second than the first. Watson did, though, spend years on patrol, and had been the department's first female captain in 1984 and first female deputy chief in 1987. At the time of her selection as chief, she was only forty years old and was serving as a station (precinct) commander.

Chief Watson received as much press coverage outside of Texas as Chief Harrington had outside of Oregon. She was appointed by a woman mayor (Kathryn Whitmire) in a state that had just elected a woman governor, the outspoken Ann Richards. She was also the protégée of Lee Brown, an advocate of community policing, at a time when it was still considered experimental by the police establishment. Many questioned whether Watson would be able to continue Brown's programs and whether her sex would make her an unacceptable leader. At the time Brown left to head the New York City Police Department, morale among Houston's cops was low, primarily due to salary disputes and to Brown's having been an outside chief recruited from Atlanta to clean up a scandal-ridden department. Mark R. Clark, the head of the patrolmen's union, stressed that Watson's up-from-the ranks history would trump the fact that she was a woman. "Police officers," he said, "from time to time have their surges of machoism. I'm guilty of it, too. But they will fall in line. This is 1990, not 1960."[9]

The department's machismo would soon be tested in a way no one had anticipated. Within weeks of her appointment, Watson announced that she was pregnant with her third child, but would take only a short maternity leave when the child was born. Interest in her philosophy of policing was instantly overshadowed by interest in her pregnancy. Harrington had become the "tarnished Penny," and now Watson became the "pistol-packin' mama."[10]

Lending additional interest to the story was the baby's father, Sergeant Robert Watson, also a member of the Houston Police Department. The two had met in 1973 when they were assigned to work in the Houston jail. Since department policies discouraged fraternization, they kept their relationship quiet until they married in 1976, on the same day she was promoted to detective. Watson and Robert did not suffer the same scrutiny as Harrington and her husband, and she often stressed, particularly in interviews with women's magazines, that her husband had encouraged her throughout her career. She pinpointed the start of her climb to the top when she and her husband were sergeants and she passed up the opportunity to take the civil service test to lieutenant because he hadn't. The next time the test was given, however, he urged her to take it.

Watson was also encouraged throughout her career by her parents. Her maternal grandfather, uncles, and a number of cousins had been police officers in her hometown of Philadelphia. Her mother had been fascinated by her relatives' police stories. Watson was less intrigued, but her mother urged her to "try it." She had intended to stay only until she could find a different government job, but she liked the work more than she had expected to. Although she thought she would be working primarily in the juvenile division, a traditional assignment for women, Watson believed the department would make better use of her degree in psychology from Texas Tech than the secretarial jobs available elsewhere. Possibly policing really was in her blood, because her younger sister also went into police work. Watson's sister also achieved a first, becoming the first woman captain in the Harris County (Texas) Sheriff's Department. Although Houston is located within Harris County, Watson did not face the same criticisms as Harrington did over family connections, since only her husband was in the same department while she was chief.

Like Harrington, Watson attracted national attention, and was the only chief featured in both *Cosmo* and *Time* within a two-month period.[11] Despite the different readerships of the magazines, both interviews centered less on Watson's ideas about policing than on her approaches to

combining the responsibilities of being a police chief with those of being a mother and a wife who outranked her husband. Watson's husband
admitted that both were concerned that her pregnancy would be an
embarrassment that would reflect poorly on women's chances to be
taken seriously for top command positions. They already had two pre-
teens, a boy and a girl, and weren't planning on a larger family, although
Watson was from a large, close family that included three sisters and two
brothers.

Watson combined her police chief, wife, and mother roles for two years.
Her tenure, like that of all big-city police chiefs, was not trouble-free and
included a number of disagreements with Mayor Whitmire over policing
strategies. In December 1991, when Whitmire had been defeated after
ten years in office, she denied Watson a pay raise, grading her at the lowest
category of evaluation—"needs improvement." The new mayor, Bob
Lanier, who during the campaign had criticized Whitmire's management
of the police department, chose not to keep Watson as chief. He stressed
that his decision had nothing to do with her sex, only that it was common for a new mayor to select a new police chief. Uncommon, though,
was Watson's decision not to retire but to remain in the department as
an assistant chief until 1992, when she was named chief in Austin, Texas,
a smaller department than Houston's, but still a large agency with about
1,000 officers. When she accepted the position in Austin, Watson made
history yet again. She became the first, and by mid-2004 remained the
only, woman to have been the chief of two large-city police departments.

Her singular status, though, did not assure Watson an easy tenure. In
Austin she faced a crisis similar to Harrington's when, in early 1993, she
fired a police officer who had been accused of using excessive force. But,
faring better than Harrington, she remained in Austin for four years, about
twice as long as she was chief in Houston. The longer tenure, smaller city,
and subdued media attention provided an opportunity to put her administrative ideas to work. Believing that a streamlined command would bring
officers closer to the community and break up the top-down management
philosophy that prevailed in policing, she eliminated ranks and reduced
the number of middle managers. Although this brought her a no-
confidence vote from the Austin Police Association, local politicians
supported her. She also shook up the traditional status differential between
detectives and police officers by delegating more decision-making to uniformed investigators and patrol officers.

All the changes Watson made were in keeping with a community policing philosophy and provided an indication of what she might have done
in Houston had less attention been paid to her pregnancy and had she
had time to implement her plans. In early 1997 she retired and joined

the U.S. Department of Justice's Office of Community Oriented Policing Services to assist cities implementing community policing strategies.[12]

Was Watson able to establish a policing legacy? Yes and no. She told *Time* at the time of her pregnancy that she wondered if there would ever be another pregnant police chief, although she attributed it as much to the ages at which chiefs are selected as to the fact that the overwhelming majority of chiefs are men. Whatever the reason, her feelings that this might be "a one-time deal" seem to have proven true.[13] In addition to having been, by 2004, the only pregnant police chief, she has been the only woman to have led two major police departments and the only woman to have led a large department in which she did not begin her career. A number of men have led more than one major police department, including Watson's mentor, Lee Brown, who led four departments in his career, beginning with Multnomah County, Oregon (in which Portland is located), where he started his career in policing, before moving to police departments in Atlanta, Houston, and New York City.

Harrington and Watson are personally almost polar opposites. Like Harrington, Watson had been denied opportunities in her career, but she rejected filing lawsuits. After she retired, she advised women to focus on self-knowledge rather than a sex-based interpretation of events. And she remained committed to a gender-blind approach to policing, refusing to attribute particular skills or abilities to either men or women. "There is probably too much emphasis given to generic titles like male and female anyway. In the final analysis," she said, "I think that it's probably more damaging than helpful."[14] Only in 2003 did she speak of the bias she faced in Austin, telling the *Dallas–Fort Worth Star–Telegram* that resentment against her had been so strong that one officer made T-shirts that characterized her in vulgar terms that she preferred not to repeat. Far more the optimist than Harrington, she called the sentiment "not typical," recalling that "We love Chief Watson" bumper stickers began to appear as a countermessage to the shirts.[15]

BEVERLY HARVARD: SHE WON THE BET

Beverly Harvard, who was chief in Atlanta from October 1994 until June 2002, joined the Atlanta Police Department in 1973, one year after Harrington finally won her promotion to detective. Because she never served in a women's bureau, as Harrington had, and was never told to make her own uniform, as Watson had been, she is a bridge between them and today's women chiefs. She was also the first, and until 2001 the only, African-American woman to lead a major-city department. Although African-American women were acting or interim chiefs in the years between 2001 and 2003, and a few led smaller departments, another African-American woman did not hold a permanent appointment in a large department until Annetta Nunn was selected chief in Birmingham in February 2003.

Harvard joined the Atlanta Police Department to win a $100 bet with her husband, Jim, a Delta Airlines employee, who had agreed with their friends that policing was not a job for a small woman with a degree in sociology. Harvard was not fulfilling a lifelong dream. A quiet woman, she seemed to relish retelling her almost accidental entry into policing.

Based in part on her sociology studies, she and Jim had talked often about the police. She did not think there was anything about the job that would prevent a woman from being good at it, but Jim didn't always agree. A conversation with friends began, as many about the police do, over someone having received a traffic ticket. From there, it led to a discussion on whether women could be effective police officers. The conversation was in the context of the Atlanta Police Department's having announced that it would begin to aggressively recruit women, a policy Harvard supported. Reflecting stereotypes of policemen, the couple's friends allowed that the right woman—large and aggressive—could do the job, but that that it wasn't a career for an average woman. Harvard had expected her husband to say that his wife could do anything she set out to do. She was disappointed that he agreed with the others that "she could never be a police officer."

At the time, Harvard, a twenty-three-year-old graduate of Atlanta's historically black Morris Brown College, was not particularly interested in becoming a police officer, but the conversation turned into the bet that changed both her life and that of her husband. Despite her studies, she had a limited knowledge of policing and the police hiring process. Showing the persistence that would help her move up the ranks, she learned the process and, like many new employees who were often assigned prior to attending to police academy, got her first taste of policing in the communications section. Even then, her interest was only minimally piqued, and she felt she would stay just long enough to learn police lingo, constitutional law, and self-defense training at the academy. Like Watson, she did not initially expect to make policing her career.

From this haphazard entry, Harvard discovered that she could put her sociology skills to use helping people. Jim, though, had his doubts and was totally unprepared for her first assignment—foot patrol from 6 P.M. to 2 A.M. in one of Atlanta's high-crime areas. Years after she became chief, she recalled that Jim was so concerned that he followed her and her partner around their beat in his car, something he stopped doing only because she feared it would get her fired.[16]

After two years on patrol, Harvard began to move up the ranks and
into other assignments, including a stint as the department's public affairs director. The public affairs post was a visible one in the early 1980s
during a rash of child murders, and Harvard handled the media frenzy
with poise that brought her notice. In 1984 she became the department's
first African-American female deputy chief, which led to assignments in
career development, criminal investigations, and the administrative services division. By the time she turned thirty-seven, she and her husband
were comfortable with her career, and they decided it was time to have a
family. Their daughter, Christa, was born in 1988. A pregnant deputy
chief in 1988 did not garner anywhere near the media attention that
would come to Watson later in Houston.

Harvard was aware that her selection would "probably open up new
opportunities for women to serve in ranking positions around the country." When she was named chief, she held the rank of deputy chief and
had been considered for the position in 1990, but lost out to Eldrin Bell,
whose retirement created the vacancy she filled, and whose position she
had been filling on an acting basis prior to being named chief. Prophet-
ically, Bell retired over differences with Atlanta Mayor Bill Campbell, who
remained mayor throughout Harvard's tenure and to whom many crit-
ics felt she paid undue deference. It had been obvious during Bell's tenure that Campbell was a mayor who maintained tight control over his
police department.

At the time of her selection as chief, Harvard described herself as
"driven by my goals, and now my goal is to be the best police chief the
Atlanta Police Department ever had." She rarely stated before or after her
appointment that it had been her goal to become the chief, but when she
learned that she was a finalist for the position, she turned down an offer
from Attorney General Janet Reno to head the DOJ's newly developed
community policing division.[17] In another indication of how closely en-
twined the careers of the pioneer women chiefs had become, and how
the first woman attorney general, who was in office from 1993 to 2000
(throughout the administration of President William J. Clinton) had
sought a high-profile woman for the community policing initiative, a similar position was subsequently filled by Watson in 1997.

Although Harvard has stated that she had "not always enjoyed approval
among her male peers," she left on her own schedule. In 2002 she declined to apply for re-appointment by Atlanta's new mayor, Shirley
Franklin, who then appointed a man from outside the department.
Harvard became assistant director of security at Atlanta's Hartsfield International Airport, working with Willie Williams, the airport's federal

security director, who had been a high-ranking police official in Philadelphia and then chief of the Los Angeles Police Department.[18]

Harvard's lengthy tenure allows for a discussion of her role as a chief
rather than solely of her symbolism as either a woman chief or an African-
American woman chief. At the time she took control, Atlanta had about
1,700 police officers and a budget of about $100 million. It had a more
severe crime problem than either Portland or Houston. In 1994 *Money*
magazine had called Atlanta the country's most violent city; and that same
year it was ranked sixth in the number of violent crimes per capita, based
on the Federal Bureau of Investigation (FBI)'s Uniform Crime Reporting system.[19]

Like any big-city chief with a lengthy tenure, Harvard oversaw and
survived a number of high-profile controversies. In the first two years of
her tenure, Atlanta hosted the Olympic Games, the Paralympics, and the
Freedom Fest (formerly Freaknik). Of the three, Freaknik was the most
controversial; it placed Atlanta in the spotlight annually, but the 1995 and
1997 celebrations were particularly difficult for Harvard. The festival drew
about 100,000 students from primarily black colleges and resembled
spring breaks that Daytona and Fort Lauderdale, Florida, had tried to
regulate when out-of-control behavior overrode the commercial and tour-
ist benefits they provided. In 1995 Freaknik turned rowdier than in past
years, resulting in about 200 arrests, mostly for disorderly conduct and
traffic violations, but some for serious offenses such as theft, weapons
concealment, and possession of narcotics. Reflecting her self-described
straitlaced background, Harvard spoke about what she believed was the
shameful way young women behaved and said that she was "mad as hell"
that women took off their clothes and allowed themselves to be fondled
by groups of men. She reported that Atlanta's rape crisis center had seen
a sharp increase in cases over the three-day event, and reminded young
women that it was more difficult to criticize men for mistreating women
when women behaved as some of the attendees had.

Harvard also had to deal with a number of corruption scandals, which
led to scrutiny of the department and of her management skills. In early
1996 an Atlanta grand jury refused to indict two police officers who had
been involved in a shoot-out with suspected robbers at a motorcycle shop,
although some eyewitnesses had claimed that one unarmed victim had
been shot at pointblank range. Harvard changed procedures for canvassing
for witnesses after it was disclosed that it took twenty days before police
interviewed the four witnesses whose version of the shooting differed from
that of the police officers. Faced with charges that the police had intentionally or inadvertently conducted a weak investigation and tried to cover
up the incident, Harvard defended the department at the same time that

she announced new rules on crime scene investigations. Although Mayor Campbell asserted his confidence in Harvard's ability to run the department, he also announced that he would reactivate the city's defunct Civilian Review Board that had been created in the 1980s after a series of shootings at public housing projects but by 1990 had been allowed to languish by Mayor Maynard Jackson.[20]

A second controversy echoed the Los Angeles Rodney King beating videotape in 1991. As in Los Angeles, the Atlanta brutality case involved white officers who were captured by a bystander's video camera in a confrontation with a black motorist during the 1997 Freaknik celebration. Taking a very different position from Los Angeles Chief Ed Davis, Harvard quickly defused the situation, but only by admitting that it was "highly questionable" whether a sergeant needed to strike Timmie Sinclair, a motorcyclist who defied a police roadblock. Despite her announcement that disciplinary action would be taken against the sergeant and another officer, Harvard faced criticism from segments of the black community. Sinclair's attorney drew attention to Harvard's sex, referring to her as "a remarkable woman," but one who needed to "put order back in law and order."[21]

Other scandals bracketed Harvard's career. The first was in 1995, only months after her appointment, when six police officers were arrested on charges ranging from shaking down drug dealers to extorting money from citizens in exchange for police protection. Although the cases stemmed from activities before she was the chief, as the incumbent, Harvard was placed in the unenviable position of having to comment on the arrests of her officers. Looking for the positive side, she stressed that the cases had come to light when other officers had reported their corrupt colleagues. "I look at it two ways," she told the public in the fall of 1995. "One, it is really sad anytime that you have police officers accused of a crime, but I think the bigger story is that we have a number of officers who felt so compelled and moved by what they were hearing going on that they came forward and spoke out."[22]

A final controversy involved crime reporting practices. Reporting crime is an inexact science. Many cities, particularly those which have held mass events where people might report crime and then leave the city, or those with large homeless populations, where it may be difficult to locate victims for follow-up information, have had their crime statistics questioned. Particularly since the mid-1990s, when crime rates became the standard by which police chiefs and even mayors were judged, the quarterly announcements of the Uniform Crime Reports by the FBI, and in particular whether certain cities' crime rates have increased or decreased, have been a source of political capital for mayors.

In Atlanta, the combined federal-state audit began in May 1998 when a former deputy chief's allegations that the department was downgrading its crime rate by improperly listing a number of cases as unfounded—meaning they could not be confirmed and therefore did not need to be counted in crime classifications—became public. The audit, released in early 1999, confirmed that a statistically significant percentage of the rapes, robberies, and auto thefts reported in 1996 had been incorrectly downgraded and that, based on a sample of crime reports, the error rate for 1996 was over 25 percent, more than double the previous year's error rate. To put the figures into perspective, what this meant in Atlanta was that 498 robberies—more than one a day—were misclassified, resulting in a claim that robberies had declined by 9 percent over the previous year, when in fact they had risen by 1 percent. Fifty-six rapes were also found to have been improperly downgraded, undercutting the city's claim that rapes had declined 11 percent from 1995, when they had actually risen by 2 percent.[23]

This type of situation frequently calls into question both a chief's integrity and management capability. If the chief doesn't know crimes are being misreported, the implication is that he or she is not aware of the department's administrative inadequacies. If the chief is aware, the implication is that crime is being intentionally downgraded to make the department look more efficient, and the city safer, than it really is. An allegation of misreporting or underreporting from within the department often stems from an officer trying to undercut the chief, which was at play in Atlanta. Earlier allegations about Atlanta's crime reporting policies, made while Harvard was acting chief, had resulted in the demotion and an $8,000 pay cut for the officer whose claims resulted in the second audit. Harvard was again successful in weathering the controversy, claiming vindication because the allegations of "gross" underreporting were not substantiated.

Many in Atlanta believed that Harvard had not been permitted to exercise full control over the department because of micromanaging by Mayor Campbell. Whether that was true or not, there was never any consideration that the new mayor would retain Harvard; she did not even re-apply for the position. The chief who replaced her, Richard Pennington, is one of a number of chiefs who have carved out national reputations as reform managers. Pennington, selected from a group of five candidates nominated by a search firm that Mayor Franklin relied on, came to Atlanta in July 2002 from New Orleans, where he had been chief for eight years. He was careful not to criticize Harvard, noting that he did not see the systemic corruption that had led to his hiring in New Orleans, where he gained a reputation for having cut crime, upgraded the department's technology, and introduced a new crime-tracking system. Despite Pennington's sidestepping comments on Harvard's tenure, an audit of the department's crime statistics released in February 2004 concluded that the department had been consistently underreporting crime since at least the mid-1990s, in part to improve the city's image for tourists and to help in the selection of the city as the site for the 1996 summer Olympics.[24] Pennington had negotiated a pay package worth more than $226,000 annually, which included a base salary of $157,000, considerably more than the $113,000 Harvard earned her last year as chief. While Harvard was earning significantly less than other Southeastern chiefs, Pennington was one of the three highest paid chiefs in the nation, although not the highest paid city official in Atlanta.[25]

Harvard is the transitional figure in women's careers as chiefs of police. Despite controversies, she had a long tenure for a big-city chief. Although she was featured in general-interest magazines aimed at African-Americans and invited to speak at women in policing gatherings, she did not closely associate herself with women in policing and seemed to concentrate primarily on cultivating local support networks. In this way, too, she was a transitional figure, certainly very different from Harrington but somewhat closer to Watson. Of the three, she was best able to become "the police chief" rather than the "woman police chief."

Ironically, it was often in association with Fulton County Sheriff Jackie Barrett, also an African-American woman, that Harvard was seen in the context of race and sex. The two were sometimes featured together, although Barrett was more likely to mention the overlapping of their careers, just as parts of their jurisdictions overlapped (Fulton County includes portions of Atlanta). Barrett said it spoke volumes about the changing demographics and power structures of the American South that two African-American women could lead major law enforcement agencies in the state. But their careers also indicate that assumptions about sisterhood can be extended too far. Although Barrett had supported Franklin, an African-American, to become Atlanta's mayor in 2002, it was Franklin who replaced Harvard with Pennington.

THE LESS WELL-KNOWN PIONEERS

One other woman has led a large-city police department, and a handful of others were interim or acting chiefs. Elaine Hedtke was chief of the Tucson, Arizona, Police Department from March 1992 to December 1993. While Harrington and Watson garnered headlines, Hedtke, an eighteen-year veteran when she was named chief of the 1,000-person (770 officers and 300 civilians) department, worked in obscurity. Her predecessor, longtime Chief Peter Ronstadt, received more press as the brother of pop star Linda Ronstadt than Hedtke did as the first woman chief.

When she was named chief, Hedtke was described by the city manager as the "perfect person for the job," a nationally recognized, progressive law enforcement executive who "understands the big picture socially and environmentally, and has excellent people and communications skills." But, like Harrington, she did not have the support of the department. The Fraternal Order of Police (the union she had once belonged to) held two rallies against her. Although none would say that it was because she was a woman, her command staff tried to undermine her leadership. Hedtke resigned to oversee Tucson's plan to annex surrounding areas that added about 215,000 residents to the city. Because the city charter required the chief to work full-time, she was named an assistant chief in charge of recruitment, training, and personnel matters. She used the position to serve out her twenty years to obtain her full pension benefits, and retired in January 1995.[26]

Carole A. Mehrling, chief of the Montgomery County (Maryland) Police Department, had a more successful tenure. From 1995 to 1999, Mehrling was the first woman to head a county police department, and during the time she was at its helm, it was the second largest department (after Atlanta), to be led by a woman.

Sonya Proctor was acting chief of the Washington, D.C., Metropolitan Police Department from mid-1997 to April 1998. She had been an assistant chief at the time she was named acting chief. Like Harrington and Watson, she was higher in rank than her husband, a patrol officer in the department. In April 1998, Charles Ramsey was brought in from the Chicago Police Department as chief, and Proctor returned to her assistant chief's position. Later that year, in September, Ramsey demoted two assistants, including Proctor. When he offered her a position as night-shift supervisor, a considerable reduction in prestige, she chose to retire after twenty-four years with the department.

Mary Bounds served as interim chief of the Cleveland Police Department, an approximately 2,000-person agency that ranks in the top twenty-five largest, from August 2001 to February 2002. At the time, Harvard was chief in Atlanta, placing two of the major-city departments in the hands of African-American women. Bounds, fifty-four at the time, was a twenty-one-year veteran who had been a precinct commander, the executive assistant to the chief, and the deputy chief of administration. She was the seventh chief that Mayor Michael White, unpopular with police, had appointed during his twelve-year tenure. Her own tenure was questionable from the first day since White was not running for re-election.

A Cleveland native, Bounds had become a police officer for economic security. The daughter of a machinist and a homemaker, she married right out of high school and bore three children before her marriage ended. She enrolled at Cuyahoga Community College and was working as a supermarket cashier when she saw a police department recruitment poster and was attracted by the salary, fringe benefits, and opportunities for advancement. While working patrol, she earned a bachelor's degree from Notre Dame College, and later a master's degree in business from Baldwin-Wallace College.

Bounds's selection as chief was an issue in the campaign to replace White; she had strong support in the black community, and one of the mayoral candidates, Raymond Pierce, a former deputy assistant secretary in the U.S. Department of Education's Office of Civil Rights, promised to retain her if he was elected. Jane Campbell, a Cuyahoga County commissioner, said only that she would review Bounds along with other city appointees. Campbell won, and on February 12, 2002, she replaced Bounds with Edward F. Lohn, another veteran Cleveland police officer who had joined the department in 1981, a year after Bounds, but had a more traditional career path, moving to the rank of sergeant in 1985, lieutenant in 1993, captain in 2000, and chief in 2002. Probably to avert political fallout from bypassing Bounds, Campbell, who is white, said the chief's selection had been made by Public Safety Director James Draper, who had been sworn in only a week earlier. Announcing that he sought a "command staff that looks like the city of Cleveland in terms of diversity," Draper asked Bounds to take charge of recruitment and training, which she agreed to do.

Bounds is one of three big-city chiefs who disproved ideas that female mayors might be more partial to female police chiefs. Although Watson was named Houston's chief by a female mayor, the same mayor later gave her a low performance rating that resulted in her leaving the post, and in 2003 Harvard was replaced by a new female mayor. Each of the more recent women chiefs was selected by a male administrator, and one, Milwaukee's Nannette Hegerty, was not supported by the sole woman member of the board that appointed her.

CHAPTER 9

Twenty-First Century Big-City Women: Is the Playing Field Finally Level?

I always thought being a police officer would be a neat job, but when I was growing up, it wasn't considered a job for a woman.
—Chief Nannette Hegerty
Milwaukee Police Department

I have a reputation for being tough, but that toughness is tempered with fairness.
—Chief Ella Bully-Cummings
Detroit Police Department

People sometimes think women think differently than men, but no matter how we think, we are professionals first. We bring all the other skills of our gender and our culture to that.
—Chief Heather Fong
San Francisco Police Department

This is truly a dream come true, but I want a swearing-in, not a coronation.
—Commissioner Kathleen O'Toole
Boston Police Department

It seemed like just another swearing in of a Boston police commissioner. Hundreds of well-wishers at New Boston Pilot Middle School watched the bagpipers and drummers and observed high-ranking officers in their dress uniforms. Commissioner O'Toole was prominent in Boston's Irish-American community and served on the Patten Commission to transform the Royal Ulster Constabulary into the Northern Ireland Police Service;

daughter Meghan was a junior at Trinity College in Ireland. The commissioner had once been an intern at the State House of Representatives and had known the mayor for many years, was a former Boston police officer who had walked a beat downtown before being laid off due to budget cuts in 1981, and had a number of family members who served in the department.

Business as usual? Not quite. This Commissioner O'Toole was named Kathleen, and the relatives who were the former members of the Boston Police Department were her husband, Dan, a retired detective, and her father-in-law. When she was sworn in on February 19, 2004, two weeks after Mayor Thomas Menino announced her selection, O'Toole became the fourth woman named to head a major-city police department since October 2003. Until she became its thirty-eighth commissioner, the Boston Police Department had been the only one of the twenty largest police departments in the nation that had never had any but white male police commissioners.

O'Toole's appointment was the fourth unforeseen police announcement within a four-month span. The surprises had begun on October 17, 2003, when the *Milwaukee Journal Sentinel* announced that Nannette Hegerty would be named chief in Milwaukee, Wisconsin, and that Milwaukee would become the largest city in the country to have a woman police chief. But before Hegerty could be sworn in on November 18, she went from chief of the largest department with a woman in charge to chief of the second largest. Two weeks earlier, Ella Bully-Cummings had become the interim chief in Detroit, a title from which the "interim" disappeared within a month.

Both Hegerty and Bully-Cummings had started their careers in their departments, left for a while, and returned in a rank lower than chief before ascending to the top spot, and both replaced unpopular chiefs. Observers were astounded that women were selected to lead departments in old, industrial, Midwestern cities, where heavily unionized police departments were not viewed as conducive to change, including accepting women as equal members of the police and fire departments. O'Toole's circumstances were somewhat different; although she had started her career in her department, she had left for a long time, and the chief she replaced was not unpopular. Yet Boston seemed as unlikely a city to select a woman to head its police department as either Milwaukee or Detroit.

Even before the dust had settled on the appointments of Hegerty and Bully-Cummings, on January 22, 2004, the San Francisco Police Commission voted to confirm Mayor Gavin Newsom's choice of Heather Fong as acting chief of the department. Fong, who replaced a chief who departed amid controversy, was urged by Newsom to apply to the committee searching for a permanent chief. She did, but by the time she was named permanent chief on April 14, 2004, she was no longer the third woman, but had been become the fourth woman chief of a big-city police department. In the interim, on February 19, 2004, O'Toole had been sworn in as Boston's commissioner.

Four women police chiefs in four major cities in four months! Between October 2003 and February 2004 women had been named the police chief by four major American cities. It had been unusual enough that four of the county's eighteen largest police departments had changed chiefs within such a short period of time. It was beyond anyone's calculation that all the new chiefs would be women.

Was this a revolution in American policing? Could it be considered a revolution when each of the chiefs had started her career in the department she now led, and three had spent the majority of their working lives in those departments? Was it just a coincidence that these women were there when their cities were looking for new chiefs, or was it that finally—after thirty years of legal equality—women had been around long enough and had proved their mettle sufficiently to receive serious consideration for some of the highest-profile police jobs in the country? Was the brass ceiling finally shattered?

This is possible for if the four women chiefs didn't represent a sea change, additional history had been made from the audience at O'Toole's swearing in. Sitting with the usual police and government dignitaries was Suffolk County (Massachusetts) Sheriff Andrea Cabral, whose appointment in November 2002 made her the first woman and only the second African-American to hold that position. Boston is located within Suffolk County, and now O'Toole and Cabral would duplicate the unusual combination of two women holding the highest-ranking law enforcement positions that Atlanta's Chief Beverly Harvard and Fulton County (Georgia) Sheriff Jackie Barrett had represented until Harvard stepped down in June 2002.

Former Portland, Oregon, Chief Penny Harrington predicted that the women would be under much closer scrutiny than male chiefs would be, although she agreed with Hegerty's view that it was impossible to calculate the importance for young girls to see women succeed in all professions. The scrutiny, though, might be more positive than Harrington suspected. The new big-city women chiefs—with the exception of Boston's O'Toole—broke their departments' brass ceilings in ways that were quite similar to men around the country and to their sister chiefs in smaller communities. Their major difference was that they were more ethnically diverse (two of the four women are members of nonwhite racial groups that wield political power in their communities) than the women leading smaller departments.

These women were not flukes or feel-good appointments. They were veteran officers who had served in a wide variety of patrol and administrative assignments, and each had a bachelor's degree and either a master's or a law degree. With the exception of O'Toole, each moved through the ranks of her department in a pattern and time frame similar to male officers, and each had held a variety of management positions before ascending to chief.

What resonated in the selection of the women was that they were chosen as managers but also as healers in departments that had undergone a series of crises. Each talked about relying on staff input and enhancing the morale and pride of the police officers, but each also had a reputation as a disciplinarian and a demanding boss. Whether this reinforced feminine stereotypes of women as communicators, conciliators, and team players, or reinforced the fact that municipal leaders now see policing less as an action-adventure film and more like the multi-million-dollar business that it is, remains to be seen. Both Hegerty's and Bully-Cummings's departments' prior chiefs were controversial, and police officers voiced satisfaction that they were leaving. Milwaukee's chief, who had spent his entire career in the department, fought openly with Mayor John Norquist. Detroit's chief, an outsider who was unpopular despite having brought Bully-Cummings back after her retirement, became involved in a controversy over an unlicensed firearm that resulted in his arrest.

If one were looking to support the view of women chiefs as healers, Bully-Cummings and Fong would come closest to filling that role. Both were selected in the wake of serious missteps by their predecessors. Of the four, two—Bully-Cummings, who retired to practice law before returning to the department, and Fong, who never left—gained all their management experience inside their departments.

NANNETTE HEGERTY: IT'S IMPORTANT TO ASK

Hegerty, fifty-two when she was selected by the Milwaukee Fire and Police Commission to become the department's seventeenth chief, replaced Arthur Jones, who seven years earlier had become its first African-American chief. Although all five members of the Fire and Police Commission are appointed by the mayor, the board selects the chief and holds oversight of the department, making Milwaukee one of the largest cities whose police chief is not directly responsible to the mayor. The vote for Hegerty was four in favor with one abstention. The abstaining commissioner was Carla Cross, who was the only woman on the board and who declined to discuss why she had abstained, noting only that since Hegerty was the board's selection, she would support the chief in every way she could.[1]

Although this lukewarm support from a woman might seem strange, women chiefs have not received particularly enthusiastic support from women in politics. Of the pioneering big-city chiefs, only one—Houston's Elizabeth (Betsy) Watson—was appointed by a woman, Mayor Kathryn Whitmire, from whom she later received a low employee evaluation. In 2002, Beverly Harvard, the first African-American woman to lead a big-city police department, did not even apply for re-appointment after the city elected its first African-American female mayor, Shirley Franklin. And Jane Campbell, the new woman mayor in Cleveland in 2002, had not retained Interim Chief Mary Bounds. One study that considered whether female mayors had an influence on the increased use of women as police officers found that there was no correlation.[2] This was not too surprising, since mayors may not have much impact on civil service hiring practices, but these few examples would indicate that women mayors may not see the police department as a major concern of their strongest supporters, or may believe that they need to prove their toughness and that a female police chief does not enhance that image.

In Milwaukee, the mayor does not have authority to unilaterally appoint or replace the chief, who serves a fixed term. Hegerty's predecessor had feuded with the mayor for years, but remained chief for his seven-year term. Before Hegerty's selection, the board changed the chief's term to four years, in the hope of minimizing conflict between the mayor and the chief. The fixed term and the appointment process in Milwaukee were the reasons Hegerty's appointment was announced so far in advance of her taking office. Mayor Norquist stepped down shortly after appointing her, and was replaced by City Council President Marvin Pratt, who became acting mayor on January 1, 2004, and who had supported Hegerty's appointment. Pratt was defeated in April in his mayoral bid, but Hegerty's job is assured for the length of her contract.

Hegerty, and most commentators, agreed that her selection had little to do with her being a woman and more to do with her having proven her management and political skills as the U.S. marshal for the Eastern District of Wisconsin, a job to which she was appointed in 1994 by President William J. Clinton and which she held until 2002, when President George W. Bush chose not to re-appoint her and instead named Waukesha County Sheriff William Kruziki to the post. There are ninety-four U.S. marshals, each appointed by the president of the United States, throughout the fifty states, Guam, the Northern Mariana Islands, Puerto Rico, and the Virgin Islands. The Marshals Service works with the federal court

system, and its services include providing court protection, prisoner transportation, and witness security, in addition to investigating and locating
federal fugitives and seizing tangible assets on behalf of the federal government. U.S. marshals are usually selected from among law enforcement
professionals who have been recommended to the president, and although
some have been re-appointed by a new president, it is more common,
particularly when there is a change in party, for the incumbent U.S.
marshal to be replaced.

Although a U.S. marshal is usually of the same party as the president,
Hegerty, while declining to specify her party affiliation, said that she had
worked for more Republicans than Democrats. How, then, did she get
to lead the Eastern District office, with its fifteen sworn officers and annual budget of $8.4 million, headquartered in Milwaukee and active in
twenty-eight Wisconsin counties?[3] Somewhat nontraditionally, she asked.
She made inquiry to Wisconsin's two Democratic senators, Herbert Kohl
and Russ Feingold, and "being in the right place at the right time, very
fortunately, I was chosen." Hegerty's approach was nontraditional not
only in its failure to respect the politics of the selection process, but also
in her willingness to ask. According to research by economists Linda
Babcock and Sara Laschever, women's careers fall behind their males colleagues' careers because they are not comfortable with asking for what
they believe they deserve. Even worse, sometimes they are so unsure of
what they deserve they don't consider negotiating at all, leading to an
"accumulation of disadvantage" by falling farther behind those, mostly
men, who are willing to ask.[4]

In Hegerty's case, asking to take over an office far smaller than most
of the assignments within the Milwaukee Police Department helped her
gain an advantage. She is a great advocate of the importance of networking
within her profession, and the eight years she spent as the U.S. marshal
gave her an opportunity to work with federal officials and numerous state
and local law enforcement leaders. When she was not re-appointed,
Hegerty returned that May to the department in her civil service rank of
captain and was placed in charge of the sensitive crimes division, which
handles a number of issues involving juveniles, including truancy, a major
problem facing Milwaukee's public schools.

Her willingness to ask rather than to wait to be asked was as important in Hegerty's selection as chief as her management and people skills.
She said that although she was initially conflicted when she learned that
she could possibly be the next chief, she discussed it with her husband
carefully because she felt that if she applied, she would get the job, and
she didn't want it to jeopardize her marriage. Her husband, George, a
former Milwaukee Police Department captain, was able to provide more

than just spousal support; he had worked as an aide for two Milwaukee chiefs and understood the demands of the job, she said, "possibly better than I did."

Hegerty believed the skills she gained outside the department were crucial in her selection. This also seemed to be true for Bully-Cummings and O'Toole, both of whom were lauded for the skills they had gained outside their departments. Boston's Mayor Menino stressed this when he described O'Toole as "both an insider and an outsider; that's a good combination."[5] Milwaukee's Mayor Norquist wasn't as glib, but said the same thing when he praised Hegerty's "great record" with the Milwaukee Police Department and with the U.S. marshals. A number of the Milwaukee commissioners also mentioned her leadership qualities, her confidence, and her experience managing a law enforcement agency as the reasons for her selection.[6]

Hegerty chose not to have her swearing-in ceremony center on her sex. She said she did not believe being a woman would affect how she would do the job. "I'm the chief," she said, "not the woman chief, although possibly women in the department feel differently." She focused instead on her twenty-seven years in law enforcement. When Hegerty joined the Milwaukee Police Department in 1976, she took a pay cut from her job as a Delta Airlines ticket agent. She had been hired as a flight attendant but wanted to return to her hometown. Since Delta did not fly from Milwaukee, she settled for a ground position that she did not find fulfilling. When she saw an ad on a local television station urging women and minorities to become police officers, she decided to try it.

She remembered that some in her recruit class, which included a handful of other women, had long-range goals, but hers was only to be the best police officer she could be. After about ten years, she felt she had done that, and she took the test for sergeant and was promoted in 1987. She became a lieutenant in 1990, and in 1991, the department's first female captain. She had received a bachelor's degree in education from the University of Wisconsin at Oshkosh prior to becoming a police officer, and, like many of the women chiefs, had continued her education, receiving a master's degree in management from Cardinal Stritch College (now Cardinal Stritch University) in 1985.

Hegerty also attended a number of law enforcement's "management finishing schools," including the Northwestern University School of Police Staff and Command and, in 1988, the Federal Bureau of Investigation's National Academy (FBINA). At the FBINA she shared a room with another woman who became a chief: Gaithersburg, Maryland's, Mary Ann Viverette. Both women made strategic moves to further their careers. Viverette left the larger Montgomery County (Maryland) Sheriff's

Department in 1978 to join the much smaller Gaithersburg department and Hegerty sought the appointment as U.S. marshal even though the office was small in comparison to the Milwaukee Police Department. Each gained from her willingness to take risks and make career changes. Viverette's department is much smaller than Hegerty's but if Viverette remains a chief until 2006 she will become the first woman president of the International Association of Chiefs of Police (IACP) in its more than 100-year history.

Hegerty became her department's first female captain in 1991, but by the time she was named chief, other women held higher rank than she did, including Deputy Chief Monica Ray, the highest ranking African-American woman, who had also achieved firsts for women, also held undergraduate and graduate degrees, and was also a graduate of the FBINA. Although Ray was not a candidate for chief, Susan Edman, another woman captain, had been, making Milwaukee the first large city in which two women were serious applicants for the chief's post. It is likely that as women continue to move up the ranks, more women will be vying against other women for top positions. It is also likely, as occurred in San Francisco, that as women chiefs shuffle their top commands, some of the winners and losers will be other women.

Even as she downplayed her role as a change agent for women, Hegerty was a symbol of how times had changed. She recalled that when she was growing up she thought being a police officer would have been "a neat job," but one that wasn't available to women at the time. But by 2003, she could be more expansive, noting that she felt she had almost been led to the position by the opportunities she'd had. "It seems to me," she said, "in looking back on my life and how I arrived here, now it almost seems like it's been my destiny and I really don't know why."

With her husband holding the Bible on which she was sworn in, Hegerty pledged to make Milwaukee a safer place to live and to draw on community support to reduce crime. Symbolically, she ended her first day as chief some ten hours later at a community meeting, where she told about fifty residents of the area that crime was not solely a police problem, but also a community problem. Although Hegerty received enthusiastic support from union leaders, she obviously had enemies. There had been an allegation, found to be untrue, that she and her husband were not fulfilling Milwaukee's requirement that members of the department live within the city. They had purchased a condominium prior to her selection as chief. The couple has no children together, but George has two adult children from a previous marriage.

Hegerty faced other controversies that were less personal. The department had just under 2,000 officers, 371 of whom were women, and a budget of about $170 million, but the budget had been stretched by overtime and morale was low due to the residency requirement and to controversies surrounding former Chief Jones. Possibly responding to claims by officers that Jones was a "bully" who considered no one but himself in setting policing priorities, Hegerty promised that she would "treat officers with respect—letting them know at every turn that I possibly can how important their job is." She also promised to meet with commanders and a transition team to work on a "business plan" before making any radical changes. Jones's unpopularity was surprising, since he had spent his entire career in the department and had early support from African-American officers. But like Portland's Harrington, he had filed many lawsuits claiming discriminatory practices, and in a strong parallel to her career, at least one lawsuit was still pending when he left.

In a city in which no single racial or ethnic group held a majority in 2004 (45 percent of residents were white, 38 percent were black, and 12 percent were Latino), the mayoral race was steeped in issues of race, and the department, too, had faced divisive issues. By February 2004 Hegerty had waded into the racial politics, promoting to captain an African-American lieutenant who had alleged that Jones had passed over him because of his associations with whites.[7] She also began to address use-of-force issues, indicating that she would replace the department's internal affairs unit, made up solely of police personnel, with a professional standards board; would consider implementing a computerized early-warning system to track problem officers; and would consider creating a community advisory board.[8] Each of these issues is devoid of gender markers, permitting her to reinforce her image as a manager rather than as a male or a female manager. But each could erode her support within the department.

ELLA BULLY-CUMMINGS: FROM A FOOT POST TO CHIEF

When Bully-Cummings was named interim chief of the 4,200-member Detroit Police Department on November 3, 2003, she became the first woman since Houston's Elizabeth (Betsy) Watson to lead one of the six largest police departments in the nation. Despite the "interim" in Bully-Cummings's title, Mayor Kwame Kilpatrick stated there would be no national search for a chief. "This is the chief of this department," he said, "we're not looking for anybody else. We want to make sure we're all engaged and moving in the right direction."[9] One month later, on December 4, without any formal announcement, he removed the "interim" from her title. She joined eight other women as chiefs in the state of

Michigan, seven in small communities and one in charge of a community college campus police department.

Although the mayor called her rise through the department "meteoric," Bully-Cummings had spent time in every rank, which resulted in favorable responses to her selection within the department. She had returned to the department at the request of the man she replaced, Jerry Oliver, an outside chief who was unpopular from the day he had arrived twenty-one months earlier. Oliver was charged by the Wayne County (in which Detroit is located) attorney with possession of an unlicensed handgun, a misdemeanor punishable by up to ninety days in jail, after federal airport authorities on October 18, 2003, found an unregistered, loaded handgun in his luggage at Detroit Metro Airport when he was traveling to a police conference in Philadelphia. He said he had bought the gun in Phoenix in 1973, while a police officer there, and claimed he was unaware that he had to register it in Michigan, but had also failed to tell airport authorities about the gun. The issue was complicated because he had not yet become a licensed, sworn police officer in Michigan. Oliver, who had fired police officers for less serious incidents, resigned and pled no contest to a civil infraction that carried a fine of between $300 and $1,000.

Oliver embodied many of the elements that make outside chiefs unpopular. He began his policing career in Phoenix, and had been chief in Pasadena, California, before going to Richmond, Virginia, in 1995. He moved to Detroit in February 2002, selected by Kilpatrick as a change agent who would impose high standards and severe discipline. He was consistently at odds with the Detroit Police Officers Association (the police union), primarily over what officers believed to be Draconian disciplinary procedures and punishments.

Bully-Cummings was the opposite. She had joined the Detroit Police Department at age nineteen, after seeing a woman in uniform when she was selling tickets at a Detroit movie theater. She began her policing career on a foot post, walking a beat, and remained until 1999 except for a period in the early 1980s when she and other new officers were laid off during the city's fiscal problems; then she worked for the *Detroit Free Press* in a variety of clerical positions before returning to the department. Since her promotion to sergeant in 1987 she had held every rank in the department, becoming a lieutenant in 1993, an inspector in 1995, a commander in 1998, and then an assistant chief in May 2002, when she returned after her retirement to practice law in 1999. As is common in large police departments, each promotion led to a change of assignment; she worked in a number of precincts in supervisory and command positions, and gained administrative experience in public information, crime prevention, training, and personnel.

Although she practiced law after her retirement and before returning to the department, Bully-Cummings was away for only three years, far less than Hegerty's eight or O'Toole's seventeen, and those in the department viewed her as an insider. It was Oliver who had persuaded her to return as the department's first female assistant chief. Forty-six when she was named chief, Bully-Cummings was one of three assistant chiefs and was the highest-ranking woman. She stressed that she was up to the challenge but that the "job is bigger than any one person, and it was only with the confidence of the mayor, the assistant chiefs, deputy chiefs, commanders, inspectors, and rank-and-file officers" that it could be done. She admitted to being "a bit numb" and "humbled" by her selection, and saw it as the "pinnacle" of her career.

Despite a reputation as a strong disciplinarian, Bully-Cummings preferred to see herself as someone who just had to push harder than her male peers. Cautiously, she allowed that men and women officers, and by extension managers, might have different styles. "I don't want to say," she added, "that women are more compassionate, humble, or sensitive, but there may be a difference in the way we view a situation." This difference, which on the street may translate into a verbal rather than a physical response, and in management may translate into a more collaborative style, may have played a part in the warm endorsement Bully-Cummings received from one of the other assistant chiefs. Walter Shoulders told the *Detroit News*: "I told her this was coming some time ago, and she didn't believe me. I know she can do the job. She's capable of doing the job. She doesn't have to look behind her as we go forward in doing the job. We've got her back." Comments by lower-ranking officers were also supportive. One sergeant told WXYZ-TV that Bully-Cummings was "just the right woman for the job" because "she had experience, a law degree, and positive leadership qualities." You know," he continued, "she is well respected. I think she will do a fine job."[10]

But Bully-Cummings wasn't always well respected. Like Annetta Nunn, chief of the Birmingham, Alabama, Police Department, Bully-Cummings became a police officer at a time when her department was actively recruiting women and minorities, who were viewed by their overwhelmingly white male colleagues as less qualified and hired only because many departments were under court orders to diversify their staffs. She remembered that some men feigned illness rather than work with her and those who would work with her had little confidence she would be able to assist them in an emergency. She worked hard, she recalled, to prove herself because she knew she would have to be "exceptional to move up through the ranks" but that she ultimately won grudging acceptance from many of her male colleagues.[11]

Her job as chief may be even more difficult; after a federal investigation into the department, city officials agreed in June 2003 to two consent decrees from the U.S. Department of Justice that called for an independent monitor to reform the department's lethal-force policies and treatment of prisoners. Although a number of deadlines had been missed by the time she took over, Bully-Cummings said she would meet every deadline within the designated five-year period. It will not be easy for her to meet her goals of professionalizing the department and reducing crime. Despite crime drops in many large cities around the nation, Detroit continued to suffer from gun violence. In January 2003 there were twenty-six homicides and sixty nonfatal shootings; a year later the numbers were thirty-five homicides and ninety shootings.[12] In February 2004, two police officers, including a woman, were killed during a traffic stop. Vowing to get illegal guns off the streets, Bully-Cummings created a task force to help reduce violence in city neighborhoods, but it has historically been this type of task force that generates citizens' complaints about police brutality. Despite this possibility, she also said she planned to resolve the more than 900 disciplinary cases that Oliver left behind.

A large measure of Bully-Cummings's support comes from her own rags-to-riches story. One of eight children of an African-American serviceman and his Japanese wife, she was born in Japan and moved with her parents to the United States when she was one. She recalled that her father was a strong disciplinarian and that the children were sheltered despite growing up in inner-city Detroit. Although neither of her parents went to college, her brothers and sisters are doctors, lawyers, and teachers, and she, too, graduated from college and law school after she joined the department. At the time she was promoted to lieutenant, she received a bachelor's degree in public administration from Madonna University, and in 1998 earned a J.D. cum laude from Detroit College of Law and Michigan State University. After she retired in 1999, she worked for a Detroit law firm, specializing in labor-management and employment discrimination cases, areas that could assist her in meeting many of the mandates of the consent decrees. Bully-Cummings is married to a former Detroit police commander, and was previously married to Wayne County's Sheriff Warren Evans.

One of the few references to Bully-Cummings's sex came not from her but from a high-ranking retired female officer. Noting that some officers believed Bully-Cummings had a reputation for standoffishness, former Commander Judy Dowling observed that women were required to maintain a "certain veneer" to survive in a male world. "From my own experience," she said, "I'm a lot more fun since I'm retired."[13]

HEATHER FONG: FROM CADET TO CHIEF

When San Francisco's Mayor Gavin Newsom appointed Heather Fong as acting chief of the police department on January 18, 2004, he urged her to apply to the committee searching for a permanent chief. Less than four months later, on April 14, Fong saw the "acting" removed from her title. Fong was reprising the "acting" position she had held for a short time in May 2003, when, while a deputy chief, she had been named the acting assistant chief (the assistant chief is one rank higher than the deputy chief).

Fong is the first Asian-surnamed woman chief of a U.S. police department and the second Asian-American chief of the San Francisco Police Department, which in 2002 was the nation's fourteenth largest department, with slightly more than 2,225 sworn officers. Her selection was accompanied not by the traditional police trappings of bagpipes and kilts that were featured at O'Toole's swearing in, but was announced in the city's Little Saigon neighborhood during the Vietnamese New Year's festival.

It was not the first time that Fong had made department history. In September 1994 she became one of the first three women captains, and in February 1996 she was one of the first two women to command a precinct when she assigned to the Chinatown district. Although San Francisco had employed policewomen since 1913, it wasn't until 1975 that women were assigned to patrol duties on the same basis as men. Fong's age prevented her from being in the first group of women patrol officers. She took the police test at only eighteen. Since the minimum age to be a police officer was twenty-one, Fong worked as a cadet until she was old enough to attend the police academy.

Fong grew up in San Francisco's North Beach area, and is not only an insider to the department, but also a local girl who succeeded beyond her expectations. She was recruited into the department by its first Asian-American chief, Fred Lau, who lived near her and mentored her career. Although she had roots in the Asian-American community and spoke fluent Cantonese and Vietnamese, her career choices were not typical of a young Asian-American girl. She attended local Catholic schools before earning a bachelor's degree from the University of San Francisco, where she later earned a master's degree in social work. While an undergraduate, she not only took the police exam and worked as a cadet, but also joined the Air Force ROTC, receiving a commission as a second lieutenant in the reserves. Fong, forty-seven at the time of her selection, recalled that she had actually planned to work as a court interpreter but found that "sitting in a room and translating looked really boring." Her father, who owned a deli in Oakland and who died before she became chief, and her mother, a legal secretary in a Chinatown law firm, supported her decision to become a police officer, in part because Chief Lau stressed the importance to the city of women and minorities joining the police department.

The situation that led to Fong's appointment was as unusual as the one that led to Bully-Cummings's selection. The department was in upheaval over a scandal that came to be known as "Fajitagate," which stemmed from a street brawl over a bag of steak fajitas that had involved three off-duty police officers in November 2002. One of the officers was the son of Assistant Chief Alex Fagan, and allegations that the incident had been covered up resulted in the indictment of Fagan and Chief Earl Sanders. It was during this time, in March 2003, that Fong had briefly been named acting chief, but when the charges against Fagan were dropped, he returned and was named chief after Sanders retired. Fong was one of the few on the command staff who had managed to stay clear of the scandal, which had occurred during the administration of Mayor Willie Brown.

When Newsom took office in 2004, he promised a new generation of leaders. Unexpectedly, many of the new leaders were women. Fong was the latest of his "women power" appointments—which included a woman criminal justice coordinator and, unusual for a city the size of San Francisco, a woman fire chief. Although many in San Francisco had commented on these and other appointments and elections of women in the city and county, Fong downplayed her sex even as she joined the other women in acknowledging their roles as trailblazers. While Newsom talked about the need for fire and police chiefs who weren't necessarily "kinder and softer," but who recognized "the importance of developing relationships," Fong maintained that although men and women may think differently, "the bottom line is, no matter how we think, we are professionals first. We bring all the other skills of our gender and our cultures to that."[14]

Fong, who spent her entire twenty-six-year career in the department, held every rank from cadet to chief, and moved easily between operational and administrative positions. In addition to patrol, she was a child abuse investigator, an instructor at the police academy, one of the two first women precinct commanders, commander of the planning division and of the special operations division (which included such high-profile units as SWAT), and deputy chief of both field operations and administration. Despite her position as the highest-ranking Asian man or woman before she was named chief, she said her "whole career has been a tryout," and the descriptions of her as modest, reserved, unassuming, straitlaced, and squeaky-clean have been criticized by some as reinforcing Asian stereotypes.

Fong, like Hegerty, moved quickly to take control of the department by making personnel changes. Even before her selection became permanent, she streamlined the top ranks by eliminating a number of positions and demoted two of four deputy chiefs, resulting in changes that called for six command staff members either to retire or to be demoted to their civil service ranks. Some of the changes involved women, a situation that will become more common as more women move through the hierarchy into management-level positions where tenure is not guaranteed and where rank is maintained at the pleasure of the chief.

KATHLEEN O'TOOLE: A SEVENTEEN-YEAR HIATUS

O'Toole is different from the other three chiefs primarily because of the time she spent away from the Boston Police Department and the variety of types of work she did while away, including interludes when she was not involved with policing at all. Her career path is similar to another high-profile police chief, Los Angeles Chief William Bratton, who was one of her earliest supporters in Boston and has remained a mentor throughout her career. Although O'Toole had been away from policing, she remained politically well-connected in Boston and she had gained a variety of management experiences in a number of police and civilian agencies, including her own consulting business. She was the only one of the chiefs whose career could be compared with that of a CEO in private industry rather than a police executive.

O'Toole was also the only one who did not take office following a period of turmoil, although she inherited a department that was undergoing labor unrest among the officers and was faced with fewer than six months to prepare for politicians, delegates, media representatives, assorted hangers-on, and protesters of all sorts who were expected to arrive in the summer of 2004 for the Democratic National Convention.

Like the other chiefs, O'Toole began her career on patrol in her department, and, like Bully-Cummings, she was laid off due to her city's budget problems in 1981. When O'Toole joined the department in 1979, she had already earned a bachelor's degree in political science from Boston College, but because the integration of women onto patrol had not been well-received by male officers, she did not feel this would add to the tenuous acceptance she and the other women received. Boston, like the other three cities, had employed policewomen for much of its history, but these women had a separate career path from male officers, who often had little contact with policewomen. In 1982, Boston had the smallest number (sixty-two) and the smallest percentage (3.7) of women of the five largest departments in the nation.[15] While she was laid off,

O'Toole did two things that influenced her later career choices. She worked at another police agency, the Massachusetts Bay Transportation Authority, the city's transit police department, which broadened her horizons beyond the Boston Police Department; and in 1982 she earned a J.D. degree from the New England School of Law, another credential that she initially told few colleagues about.

In 1986 William Bratton, whose career also had begun in the Boston Police Department, was named chief of yet another police department within Boston—the Metropolitan Police Department, which was the third largest department in the state after the Boston Police Department and the Massachusetts State Police. A division of the Metropolitan District Commission, the department patrolled parks, reservoirs, beaches, parkways, and highways in the Greater Boston area. Bratton believed that O'Toole, by then a sergeant, could help him reform what he called "the worst police department in America." He made her a deputy superintendent, basically his second in command, because he believed her knowledge of the legislative process from the days she had worked as an intern would help in getting funds to equip the department. He was right. The department received more than $3.5 million in state funding, and by 1989 the State Police wanted to take over the 600-person department.[16] Bratton left in April 1990 to become chief of New York City's Transit Police, and O'Toole replaced him as superintendent of the Metropolitan Police, becoming the first female chief of a major department on the East Coast.

O'Toole then moved from government policing to private security, working as an investigator for Digital Equipment Corp., but in 1992, after the State Police had been successful in taking over the Metropolitan Police, O'Toole returned to government service with the title of lieutenant colonel in the State Police, making her one of the highest-ranking women in the nation in a state police agency. Two years later, she moved on again, after Governor William Weld named her secretary of the Office of Public Safety, a cabinet-level umbrella agency with oversight of twenty criminal justice agencies with more than 10,000 employees and an operating budget of more than $1 million. Coincidentally, another former high-ranking woman, New York City's Jane Perlov, held this position from 1998 until 2001, when she was named chief of the Raleigh, North Carolina, Police Department.

In yet another unusual career twist, O'Toole left policing again in 1998 to become head of Boston College's Alumni Association and was also invited that year to serve on the Patten Commission on Policing in Northern Ireland, which played a major role in restructuring the Royal Ulster Constabulary as part of the peace process between Northern Ireland's

Protestant and Catholic populations. In 1999 she was appointed by Mayor Menino, like Bratton a long-time mentor, to a commission that was examining the Boston Fire Department in light of allegations of racial and gender discrimination. In 2000, Menino appointed her to another commission, this one involving waterfront development. That same year she founded O'Toole Associates, an international consulting firm specializing in public affairs and crisis management.

Hegerty had taken a pay cut to become a police officer when she joined the Milwaukee Police Department, but O'Toole took a pay cut to become Boston's $160,000 commissioner, although she assured everyone that it was "dream job." O'Toole is the only police commissioner—male or female—who took a leave of absence from her department as a sergeant and returned seventeen years later as the commissioner. Despite the length of her absence, she was greeted enthusiastically by Boston's three police unions.

IS THE PLAYING FIELD FINALLY LEVEL?

The emergence of four women as major-city police chiefs within months asks the question "Is the playing field finally level?" The only one of the chiefs to tackle this question directly, Hegerty, thought it was, and that if it wasn't quite there yet, it was certainly getting close. But the answer may be somewhat more complex. Writing about successful businesswomen, Virginia O'Brien observed that women of different ages had different expectations and worldviews based on the opportunities open to them. She suggested that it was reasonable to assume that it took twenty-five or thirty years to grow a CEO, since women need to have had positive experiences in the workplace and must believe they have influence over a company's agenda before they can aspire to top rank. Younger women, she observed, had faced fewer barriers; their expectations were loftier; they may have had female mentors or role models; and they felt comfortable making use of both female and male networks.[17]

Although the numbers are still small, there have now been enough women that it is safe to make some generalizations about the careers of women who have been CEOs of large police departments. Even with their obvious differences from private industry, many of O'Brien's suggestions can be observed in the business of policing. The average length of service of the big-city women chiefs was similar to that of the women in industry; each had more than twenty years in policing. None of these women was the first on patrol in her department, but some were the first in various supervisory ranks, indicating that they took full advantage of promotion opportunities throughout their careers.

Each felt comfortable making use of networks, although their networks were primarily within the policing profession. The two women who were members of ethnic minorities were strongly supported by those communities, and O'Toole had roots in Boston's influential Irish-American community. Two of the women, O'Toole and Fong, had powerful mentors; the other two, Bully-Cummings and Hegerty, were less directly influenced by others. In all cases, though, contrary to O'Brien's suggestion that modern women leaders might have had women mentors, this was not the case for the four women police chiefs. Like the smaller city chiefs, their mentors were men. This is not surprising, since even the best and brightest police officers must depend on more than civil service testing to move into management. Assignments and ranks above civil service (sergeant or lieutenant in small departments, captain or higher in major-city departments) create opportunities for even greater upward mobility, and promotion to these is most often determined by those in even higher ranks. As long as men predominate in the departments, male mentors will play pivotal roles in women's career advancement.

Two of the women, O'Toole and Fong, had particularly powerful, high-level mentors, Bratton and Lau, early in their careers. O'Toole had demonstrated drive and risk-taking throughout her career, but it was Bratton who gave her, then one of many Boston Police Department sergeants, a high enough rank to allow her to wield power and authority commensurate with her abilities. O'Toole also followed in Bratton's footsteps by "learning the men's game" of taking risks[18] by making career moves that most would have seen as moving away from, rather than closer to, a police commissioner's badge. Bratton's moves included not only his stints as chief in Boston, but also his time leading first the New York City Transit Police Department, then the New York City Police Department (NYPD), and the Los Angeles Police Department (LAPD). There were various private-sector positions between some of these assignments, and he, too, led a lucrative consulting business before returning to the public sector as the LAPD's chief. O'Toole had also known the mayor who appointed her since her days as an undergraduate intern with the Massachusetts state legislature. Although Fong's original mentor, former Chief Lau, had retired, his influence remained strong. Fong, who had a reputation in the department for careful deliberation rather than risk-taking, had already shown, though, that she, too, was not risk-averse by entering what for a young Asian-American woman was an unusual career: policing.

While it might be a stretch to call Bully-Cummings's predecessor, Chief Oliver, a mentor, since they had worked together for only twenty-one months, his bringing her back into the Detroit Police Department as its highest-ranking woman positioned her for consideration for the top job when his own misstep led to his resignation. And she did remind those who were happy to see him go, that it was he who had convinced her to return to help "reform and rebuild the department," and that she planned to continue the changes he had set in motion. Hegerty did not mention a specific mentor, saying only that she had always been looked on favorably, had received support throughout her career, and had never particularly felt she had to prove herself only because she was a woman. She, too, displayed risk-taking behavior when she applied for the position of U.S. marshal, and was able to rely on her husband for an accurate picture of what it might mean to apply for and become the chief.

The women who led large departments, whether chiefs or sheriffs, were well educated; all had either a master's degree or a law degree. Law school graduates included Bully-Cummings, O'Toole, Sheriff Margo Frasier of Travis County (Texas), and Suffolk County Sheriff Cabral. Although O'Toole never practiced law, each of the others did so prior to coming to her present position, and O'Toole, Bully-Cummings, and Frasier earned their law degrees while working in law enforcement. This high level of education has not been seen among the big-city male chiefs, so it was difficult to determine whether it marked the beginning of a shift from chiefs who are the toughest guys in the valley to those who are more sophisticated managers, or whether it was a continuation of the historical artifact of women in policing having to be better educated to get to the same place men have gotten.

With the possible exception of O'Toole, obvious similarities in the careers of the big-city women chiefs can be discerned, but the selection of a chief of police is a singularly local event. The reason a particular person is selected, and the length of each chief's tenure, is too idiosyncratic to make any but the broadest generalizations. Each jurisdiction is seeking to meet local needs, and a large number of stakeholders may be involved in the process. Among those who might have a direct say in the selection of a chief are mayors, city managers, and city council members; search committees; and outside search firms. Those with indirect influence include the media, labor unions representing police officers and other ranks covered by union agreements (in the largest departments, police officers, sergeants, lieutenants, and even captains might be represented by separate unions), and various special-interest groups, including chambers of commerce, associations representing ethnic or racial minorities, and influential leaders of a community's major industry or industries.[19]

Just as the factors that influence the selection are difficult to discern, so are those that influence a chief's departure. The short tenures and high turnover rates of police chiefs, particularly in large cities, are well documented. Studies in the 1990s found that high turnover was "the rule rather than the exception," and that in the mid-1990s tenure of metropolitan chiefs fell from 5.5 years to between 3.5 and 4.5 years. A 1997 study by the International Association of Chiefs of Police (IACP) estimated that the average tenure for major-city chiefs was 2.5 years, while the Police Executive Research Forum (PERF) reported that the average tenure for chiefs whose jurisdictions encompassed more than 500,000 residents was just below five years. PERF also found that only about 25 percent of the chiefs had employment contracts or agreements, which meant that 75 percent could be asked to leave virtually overnight for practically any reason.[20] Thus, the reason for anyone's arriving or departing—voluntarily or otherwise—might be impossible to discern if the individual or the media did not make an issue of it.

If the career paths of the twenty-first century big-city women chiefs follow the patterns of their male colleagues, their tenures may be short. Only Hegerty is guaranteed her full four-year term. Each, though, is guaranteed a place in women's more than hundred-year history of breaking the brass ceiling.

CHAPTER 10

Women Police Chiefs and Sheriffs: A Collective Portrait

Each of us is her own woman, but we also need to learn from each other's stories.

—Chief Diane Skoog, ret.
Carver, Massachusetts, Police Department (1990–2002)
Executive Director, National Association of Women
Law Enforcement Executives

I'm always so pleased when I go to a conference and meet another female chief. The men are great, but it is nice to be with another woman sometimes.

—Chief Jeanne Miller
Reynoldsburg, Ohio, Police Department

There are more of us than people realize. We need to get past this "first" thing.

—Chief Ann Glavin
California State University at Northridge Police Department

When I heard the women were going to meet at the National Sheriffs' Association, I wasn't sure there was a need, but it was terrific to meet the other women and find out about who they are and how they also got to be sheriffs.

—Sheriff Carolyn "Bunny" Welsh
Chester County (Pennsylvania) Sheriff's Department

With approximately 18,000 police departments in the United States, it is not an exaggeration to say that a chief or sheriff might know very little about her counterparts across her state, and certainly across the nation.

About 200 women—157 police chiefs and 25 sheriffs—held office at the end of 2000. The numbers have increased since then. The chiefs led a variety of types of agencies; all but two of the sheriffs were elected county officials. The collective portrait of the women is based on questionnaires completed by ninety-six chiefs (61 percent of those sent the questionnaire) and twenty-one sheriffs (84 percent). The response percentages, particularly for the sheriffs, were very high, and provided a rich view of the women.

Each of the women surveyed was still in office in January 2001, but the vagaries of the political system have resulted in some no longer holding their positions. Some have retired, and some of the chiefs have gone on to lead other agencies. The appointment pattern of women chiefs also shifted drastically at the end of 2003 and continued into 2004, with the selection of women chiefs in four of the twenty largest police departments in the nation (Detroit, San Francisco, Boston, and Milwaukee).

Although the selection of these chiefs changed the information about the sizes of departments led by women, each of the big-city appointees had a career pattern that was similar to that of the small department chiefs. Each began her career in the agency she now led, although, interestingly, three of the four left at some point in their career for other employment. In this way, they combine the two most obvious career patterns for chiefs: either starting a career in the agency of which she ultimately became chief, or moving to a different agency, sometimes at the start of a career but more often after achieving a certain rank, and then being hired as chief in a totally new agency.

The most obvious difference between the new big-city chiefs and the smaller-city chiefs was the attention paid by the media to them and the intensity of the problems they faced. The policing adages "bigger city, bigger headaches" and "more cops, more problems" often hold true. In large cities more can go wrong; more police officers on the streets multiply the possibilities for mistakes, situations often have greater volatility when they take on political or racial overtones, and media competition can lead to small problems getting magnified into major crises. The three women pioneers in large agencies—Penny Harrington in Portland, Oregon (1985–1986), Elizabeth "Betsy" Watson in Houston (1990–1992) and then in Austin (1992–1997), and Beverly Harvard in Atlanta (1994–2002)—were too few to provide a guideline to whether the later appointments heralded a major shift in the culture of policing or merely reflected that there was a generation of women in ranks to be considered for CEO positions in major departments. While the selections of these women were important developments by which to measure women's acceptance, the localized nature of policing meant that it was equally important to consider what was happening out of the media limelight, where the vast policing of America takes place.

WHY SO MANY DEPARTMENTS?

If all the women profiled in *Breaking the Brass Ceiling* were the CEOs of their departments, why were their titles and career paths different? A brief history of policing, women's entry into policing, and the types of departments and their rank structures will help to navigate the overlapping jurisdictions in American law enforcement.

Sheriffs' and police departments share a basic responsibility for crime prevention and apprehension of offenders. They are made up primarily of sworn officers (the phrase used to denote someone who has the legal authority to detain and arrest; who carries a firearm; and who has legal authority to use force, including shooting someone under certainly pre-scribed conditions). Both also employ civilians (nonsworn, unarmed people) who bring a variety of skills for which police authority is not con-sidered essential. Although civilians are important to police and sheriffs' departments, in policing, the size of a department, sometimes called its "strength," refers to the number of sworn officers in the department. While most of the sworn officers are in the rank of police officer, the to-tal strength of a department includes sworn officers in all ranks, up to and including the chief or the sheriff. Thus, "police officer" may mean one of two things. It is anyone in the entry-level rank called a "police officer," or it may refer generically to anyone with authority as a sworn officer, regardless of rank. Before 1973, most police departments had "policemen" (or "patrolmen") and "policewomen," but in response to legal changes that mandated that men and women be hired on an equal basis, many departments changed the title of their entry level position to "police officer." Sworn status is less important in sheriffs' departments, particularly in those that do not respond to citizens' calls for police ser-vice and are involved primarily in jail operations and court security.

The rank structures are quite similar, although sheriffs' officers' titles can be confusing. The lowest-ranking officer in most sheriffs' departments is called a "deputy sheriff." In this case, "deputy" does not mean "assis-tant to" but means the same as "police officer" does in a police depart-ment. The person who reports directly to the sheriff and is immediately below the sheriff may be called either the chief of the department or the "undersheriff." Other, intermediate ranks in sheriffs' departments are simi-lar to those in police departments, where the lowest rank is police officer, followed sometimes by corporal or master police officer, and then by the ranks of sergeant, lieutenant, captain, inspector, major, assistant or deputy chief, and then chief. The larger the department, the more ranks there will be. Regardless of the number of ranks, the organization is always a pyramid. The vast majority of the employees are in the lowest rank, and there are fewer people in each higher rank than in the one below it.

"Detective"—or "investigator" in some parts of the country—denotes someone who works out of uniform. Sometimes it is a rank obtained by civil service test or by nonobjective mechanisms such as breaking a big case or establishing a record as an officer who makes numerous arrests for serious crimes. In other jurisdictions, it only designates that an officer is working out of uniform—or in "plainclothes" (what police call any assignment out of uniform). To further confuse things, not all plainclothes officers are detectives. Most television shows, including two of the most popular, *Law & Order* and *NYPD Blue*, were about detectives. The show most associated with women officers, *Cagney and Lacey*, was also about detectives.

The highest rank can be even more complicated than lower ranks. In some jurisdictions, there is a rank or title of commissioner or superintendent. Thus, for example, in New York City, *Commissioner* William Bratton was the head of the New York City Police Department (NYPD); but in the Los Angeles Police Department (LAPD) his title was *Chief* Bratton. The titles are different, but in these cases, both denote CEO status, although often in large cities the title "commissioner" indicates that the holder of the position is not considered a sworn member of the force even though he or she came from the ranks of the police and usually carries a badge and a firearm. In New York, the commissioner never wears a uniform; in Los Angeles the chief often does. Sometimes this reflects the history and culture of the department; sometimes it is at the chief's discretion. Not all chiefs are actually the top cops in their departments. For instance, in the NYPD there are about a dozen people with the rank of chief; four of them in 2004 were women. All held important management roles, but none was the CEO of the department, a status held only by the commissioner.

Some cities also employ a public safety director, who is most often a civilian manager to whom both the police chief and the fire chief report. Smaller agencies have shorter command structures with fewer ranks. Many of the women featured in *Breaking the Brass Ceiling* went from captain to chief. This does not mean they skipped ranks; it means they were in agencies where captain was the highest rank directly below the chief. In Milwaukee, there are ranks between captain and chief, so when Nannette Hegerty was selected as chief, she did skip a number of ranks. Although the ranks are different from private employment, the principles are not. Nor are police organizations dissimilar to small or large companies. In a small "mom and pop" store the employees are fewer in number and are known individually by the owners, just as in a small police department the chief will know virtually all employees by name, and if she came up the ranks in that department, she will very likely have worked with most of them. In a corporation like Wal-Mart, a regional store manager is less likely to be involved regularly with either store sales associates or with corporate-level directors and vice presidents, just as a sergeant or lieutenant in the New York City, Chicago, or Los Angeles police department is unlikely to have direct contact with the police chief or commissioner.

Sheriffs' Departments

Sheriffs are the nation's oldest law enforcement officers. They are descended from the British's crown's "shire reeve," the chief law enforcement officer who was also a civil administrator. This history is reflected in today's sheriffs, many of whom also collect taxes and auction off property against which there are tax liens. Although some sheriffs' departments undertake traditional policing functions, many do not, and are primarily involved in court-related activities, such as serving court papers, protecting court officials, and providing courthouse security. Equally important is the sheriff's role in managing the local jail.

In addition to England, the Danes also had an official known as a "reeve," and a similar official existed in Holland. When the Dutch government organized a court system in New Amsterdam (now New York City) in 1653, the *schout* was designated to prosecute cases (as a county attorney does today) and to execute the court's orders and judgments. The first two sheriffs in North America were appointed by King Charles I in 1634: William Stone in Accomac County (Virginia) and Lord William Baldridge in Saint Mary's County (Maryland). Although English sheriffs were appointed by the crown, in the United States the sheriff became an elected official as early as 1776, when Maryland first elected them for two-year terms.

Most of the approximately 3,000 sheriffs' departments are in suburban or rural counties, but the largest offices are in urban areas. The two largest in 2000 were the Los Angeles County Sheriff's Office, with close to 8,500 officers, and Cook County (Illinois), with somewhat more than 5,500 officers. Four women—Laurie Smith, sheriff of Santa Clara County (California); Margo Frasier, sheriff of Travis County (Texas); Beth Lundy, sheriff of Calcasieu Parish (Louisiana, where counties are called parishes); and Jackie Barrett, sheriff of Fulton County (Georgia)—have been elected to run large sheriffs' departments. Women make up about 1 percent of the nation's sheriffs.

In 2000, women made up about 12.5 percent of the sworn officers in sheriffs' departments, a *decrease* of about 1,200 officers since 1990, in spite of an increase of more than 23,000 full-time sworn officers during the decade.[1] There are a number of factors that may have accounted for this. Since the number of women in police departments was increasing, women may have preferred more varied assignments than the custodial positions that often make up a large portion of deputy sheriffs' duties. They may also have preferred the civil service protections of a police department and the possibility of a more generous benefits plan than is offered in many sheriffs' departments, where many officers continue to serve at the pleasure of the sheriff and are subject to being replaced after each election.

The figures may also have indicated that the lawsuits that assured women of equal pay and barred assigning them solely to women's jails have led some sheriffs to conclude that they could replace female deputies with civilians, who are frequently lower in prestige and in salary. Women have continued to work in sheriffs' departments in a variety of clerical positions and as dispatchers, answering telephone calls from members of the public and assigning officers in the field to answer the calls, based on the type of incident reported or the proximity of the officer dispatched. Although it is possible for women to run successfully for sheriff without having served in lower ranks, the decreasing numbers of women, particularly in large sheriffs' departments, who seem to be involved in patrol duties may make it harder for upcoming women to establish themselves as serious candidates for the position. This may be offset, though, by women who attained rank in police departments deciding to run for sheriff.

Police Departments

Although there are far more police departments than sheriffs' departments, they are a more recent law enforcement invention. New York City established the first agency that we would today recognize as a police department in 1845. Other cities soon converted their separate day and night patrols into twenty-four-hour police departments, including New Orleans and Cincinnati in 1852, Boston and Philadelphia in 1854, Chicago in 1855, and Baltimore and Newark, New Jersey, in 1857. By the end of the 1880s, virtually every large city had a department based in part on the London Metropolitan Police, which had been reorganized in 1829 by Sir Robert Peel. (It is because of Peel's influence that English police are known as bobbies.) The similarities between the U.S. and the London police, though, were superficial. In the United States, police were far more localized than in England. Each department was organized by local politicians and was under local control, and each has remained that way to the present.

The responsibilities of the police were diverse. They included keeping the streets free of roaming animals, licensing pets and livestock, returning runaway animals to their owners, cleaning the streets, standing by until the dead and dying were removed to either the morgue or the hospital, directing traffic, fighting fires, inspecting buildings, and supervising elections. In addition, they often cared for transients, tramps, and homeless people, frequently maintaining soup kitchens and opening their station houses at night to vagrants with no place to stay, and they sometimes found time to engage in what we today consider more traditional police activities, including maintaining order, preventing crime, protecting life and property, suppressing vice, and patrolling the streets. By the 1880s it was common for American police to be armed and uniformed, and by the early years of the twentieth century, the development of other municipal services freed them from some of their peripheral roles.

Policing in the United States is more localized than anywhere else in the world. As the population moved west, each town formed its own police force, creating a distinctly local service. Even as the nation grew and other tasks were taken over by the county, state or federal government, the desires of local politicians to maintain control of the police meshed with the fears of a largely immigrant population that a well-organized, centralized or national police force would inhibit personal liberties. Since many immigrants were in flight from their home countries, they wanted protection from crime and disorder, but they did not want a large, well-organized federal police force monitoring their thoughts and activities. The inefficiencies that came with local authority and the ability to exercise local control over the priorities of the police fit the desires of both politicians and average citizens equally well, even if for different reasons.

Most other countries have a large national police force, often augmented by a small number of regional or specialized police forces, but the United States has so many police forces that even the government is unsure how to count them. If one includes only forces that are within geographically defined, although overlapping, political entities (cities, counties, or states), the number is approximately 15,750. This includes the 3,000 sheriffs' departments and the 49 state police agencies (Hawaii is the only state without any state-level policing). There are an additional 2,000 special-jurisdiction police departments, which include railroad and transit, parks districts, colleges and universities, airports, and others specified in state or local laws. The number does not include federal agencies, where policing is also fragmented. Contrary to the beliefs of many, the Federal Bureau of Investigation (FBI) is not a national police force, and is only one—albeit the best-known—of about seventy federal police agencies.

The approximately 18,000 police departments, a staggering number of mostly small, overlapping agencies, employ nearly 800,000 full-time sworn officers, more than half in local (city, town, or village) police departments.[2] Since each is independent of the others, each has a chief of its own, resulting in about 18,000 people who have the right to call themselves the chief of police (or the sheriff in the case of the 3,000 sheriffs' departments). Women make up slightly more than 1 percent (about 200) of these police chiefs.

Police chiefs, although once elected in a few parts of the country, are virtually all appointed by the mayor or city manager of a city, town, or village, although a few counties have police departments in addition to sheriffs' departments. Virtually all chiefs, whether from within or from outside their departments, have been police officers. The phrase "outsider" means from outside the particular department, not from outside policing.

Despite the media's focus on departments in New York City, Los Angeles, San Francisco, Washington, D.C., and Baltimore (all of which have been chronicled on television dramas and a few comedies), most police departments are small; far more than half are made up of fewer than fifty police officers; fewer than fifty employ more than 1,000 officers. Regardless of the size of the department, these officers provide patrol, investigation, traffic control, and other services within their city, town, village, or county.

The largest police force in the country is New York City's. At its largest, in 2002, the department contained more than 40,000 personnel; by 2003 this had fallen to about 36,000. This was disproportionate to all other departments; the second largest department, Chicago, had somewhat fewer than 14,000 sworn officers in 2000. After these, the numbers dropped considerably. These were the only two departments with more than 10,000 officers. The next three largest—Los Angeles, Philadelphia, and Houston—ranged from fewer than 9,500 to fewer than 5,500.

Some areas had county police departments that developed primarily in populous suburban areas with no large cities but with a need for coordinated policing. Two of the five largest county departments were east of New York City in the adjacent Long Island counties of Nassau and Suffolk; each had about 3,000 officers.

The first large county police department to have a woman chief was Montgomery County, Maryland, where Carole A. Mehrling, who had spent her entire career in the department, was chief from March 1995 until 1999, when she retired after twenty-five years with the department. When she joined the department in 1971, she was assigned to its all-female juvenile aid bureau, the only place women could work in the 250-officer department. When restrictions on women's roles were lifted, she became a corporal in the all-male narcotics division, but her assignment as an undercover officer was still somewhat traditional, allowing her, as a woman, to go places that male officers couldn't, and to add an element of surprise to a drug transaction. By the time she was named chief, the department had grown to almost 950 officers, indicative of the growth of the county, a suburb of Washington, D.C. She was the first female chief in the county, and the department she led was then the second-largest with a woman CEO.

Kim Ward, who began her career with the Baltimore County (Maryland) Police Department, was a thirteen-year veteran with the rank of colonel when she was selected in 1994 to lead the department, which was composed of about 2,000 people, including more than 1,700 sworn officers and about 300 civilians. Ward had previously been a teacher, and in 2002 held a bachelor's degree in behavioral science and a master's in education. In January 2004, Suzanne Devlin was named chief of the Fairfax County (Virginia) Police Department, a suburban county of about 1 million people south of Washington, D.C.

The other category of geographically based agencies is the state police. All states except Hawaii have a statewide police agency. There are three basic types of state police agencies. The most common are "full service" departments that, in addition to patrolling state highways, carry out the functions of a local police department in rural and unincorporated areas, and that also provide training, expertise, and laboratory support for smaller police agencies within their state. Most, but not all, are located in the Northeast and the Midwest; examples are Massachusetts, New Jersey, Michigan, Indiana, and Minnesota (the last is the only one of this group to have been led by a woman).

State police in twelve states are limited to patrol of state and interstate roadways, and they are normally called highway patrols. The nation's largest highway patrol is the California Highway Patrol (CHiP), which employs about 10,000 people, more than 6,500 of whom are sworn police officers. Some other states with highway patrols are Florida, Mississippi, Missouri, Utah, and Wyoming. Some states also have investigative agencies whose officers work primarily detecting frauds of various types. Two agencies that fit this model are the Florida Department of Law Enforcement (a separate agency from the Florida Highway Patrol) and the Georgia Bureau of Investigation (separate from the Georgia Department of Public Safety).

The full-service and highway patrol state police agencies tend to be very military in their organizational structures and in the training, style, and bearing of their officers. Many call their police officers "troopers," and they are likely to use the military ranks of corporal, master sergeant, and major. The head of the agency may carry the rank of superintendent or colonel. State police were among the last agencies to admit women on an equal basis, and with few exceptions they have lower percentages of women officers than the other types of law enforcement agencies.

Police forces also exist for transit, park, or airport districts, and many colleges and universities also have their own police forces. As the legal responsibilities of colleges and universities for the safety of their staffs and students have increased, so has the number of college and university police departments. By 1999, there were more than 700 college and university police departments, some of which were larger and better equipped than the forces of the towns in which their campuses were located. College and university policing has proven to be female-friendly. By the end of 2000, colleges and universities employed more than 10,000 police officers, and an increasing number of forces were headed by women. Almost half of the women who responded to the survey were college or university police chiefs.

Many Native American tribes have their own forces that provide patrol and other police services on the reservations; these are collectively known as tribal police, and most, though not all, of the officers are themselves Native Americans. In 2000, 171 tribes operated their own law enforcement agencies; these employed almost 3,500 full-time personnel, of whom 67 percent (2,303) were sworn police officers. Most of these departments were small; only seven employed more than fifty full-time sworn officers, and fifty-two tribal forces had fewer than five officers. The two largest departments were both in Arizona: the Navajo Nation Department of Law Enforcement and the Tohono O'Odham Tribal Police Department.[3] Two of the respondents identified themselves as Native American and were chief of a tribal police force; one force had fewer than ten officers, and the other, 350.

A SNAPSHOT IN TIME

The inability of statistics to pinpoint the successes of individual women chiefs or sheriffs was part of the rationale for *Breaking the Brass Ceiling:*

to document the number of women chiefs and sheriffs before determining that there was a sizable enough number to undertake a mail survey and interviews. It is difficult to locate women chiefs, most of whom until the end of 2003 were in small police departments or in departments, such as colleges and universities or airport and transit departments, that rarely are included in statistical compilations of police agencies.

Counting sheriffs was easier than counting chiefs because sheriffs are elected for specified terms, generally two or four years. Chiefs, though, may have short tenures. In policing, a chief is never more than one scandal away from dismissal. This is somewhat similar to business, where a company president or chief operating officer may be dependent on the year's financial reports to maintain her position. Yet some chiefs, particularly in small communities, like presidents of small companies, may retain their positions for a decade or more, as long as local politicians and citizens (in the case of police chiefs) and boards of directors and shareholders (in the case of company presidents) maintain confidence in their leadership.

Long tenures are less likely in large cities, in part because more can go wrong, but often because frequent changes at the mayoral level result in each new administrator bringing in a new police commissioner. Despite this, Beverly Harvard, Atlanta's female chief, remained in the position from 1994 to 2002. Since sheriffs are elected for two or four years, they can be assured of remaining in office except under the most extreme conditions.

Each woman chief or sheriff had a different story to tell of her climb to the top, but there are a number of ways in which they also mirrored all women in policing today. This collective portrait, based on data gathered in 2001 and 2002 from questionnaires completed by women police chiefs and sheriffs, and in interviews with many of the women, provides a context into which to place those individual stories. All statistical findings have been rounded off to the closest percentage point.

Age

A number of the police chiefs were quite young; the sheriffs tended to be somewhat older. While the youngest chief was twenty-eight and two were under thirty, the youngest sheriff was thirty-six, and only three were under forty. Because of these few very young chiefs, the age range of the chiefs was wider than that of the sheriffs; the oldest was fifty-eight, but twenty-one of the women were between fifty and fifty-eight, resulting in an average age of 45.6 years. The sheriffs were clustered in their mid-forties to mid-fifties; the oldest was fifty-seven, resulting in an average age of 46.5, not quite a year older than the average of the chiefs, even though their individual ages were much closer together. The youngest chiefs were in the smallest departments. Age and department size were not as closely correlated for the sheriffs.

Since sheriffs must face an electorate that may be skeptical of a woman's ability to fill the position, it was not surprising that the women were older and had to be quite accomplished in either law enforcement or the career they were presenting to voters as the foundation for their election. It is unlikely that voters could be swayed to elect anyone—male or female—as young as twenty-eight (the age of the youngest chief) to a position that often carried the designation of chief law enforcement officer of the county.

Type of Agency

There was far greater variety in the types of agencies the police chiefs led than those of the sheriffs. This was anticipated. The overwhelming majority of sheriffs' departments are county departments—and the vast majority of sheriffs are elected. Only a few states' legal codes provide for sheriffs at any other level of government. Although jurisdiction did not affect the size of the agency, it did affect the work of the office. Charlottesville, Virginia's, Cornelia D. Johnson, a city sheriff, led one of the smaller offices, with ten employees assigned to corrections or civil court functions. None were sworn police officers, and none patrolled or answered calls for service from the community, roles that were filled by that city's police department. At age fifty-seven, Johnson was the oldest sheriff and the only African-American sheriff who completed the questionnaire, although both she and Fulton County's Barrett, who is also African-American, were interviewed.

The overwhelming majority of the chiefs were in charge of either municipal or college and university police departments. Forty-eight (49 percent) led municipal police departments, and the next largest group (forty chiefs, 42 percent) led college and university departments that employed full-time, sworn police officers. Of the eight additional respondents, two were county chiefs, two were airport authority chiefs, two were tribal chiefs, and two were state police chiefs. The two state police chiefs, although only 2 percent of the total, are the only two women ever to have led state police agencies; one has since retired.

Size of Agency

What business and policing have in common is that power is often attributed to the size of the agency you lead. In the case of business, this is measured by dollars; in policing, it is more likely to be measured by number of personnel. Just as *Fortune* magazine deemed Hewlett-Packard's Carleton S. (Carly) Fiorina as the most powerful businesswoman in 2003 because she led a $72 billion company, police chiefs and sheriffs tend to receive media coverage and at least some deference from their peers based on the size of the department and the aura that surrounds big-city policing.

Although they were the newest women chiefs, Detroit's Ella Bully-Cummings, San Francisco's Heather Fong, Boston's Kathleen O'Toole, and Milwaukee's Nannette Hegerty were immediately catapulted into similar prominence because they were the only women in mid-2004 to lead municipal police departments that were ranked in the police equivalent of *Fortune*'s Top 50. In 2000, the Detroit Police Department was the nation's sixth largest, with more than 4,000 sworn officers; the San Francisco Police Department the fourteenth, largest with about 2,225 sworn officers; the Boston Police Department the sixteenth largest, with slightly over 2,000 sworn officers; and the Milwaukee Police Department the eighteenth largest, with a sworn staff of just below 2,000. Reinforcing the central preoccupation with big-city policing, Santa Clara County's Sheriff Smith is less well-known in policing than the women chiefs, even though her agency is about the same size as Milwaukee's police department.

Despite the emergence of women leading large agencies, most of the women chiefs, like most male chiefs, led small police departments. Small is a relative concept, and is often defined as fewer than twenty-five police officers. Midsize agencies are often defined as more than 25 up to about 100 total staff. For example, in California, about 60 percent fall within this definition.[4] Size is complicated by jurisdiction. Some very small towns have very small police departments. One of the women chiefs was the sole full-time member of her department. At the same time, college and university, airport, or transit agencies may be made up of hundreds of sworn officers but are often overlooked because they cross municipal or county boundaries.

Although large cities have been more aggressive in recruiting women than small departments have been, the number of promotions it takes to reach the top and a number of civil service and union constraints make it more difficult to negotiate the rungs of a large agency. While small agencies have been perceived as less welcoming toward women than large ones, at least some of these small departments are giving women the chance to take charge. Overriding this apparent contradiction may be the smaller talent pools in small agencies. This, combined with fewer ranks to chief, may work to the advantage of the women who make their careers in these departments.

Education

Women at the top of policing are well-educated. Of the eighty-four chiefs who reported their highest education level, three (4 percent) listed a doctorate of law degree, thirty-five (42 percent) listed a master's degree, thirty-seven (44 percent) listed a bachelor's degree, three (4 percent) listed an associate's (two-year) degree, and six (7 percent) listed a high school diploma. The women were ahead of the rising standards for chiefs of police. Today most large cities, suburban areas, and smaller towns with white-collar or college communities are looking for a chief with at least a bachelor's degree, but many of the women far exceeded that requirement. The women with only high school educations were clustered in departments with fewer than fifteen officers, although, again reflecting that most police departments are small, many of the women with bachelor's degrees were also leading small departments.

The sheriffs presented a startling difference from the stereotypes of the back-slapping politicos portrayed in films as county sheriffs in rural America. Of the fifteen women who provided information on their educations, 66 percent had at least a bachelor's degree, including five with four-year degrees, two with a master's degree, one with a nursing degree, and one (Travis County [Texas] Sheriff Margo Frasier) with a J.D. Suffolk County (Massachusetts) Sheriff Andrea Cabal, appointed in 2002 by acting Governor Jane Swift, is also an attorney, as are Detroit's Bully-Cummings and Boston's O'Toole. Of the sheriffs who did not have a four-year degree, two had an associate's degree and only three, including Charlotteville's Johnson, who had been a popular police officer in her city prior to her election, had only a high school diploma.

Relatively little information exists on the education levels of police chiefs, and even less on sheriffs. Since the small amount of research on the education levels of chiefs has centered on large agencies, comparisons are difficult, but preliminary analysis indicates that women chiefs have a wider range of academic backgrounds than men chiefs. Most of the men queried in a 1998 survey[5] had a degree in criminology, criminal justice, justice administration, public policy, political science, or government. Women chiefs had degrees in all these disciplines as well as in English, history, education, nursing, or health- and recreation-related fields. The same was true of the sheriffs; of the fourteen who indicated their college majors, only five studied criminal justice or a related field. This may have indicated that some of the women had not anticipated a policing career, or it might have reflected that the men attended school while already in policing, with an eye toward upward mobility, while more of the women completed their education and then chose a policing career.

Race

One area in which neither the chiefs nor the sheriffs were diverse was race. Of the ninety-four police chiefs who indicated their race or ethnicity, eighty-four (88 percent) were white, four (5 percent) were African-American, three (4 percent) were Hispanic or had a Hispanic surname, one (1 percent) was Native American, and two (2 percent) indicated "other" without supplying details (although one of these was a tribal chief and might have been Native American). The sheriffs were even less racially diverse. Of the twenty-one sheriffs who indicated their race, all but two were white; one (the city sheriff) was African-American, and one checked "other."

This portion of the study seemed disproportionately influenced by who chose to complete the survey, and it indicated how a collective portrait may not always capture what is happening. In addition to Atlanta's Beverly Harvard, African-American women who have been a chief of police include Evelyn B. Hicks, appointed in Opa-Locka, Florida, in 1995; Ivin B. Lee, appointed in Dunbar, West Virginia, in 1996; and interim or acting chiefs Sonya Proctor, in Washington, D.C., and Mary Bounds in Cleveland.[6] Two of the three chiefs named to lead a large municipal department in 2003 were African-American: Annetta Nunn in Birmingham, Alabama, and Ella Bully-Cummings in Detroit (her father is African-American and her mother is Japanese). One, Heather Fong, was the first Asian-surnamed woman to lead a police department.

The racial breakdown of women at the top was not reflective of women in law enforcement at all ranks and was influenced by the number of women chiefs in small police agencies. The numbers of minority women, particularly African-American women, have been increasing annually in large-city police departments but have remained static—in some cases nonexistent—in very small departments, often in communities with few or no minority residents. As more women move to the top of large police agencies, it is likely that more women chiefs will be nonwhite, although a larger applicant pool doesn't ensure this will be so. In larger departments, there are more ranks to travel through before the top spot becomes a realistic option, there are more people in higher ranks vying for upward mobility, and there are more specialist assignments or opportunities along the way that may decrease the desire for the chief's job. This may lead middle-ranking officers to decide that heading a special unit as a captain, an inspector, or a deputy chief provides sufficient ego gratification without the pressures and fishbowl existence that accompany the position of police chief or sheriff.

Marital Status

The women were very open about their personal lives. Two of the pioneer women chiefs, Portland's Harrington and Houston's Watson from 1990 to 1992, were married to lower-ranking men in their departments during their tenures as chief. Harrington faced criticism because not only her husband, but also her sister and brother-in-law were employed in the department while she was chief. Watson received less criticism over her husband but he became the focus of curiosity when she announced during her tenure that she was pregnant. Reinforcing that concerns about spouses' positions in their agencies continued to challenge women CEOs, Santa Clara County's Sheriff Smith felt it necessary, after her 1998 election, to assure constituents that her reorganization would not include appointing her husband, a retired San Jose police supervisor, as her undersheriff.

All but one of the chiefs indicated her marital status at the time she entered policing, and ninety-one indicated marital status at the time they completed the survey. The two largest categories when the women entered policing were single (fifty-seven women) and married (twenty-six). Four were cohabiting (defined as living with someone to whom they were not married; they were not asked whether this was a man or a woman), and eight were divorced. Many of the women's living arrangements had changed by the time they became chief. Although the two largest categories were still single and married, they had been reversed (thirty-eight married and twenty-four single). The four large-city chiefs appointed in 2003 and 2004 fit within this pattern; three were married and one was single. The number of women who were divorced had doubled from eight to sixteen, and the number cohabiting had increased threefold, from four to twelve. One chief was a widow.

Comparable data for the sheriffs indicated much less change in their marital status. This might be attributed to the fact they were somewhat older. Also, it is possible that their lives needed greater stability so that they could establish a political base in the county prior to running for office. Fourteen of the twenty-one sheriffs were married before they entered law enforcement, and fourteen of twenty (one did not reply) were married at the time they completed the questionnaire, although only nine indicated "married" at both periods in their lives. Even this was subject to interpretation, and there was no way of knowing whether "married" at both times meant "married to the same person." Two sheriffs specifically explained that they were married to the same man as when their careers had begun, and one indicated that she had divorced and subsequently remarried the same man four years later. The others were less specific.

Many of the women had a partner who was also in policing. Of the chiefs who replied, thirty-one answered yes and thirty-nine answered no. The three married big-city chiefs were married to retired members of the departments they led. One of the three, Bully-Cummings, was divorced; her previous husband was also in law enforcement, and at the time of her appointment was the sheriff of Wayne County (in which Detroit is located). Nine of the chiefs had at sometime worked in the same department as their partner. Carrboro, North Carolina, Chief Hutchison, the only chief who specified that she was cohabiting with a woman, indicated that her partner was not in policing; in fact, her partner is a stay-at-home mother to the couple's two children.

Dual policing careers were much less prevalent among the sheriffs. Five who lived with a partner or spouse reported the person had been in policing. As with their marital status, a number of the sheriffs wrote explanations. Only one of the partners or spouses of the sheriffs worked in any of the sheriffs' agencies, and he had been her first patrol supervisor. Santa Clara County's Smith met her husband in her current agency, but he had left many years earlier to work elsewhere in policing and was now retired.

Career Paths: Twists and Turns

Although police officers at lower ranks generally spend their entire career in a single agency, this was not so for many chiefs and sheriffs. Some sheriffs' departments are not covered by civil service regulations; this allows a sheriff to bring in his or her own staff at almost any level within the agency, but police departments tend to be more rigid. In some municipal departments, the chief is the only person who can be hired at any rank other than entry-level police officer. Other agencies permit some midpoint (lateral) entry, but often only at specific points in the rank structure. This means that most people stay with the same agency for their entire career, while others—often those who aspire to chief or sheriff— must make strategic moves along the way.

Only about one third of the chiefs (thirty-three) led the department in which they had begun their policing career. Among these single-agency chiefs, twenty-one (63 percent) were the first woman in their department, and twenty-eight (84 percent) were also the first woman supervisor. The figures on single-agency chiefs have been altered dramatically by the four new big-city chiefs. Each is chief of the agency in which she began her career, although three of the four had left at some point for other opportunities. Although many male chiefs of large departments have been outsiders, this trend to what could be called "insider outsiders" has not been discerned among men. Whether it was merely a coincidence or a developing pattern that may or may not be unique to women is interesting to consider as future appointments are made.

Of the sixty-three chiefs who were not in their original agency, half had moved once, nineteen had moved twice, eight had moved three times, and one, a college or university chief, had moved five times during her career. This mobility was unexpected, since it contradicted indications in the private sector and among federal government employees that managers, whether men or women, have become less willing to relocate in an age of two-career families. The findings may have been skewed by the existence of a small number of women who were committed to reaching the top and were willing to go wherever the opportunities opened up.

Accepting a position as chief may also lead to forced mobility. Chiefs' positions have few tenure guarantees; a chief may be fired quickly or may decide to apply for another position elsewhere. Twelve of the women surveyed had moved to their current chief's position from a chief's position elsewhere. As more women become chiefs, it is anticipated that this phenomenon will increase; in 2002, at least six women chiefs moved from one top spot to another, and this trend has continued.

For sheriffs, mobility can mean coming from another profession in addition to coming from another law enforcement agency. One sheriff, who openly talked about her own career and her private life, requested anonymity only when she spoke about police chiefs. "Chiefs," she said, "are like rolling stones, they go to conferences always looking to see where there are openings in larger departments, or better-paying departments. We sheriffs can't do that; we have to have roots in our communities if we expect people to vote for us. We can be different, we can be minorities, we can be women, but we can't be strangers."

Reinforcing her observations, twenty of the twenty-one sheriffs were elected officials. Only three of the eighteen who responded (slightly more than 14 percent) had worked in two or more agencies before being elected sheriff; nine (just under 43 percent) had spent their entire career in their present department. Eight (38 percent) did not have prior law enforcement experience but had been active in their communities in other areas. This was surprising, because it had been anticipated that only a woman with a law enforcement background would have been able to counter claims that the job of a sheriff was inherently masculine due to its "top cop" image.

Tenure: Length of Time in Office

Tenure issues are very different for chiefs and sheriffs. Chiefs are appointed, and even when they have employment contracts, they may be—

and often are—asked to leave or they decide to leave suddenly. The causes can include a series of negative events in the community, possibly incidents involving shootings by police officers or real or perceived racial insensitivity; a corruption scandal that might have begun under a previous administration but becomes public under the current regime; or a more general philosophical disagreement with the elected official who appointed the chief. Recognizing this, Minnetonka, Minnesota, Chief Joy Rickla, who has held a number of management and CEO positions in Minnesota law enforcement agencies, has advised women who want to be chiefs to remember that in addition to professional concerns, they must get their finances in order because "you could find yourself without a job literally overnight."

This is not a concern of sheriffs, who are elected for either two- or four-year terms (four years is the most common) and can be ousted only by voters, unless they choose to step down or become involved in illegal activities. Generally, the decision whether to run again is made by the sheriff and can be made months—even years—before a term of office ends, allowing for post-career planning. Many of the women sheriffs were new; eight (38 percent) had not yet reached, or were just at, the halfway mark of a four-year term; four were past the halfway mark; and four (19 percent) were completing their first term and were planning their re-election campaign. Two were in their second term, and two had been elected three times. Thus, their tenures as sheriff ranged from one who had been in office not quite half a year to the two who had twelve years or more. The two most senior women had recently been re-elected for the third time, but thirteen years in office was the maximum tenure.

There were far wider variances in the number of years each woman had served as chief. One municipal chief was still in her first year, while one university chief was in her twenty-fifth year. Despite this, because most of the women were relatively new CEOs; the median tenure for chiefs was three years, not all that different from the sheriffs.

Epilogue

Breaking the Brass Ceiling has documented the experiences of women police chiefs and sheriffs who have reached the top of their profession. Based primarily on interviews and questionnaires, it relates their stories from their days on patrol to their ascendancy to CEO status. It has focused on the women who have caught the brass ring and have broken through to the top in a historically and stereotypically male world, in a business where rank is literally signified by wearing brass—in the shape of stars, bars, and badges—and where those brass insignias are a constant, visible symbol of one's achievements in the organization. It has broached the subject of whether the playing field for women is finally level.

One chief, Milwaukee's Nannette Hegerty, thought it was level—or at least close—but others have not been so confident. Even Hegerty hedged, noting that the numbers and percentages of women in policing at all ranks will most likely never equal the numbers and percentages of men. She attributed this to women having different dreams than men and different realities in their lives. Other chiefs and sheriffs were less direct, noting sometimes that women might approach an issue differently, might solve a problem differently, but that basically as long as the tasks were completed, that was all that mattered. Certainly, their own careers seemed to support this analysis.

Estimated in 1994 to be no more than 100, the number of women police chiefs more than doubled in a decade. The increases for women sheriffs were even greater. From single digits in 1994, they have increased to about thirty—still a small number, and, like the women chiefs, just slightly more than 1 percent of the total universe. Much of the increase has occurred since 2000, presaging that it will continue.

But numbers, as always, tell only part of the story. By 2004 women led major police and sheriffs' departments in more than purely token numbers. Women led four of the eighteen largest police departments and four of the twenty-five largest sheriffs' departments in the nation. The women's careers were remarkably similar to those of their male peers, with the sole exception that none except Elizabeth (Betsy) Watson, who went from the Houston Police Department to the Austin Police Department, had been chief in a big-city department other than where she had begun her career, and none had yet followed in the footsteps of a handful of men who have established a pattern of moving from one large department to another.[1] This may change as more women in more agencies, particularly larger ones, create a pool of applicants for consideration for positions around the country.

Despite the perceived preference of cities for selecting chiefs from inside the police department, more than two-thirds of the women chiefs were outsiders, defined as not having spent their entire career in the department in which they became chief. As with so much of policing, though, this, too, can be misleading, since many of the chiefs joined their current departments early in their career, after leaving other agencies. Some, just like their male colleagues, moved to their agency specifically to accept the position of chief.

As elected rather than appointed CEOs, sheriffs had an opportunity to present to the voters a different set of skills than those seeking a police chief might have been searching for. Despite this, each of the women sheriffs who was elected to run a large department, especially one whose deputies had patrol and arrest authority, had some background in law enforcement. Here, too, the sheriffs were similar to their male peers.

The similarities between men and women police chiefs and men and women sheriffs were striking except in education levels. Although there are strong indications that police chiefs appointed since the late 1990s were far better educated than their predecessors, the women chiefs and sheriffs—particularly those in large agencies—were exceptional in their educational levels. Each had earned a master's degree or a J.D.

Should this be viewed positively or negatively? At first glance, it would appear solely positive. Who wouldn't want the leader of one of the most important government services not to be as well educated as possible? Also, might this represent a move away from movie and television cops, often all brawn and little brain, in favor of well-spoken, educated professionals who are truly managers rather than merely top cops? At second glance, though, does it mean that women are still being held to a higher standard, expected to have more impressive credentials for the same position? Even if this were true, would it represent a step forward for policing? Isn't a résumé centered on education and management training more impressive than one that lists the number of arrests made or doors kicked in? Since virtually the only difference the women would concede in their styles of policing is their lesser physical strength, any shift from brawn to brains can only benefit them.

In shattering the brass ceiling, the women have also been successful in sidestepping the so-called glass walls that often inhibit women in business. Recent chiefs have sufficient patrol experience to quiet the criticisms of all but the most macho men that they have not proven themselves on the street—an important rite of passage in policing. They have also been successful in turning "softer" assignments in training, personnel, public affairs, and administration into pluses. They need not be the toughest guy—or even the toughest gal—in the valley to succeed. Today's chiefs and sheriffs must be armed not only with patrol experience, but with administrative expertise and advanced training and education as well. Surprisingly, if women running for sheriff lacked one of the three, the patrol experience was often seen as less important than the other two.

But women chiefs and sheriffs, like so many successful women, have made trade-offs. They, too, have found that high professional achievement and domestic responsibilities rarely mix. Many of the women were single, particularly those who had moved around to enhance their career, and few had more than two children. Of those who were married and had made strategic career twists and turns that involved physical moves from their hometown or career starting point, many were married to men who had also had a policing career. The women overcame societal constraints on men's unwillingness or inability to be a trailing spouse who moved for his wife's career in part due to their choice of partners. Many of them were married to men who had worked in the same police department and whom they had met in the course of work. But since the men were usually older, many had taken advantage of police pensions that permit retiring while still quite young, and therefore had few career concerns of their own. Married women rarely had more than two children, which minimized the family and child care concerns that sidetrack the careers of many women in management.

In addition to documenting the successes of women in law enforcement, *Breaking the Brass Ceiling* sought to demystify policing for general readers. Why are there so many different types of police agencies? What are their jurisdictions, and how do they interact with one another? Who are the women who go into policing? Why do they go there? What do they do once they get there? Who assists them and who resists them? Why do some of their peers still see them as temporary interlopers who will one day disappear, even though they have policed for more than 100

years? Many of these questions have been answered by the women themselves and through comparisons with women in other fields.

WHY SO FEW?

Readers may still be left asking themselves, "Why so few?" Answers are
many. Women seem to be less interested in policing careers than men.
Whether the reasons lie in society or in police departments' unwillingness to embrace equality is a debate to be conducted elsewhere. Regardless of one's viewpoint, it does not appear that women will ever be present
in policing in the same percentages as in the general population or in the
labor force. If the numbers at the bottom stay low, so will the numbers
at the top. A number of women chiefs were not only the first woman in
their department; they were the only woman, up to and including the
time they became chief. While this may undercut some of the concern
about recruitment and retention of women officers, it reinforces the fact
that the pipeline of women to promote will rarely be full, and certainly
never bursting at the seams.

Crucial decisions that may affect the ability to move into management
must be made early in one's career. Most of the women, particularly those
in larger agencies, were promoted for the first or second time (to sergeant
or lieutenant) within ten years of when they began their careers. The vagaries of when and how often civil service tests will be given, and the
requirements that applicants for promotion normally have at least some
minimum number of years in each lower rank, mean that careers cannot
be left to chance. If a police officer decides to pass up a test for sergeant
three or four years into her career, she will be ineligible for the test that
may be given for lieutenant three or four years later. Thus, skipping the
first promotional opportunity may put a candidate as much as a decade
behind in making rank, possibly precluding any chance to be considered
for executive-level positions later in her career.

Since women are more likely to postpone such decisions, often for family and child care reasons; are less likely to negotiate better conditions or
assignments; and are more likely than men to attribute their successes to
luck, more women will have to begin to position themselves for upward
mobility earlier in their careers in order for substantially greater numbers
to become chiefs.

Increasing the numbers of women in upper management in addition
to those who are already chiefs will increase the pool of women who are
likely to receive serious consideration for job vacancies. Whether an internal or an external selection, a person considered for a chief's job must
have achieved at least midlevel, if not executive-level, rank in some po-

lice department. This is why the decision to forgo a promotion early in a career can affect the entire climb through the ranks.

The size of a city also influences the applicant pool for the chief's badge. The larger the city, the less likely an outside applicant will be considered. Although it is hard to quantify, most cities prefer inside candidates unless there has been a scandal. Inside candidates are known to local politicians and civic groups, and they are knowledgeable about the city. They know the police department, particularly its strengths and weaknesses, and its dynamic leaders. There is also a level of city pride in being able to select a "homegrown" talent rather than turn to an administrator who developed his or her policing skills elsewhere.

Because the selection of outside chiefs has often come after a department has been racked by scandals or by community problems, turning to an outsider may send a negative message to officers or citizens that there is something wrong with the police department. To overcome this, an outside applicant must have an established reputation and experience as a chief, or at least as a second in command. It is unlikely that the chief of a 100-person agency will be named to lead one of 1,000 people, resulting in larger departments having smaller applicant pools.

As more women become chiefs, more will be in positions to "trade up." A number of women in recent years have begun to make multiple career moves as chiefs, and it is likely this trend will accelerate. One of the biggest considerations for becoming a chief is already being one. A chief may also consider running for sheriff, since it is not uncommon for police executives with a local following to translate that support into a campaign.

The increasing number of women chiefs and sheriffs seems also to have enhanced their credibility with the media. No longer treated like curiosities, they are able to build professional records without all the pitfalls of tokenism. Without the frenzied, "gee whiz" media coverage, women chiefs have been able to avoid the hoopla that many mayors and city managers are not eager to undergo, and women candidates for sheriff have been able to concentrate on advising voters of their abilities to manage multimillion-dollar agencies. There are sufficient pitfalls for a politician selecting a police chief without undue attention being paid to the sex of the candidate.

The localized nature of the police chief selection process and the vagaries of a sheriff's election process make it unwise to predict too far into the future, but all indications are pointing to increases in the numbers of women police chiefs and sheriffs. Instead of asking "Why so few?" the question sometime soon may become "Why not even more?"

Notes

CHAPTER 1

1. Scott McCabe, "Riviera Loses Try to Hire Black Female Police Chief," *Palm Beach Post*, Jan. 5, 2002, p. 4B; "Ex Miramar Chief to Head North Miami Police Force," *Miami Herald*, Jan. 6, 2002, p. 2BR.

2. Ann Longmore-Etheridge, "Leadership in a Time of Change," *Security Management*, Jan. 2004, pp. 79–86.

3. "Again a First," *Law Enforcement News*, Feb. 4, 1995, p. 4; Trenton Daniel, "Opa-Locka—'Baghdad of the South'—Striving to Change Its Image," retrieved Feb. 9, 2004, from *Miami Herald*, http://www.herald.com.

4. "Douglas, Wyoming, Gets First Woman Chief," Associated Press, retrieved June 10, 2003, from http://www.sameshield.com.

5. Lee was one of the women featured in the traveling exhibition of the Behring Center of the Smithsonian Institution's National Museum of American History, "Serving Home and Community: Women of Southern Appalachia," which toured until Nov. 23, 2003; Pat Lawrence, "Rights and Wrongs," *Woman's Views*, Jan. 2003, retrieved Mar. 9, 2004, from http://search.netscape.com/ns/boomframe.jsp?query+Ivin+Lee.

6. Brian A. Reaves & Andrew L. Goldberg, *Local Police Departments, 1997* (Washington, DC: Bureau of Justice Statistics, 2000), p. 5.

7. Bernard Cohen & Jan M. Chaiken, *Police Background Characteristics and Performance* (Lexington, MA: Lexington Books, 1973); Charles D. Hale & Wilson R. Wilson, *Personal Characteristics of Assaulted and Non-Assaulted Officers* (Norman: Bureau of Government Research, University of Oklahoma, 1974).

8. "Los Angeles: The Christopher Commission Report," retrieved Apr. 23, 2004, from http://www.hrw.org/reports98/police/uspo75.htm; Zev Yaroslavsky & Katherine Spillar, "More Women in the Ranks Would Stem LAPD Brutality," *Los Angeles Times*, Oct. 2, 2002, retrieved Apr. 11, 2004, from http://www.womenandpolicing.org.

9. "Never Too Late," *Law Enforcement News*, July 20, 1995, p. 4.

10. Tamar Lewin, "Equal Pay for Equal Work Is No. 1 Goal of Women," *New York Times*, Sept. 5, 1997, p. A20.

11. "New M.I.T. Police Chief Is Ready for Stern Tests," *New York Times*, Nov. 29, 1987, p. 68.

12. Psychological journals and women's journals are filled with articles that indicate that gender stereotypes have continued despite the greater opportunities for women in what were once viewed as men's fields. See Margaret Mooney Marini & Mary C. Brinton, "Sex Typing in Occupational Socialization," in Barbara Reskin, ed., *Sex Segregation in the Workplace*, pp. 192–232 (Washington, DC: National Academy Press, 1984). Barrie Thorne, *Gender Play: Girls and Boys in School* (New Brunswick, NJ: Rutgers University Press, 1993), describes how this behavior begins early in life and is reinforced by one's peers.

13. "Jobs and Salaries, 2001: A Sampler," *New York Times*, Oct. 29, 2002, p. G1.

14. George T. Felkenes & Jean Reith Schroedel, "A Case Study of Minority Women in Policing," *Women & Criminal Justice* 4, no. 2 (1993): 76, 83.

15. Williams has written extensively about men in traditionally women's fields, particularly nursing. See Christine L. Williams, *Still a Man's World: Men Who Do "Women's Work"* (Berkeley: University of California Press, 1995).

16. M. Steven Meagher & Nancy A. Yentes, "Choosing a Career in Policing: A Comparison of Male and Female Perceptions," *Journal of Police Science and Administration* 14, no. 4 (1986): 320–327.

17. William M. Timmons & Brad E. Hainsworth, "Attracting and Retaining Females in Law Enforcement: Sex-Based Problems of Women Cops in 1988," *International Journal of Offender Therapy and Comparative Criminology* 33 (Dec. 1989): 197–207.

CHAPTER 2

1. "Calumet City Gets First Female Chief," *Daily Southtown*, May 11, 2003, retrieved June 10, 2003, from http://www.sameshield.com.

2. Paul Zielbauer, "Police Chief, under Fire, Is Demoted in Hartford," *New York Times*, July 18, 2000, p. B5.

3. "Green Pasture," *Law Enforcement News*, Jan. 15/31, 1999, p. 7.

4. "Mr. & Mrs. Chief," *Law Enforcement News*, Sept. 15/30, 2003, p. 4.

5. "Goddess with a Gun," *Palo Alto Weekly*, Feb. 12, 2003, retrieved Nov. 15, 2003, from http://www.paloaltoonline.com/weekly/morgue/2002/2003_02_12.chieflynne6.html.

6. *WomenPolice*, Spring 2002, p. 24.

7. "Still First," *Law Enforcement News*, Sept. 15/30, 2002, p. 4.

8. "The Old Switcheroo," *Law Enforcement News*, May 31, 2001, p. 4.

9. "Major Addition," *Law Enforcement News*, Oct. 15, 1997, p. 4.

10. Sheila Schmitt, "'Sheriff Mom': Women Are Gaining in Numbers in a Traditionally Male Post," *Law and Order*, Jan. 1996, p. 65.

11. James E. Booker, "Top Drawer Stuff," *Carib News*, week ending Dec. 28, 1999, p. 48.

12. Francie Latour, "Next Sheriff Seen Facing Uphill Battle," *Boston Globe*, Nov. 16, 2002, p. B1.

13. Leonard F. Fuld, *Police Administration* (New York: G.P. Putnam's, 1909; repr. Montclair, NJ: Patterson Smith, 1971), p. 420.

14. Matthew J. Hickman & Brian A. Reaves, *Local Police Departments, 2000* (Washington, DC: U.S. Department of Justice, 2003), p. 1.

15. Matthew J. Hickman & Brian A. Reaves, *Sheriffs' Offices, 2000* (Washington, DC: U.S. Department of Justice, 2003), pp. iii, 7.

16. Fox Butterfield, "Study Finds 2.6% Increase in U.S. Prison Population," *New York Times*, July 28, 2003, p. A12.

17. Numbers and percentages were developed based on data from Hickman & Reaves, *Local Police Departments, 2000* and Brian A. Reaves & Matthew J. Hickman, *Police Departments in Large Cities, 1990–2000* (Washington, DC: U.S. Department of Justice, 2002).

18. *Equality Denied: The Status of Women in Policing: 2001* (Los Angeles: National Center for Women & Policing/The Feminist Majority, 2002).

19. Cheryl Winokur Munk, "Women Still Minority on Boards of Most Fortune 500 Companies," *Wall Street Journal*, Dec. 10, 2003, p. 7A.

20. Susan Saulny, "A Much-Threatened Judge Resigns to Be a Partner in a Private Firm," *New York Times*, Oct. 1, 2003, p. B2.

21. Robert D. McFadden, "Fairstein Is to Retire as Prosecutor of Sex Crimes," *New York Times*, Dec. 18, 2001, p. D4.

22. Barbara Nelson Pavin, "The First Years: What Should a Female Superintendent Know Beforehand?", in C. Cryss Brunner, ed., *Sacred Dreams: Women and the Superintendency*, pp. 105–123 (Albany: State University of New York Press, 1999).

23. Estelle Kamler & Carol Shakeshaft, "The Role of Search Consultants in the Career Paths of Women Superintendents," in C. Cryss Brunner, ed., *Sacred Dreams*, pp. 51–52 (Albany: State University of New York Press, 1999).

24. The author can attest to such questions. When I was a captain in 1979, I was asked by a secretary if she could call me "Captain Dorothy" rather than "Captain Schulz." "Only if my colleagues are called Captain J.J. and Lieutenant Phil," I replied.

CHAPTER 3

1. The author interviewed more than half a dozen people in 2003 and 2004 who remembered hearing about Chief Overturf, including her granddaughter Mildred Fitzgerrell. A number of them sent recollections and clippings from area newspapers, including "Woman Police Chief Issue at Election," *Zeigler News*, Apr. 15, 1921, n.p.; "Mrs. Laundsbury Is Policewoman," *Zeigler News*, Nov. 6, 1925, p. 1; and "Policewomen Nothing New," probably *Benton Evening News*, Aug. 19, 1982, n.p. See also "Woman Police Chief Captures Two Bandits," *New York Times*, Feb. 17, 1921, p. 2.

2. This version of Spenser's career, attributed to a juvenile court referee in Cincinnati, Ohio, can be found in Chloe Owings, *Women Police: A Study of the Development and Status of the Women Police Movement* (New York: Hitchcock, 1925), p. 105.

3. Dorothy Moses Schulz, *From Social Worker to Crimefighter: Women in United States Municipal Policing* (Westport, CT: Praeger, 1995), pp. 30–31; "Made Good as Police Chief, She's to Be Promoted," *Columbus* (Ohio) *Evening Dispatch*, Feb. 28,

1921, p. 1; *Bridge to the Past: A History of Milford, Ohio* (Milford, OH: Greater Milford Area Historical Society, n.d).

4. "Woman Appointed Police Head in Cumberland, MD," *National Police Journal*, May 1921, p. 30; "Women to Run Kansas Town: Two Grandmothers at Head," *New York Times*, Apr. 7, 1921, p. 19.

5. *The Woman Citizen*, Apr. 26, 1919, p. 1015; "Few Women Have Run for Fargo City Offices," *Fargo Forum*, Apr. 13, 1974, n.p.

6. E-mail to author and newspaper clippings on Wilder from Steve Stark, executive director, Cass County Historical Society, Bonanzaville, ND, July 23, 2003; "First, Again," *Law Enforcement News*, Feb. 28, 1997, p. 5.

7. "Region 7 News," *WomenPolice*, Spring 2004, p. 19.

8. "Mother Made Police Boss," *Cincinnati Post*, Mar. 16, 1926, n.p.

9. Molly A. McIntyre, "From the Top," *Police Product News*, Jan. 1980, p. 24.

10. "International Police Vehicle Design Contest, 1993," *Law and Order*, July 1993, p. 23; "New Cops on the Block," *U.S. News & World Report*, Aug. 2, 1993, pp. 22–25; "Agreeing in Part," *Law Enforcement News*, Apr. 30, 1995, pp. 4–5.

11. Chief Lott was interviewed by the author in January 2004; she also sent the author clippings about her career.

12. E-mails to author from Detective Jack Carter, Coalinga Police Department, winter 2003/2004.

13. Arlene Saffron, "Chief Shot in Front of Family," *American Police Beat*, Nov. 1998, p. 1; Craig W. Floyd, "No Privilege with Rank," *American Police Beat*, Sept. 2001, pp. 60–61.

14. A. Vance Stickley, "Women in Command," *WomenPolice*, June 1988, pp. 8–9; and "Women in Command," *WomenPolice*, Sept. 1988, pp. 8–9, 15.

15. Mary Mihaly, "Chief Sally," *Cleveland*, Dec. 1987, pp. 158–161, 235.

16. Kristal Leebrick, "Looking for a Mentor: Women in Law Enforcement Lack Female Role Models," *Minnesota Police Chief*, Mar. 1991, pp. 17–19. Information about Beise and Gagnon was provided to the author by their departments in March 2004.

17. Stickley, "Women in Command," Sept. 1988, pp. 8–9. Information about Mackwardt and Guidry was provided to the author by Clute Police Chief Mark Wicker in March 2004.

18. "Becoming Chief of Police: Career Advancement among Texas Police Chiefs," *TELEMASP Bulletin* 9, no. 1 (Jan./Feb. 2002): pp. 1–7.

19. "Memorial: In Memory of Mary Mabyn Voswinkle Bard," retrieved Mar. 1, 2001, from http://rupd.rice.edu/Mary.html; "Rice University Police Department," retrieved Mar. 1, 2001, from http://rupd.rice.edu/about.html.

20. John J. Sloan III, Mark M. Lanier, & Deborah L. Beer, "Policing the Contemporary University Campus: Challenging Traditional Organizational Models," *Journal of Security Administration* 23, no. 2 (June 2000): 1–23; "Campus Law Enforcement Statistics," Bureau of Justice Statistics, retrieved Sept. 2, 2003, from http://www.cjp.usdoj.gov/bjs.cample.htm; Craig W. Floyd, "Lives on the Line," *American Police Beat*, Dec. 2003, pp. 46–47.

21. "SWAT Team for Berkeley," *New York Times*, Sept. 28, 1994, p. B8; "Campus SWAT Team," *New York Times*, Oct. 9, 1994, sec. 6, p. 18.

22. "Lakewood Chief Follows Her Calling to Be Top Cop," Arlington Heights, IL, *Daily Herald*, July 15, 1996, p. 3.

CHAPTER 4

1. Eleanor Clift & Tom Brazaitis, *Madam President: Shattering the Last Glass Ceiling* (New York: Scribner, 2000), p. 25.

2. Elisabeth Bumiller, "Trusted Advisor's Memoir Lifts Curtain a Bit," *New York Times*, Apr. 1, 2004, p. A20.

3. Felice N. Schwartz, "Management Women and the New Facts of Life," *Harvard Business Review*, Jan.–Feb., 1989, p. 65.

4. See, for instance, Veronica Chambers, *Having It All?: Black Women and Success* (New York: Doubleday, 2003); Sylvia Ann Hewlett, *Creating a Life: Professional Women and the Quest for Children* (New York: Talk Miramax Books, 2002); Elizabeth Becker, "Motherhood Deters Women from Army's Highest Ranks," *New York Times*, Nov. 20, 1999, p. 1; "Pregnancy and the Chief," *Time*, June 18, 1990, p. 23.

5. "Women in Command: Breaking Through the Brass Ceiling," at the Canadian Police College, Ottawa, Ontario, Canada, on Oct. 27, 2003. The author was a panelist with Boniface and Clément.

6. Among the authors raising these issues are Virgina Valian, *Why So Slow?: The Advancement of Women* (Cambridge, MA: MIT Press, 1998); Hewlett, *Creating a Life;* and Allison Pearson, *I Don't Know How She Does It: The Life of Kate Reddy, Working Mother* (New York: Knopf, 2002).

7. Linda Wirth, *Breaking Through the Glass Ceiling: Women in Management* (London: International Labour Office, 2001).

8. Aileen Jacobson, *Women in Charge: Dilemmas of Women in Authority* (New York: Van Nostrand Reinhold, 1985), p. 17.

9. "Swearing-in for San Mateo's New Police Chief," *San Francisco Chronicle*, May 2, 2000, p. A14; Andy Altman-Ohr, "San Mateo Police Chief Gets Sworn In with Brachah," *J, the Jewish News Weekly of Northern California*, Aug. 25, 2000, retrieved Mar. 23, 2004, from http://www.jewishsf.com/content/2-0-/module/displaystory/short_id.

10. Dorothy Moses Schulz, "California Dreaming: Leading the Way to Gender-Free Police Management?" *Criminal Justice the Americas*, June–July 1994, pp. 1, 8–11.

11. Linda Taaffe, "Just the Facts, Ma'am," *Los Altos Town Crier*, Sept. 5, 2001, retrieved Mar. 23, 2004, from http://latc.com/2001/09/05/news/coverstol/print.html.

12. Kathie Kudlo, "End of the Line of Duty for Campus Police Chief," *The Poly Post*, Mar. 23, 2004, retrieved Mar. 23, 2004, from http://www.thepolypost.com/strong.php?story=852; Schulz, "California Dreaming," pp. 1, 8–11.

13. Rosabeth M. Kanter, *Men and Women of the Corporation* (New York: Basic Books, 1977).

14. "From Patrol to VP," *Philadelphia Daily News*, Apr. 16, 2002, retrieved Apr. 18, 2002, from http://www.philly.com.

15. "Officers Say New Boss Is Asking Too Much," *American Police Beat*, Jan. 2004, p. 60; "Some Officers Say They Hate Their Jobs," *American Police Beat*, Feb. 2004, p. 4.

16. Shaila K. Dewan, "New York's Gospel of Policing by Data Spreads across U.S.," *New York Times*, Apr. 28, 2004, pp. 1, B6.

CHAPTER 5

1. Susan E. Martin, "The Effectiveness of Affirmative Action: The Case of Women in Policing," *Justice Quarterly* 8 (1991): 489–504.

2. "Then There Was Nunn," *Law Enforcement News*, Mar. 15/31, 2003, p. 4; Benjamin Nicolet, "Mayor Picks Nunn as Chief," *Birmingham News*, Feb. 12, 2003, pp. 1A, 2A.

3. Jack E. Enter, "The Rise to the Top: An Analysis of Police Chief Career Patterns," *Journal of Police Science and Administration* 14, no. 4 (1986): 334–346.

4. Mark L. Dantzker, "Identifying Employment Criteria and Requisite Skills for the Position of Police Chief: Preliminary Findings," *Police Forum* 4, no. 3 (1994): 9–12; Mark L. Dantzker, "The Position of Municipal Police Chief: An Examination of Selection Criteria and Requisite Skills," *Police Studies* 19, no. 1 (1996): 1–17.

5. Steven Krull, *What Criteria Will Be Used to Select Police Chiefs in Mid-Sized Agencies by the Year 2005?* (Sacramento, CA: Command College Class XIX, Police Officer Standards and Training, 1995), pp. 12, 86.

6. "Becoming Chief of Police: Career Advancement among Texas Police Chiefs," *TELEMAS Bulletin* 9, no. 1 (Jan./Feb. 2002): 1–7.

7. Carol Robinson, "Mayor May Reveal New Police Chief Today, Black Female Deputy Chief a Front-Runner," *Birmingham News*, Feb. 11, 2003, p. 1.

8. Nicolet, "Mayor Picks Nunn as Chief."

9. Eleanor Clift & Tom Brazaitis, *Madam President: Shattering the Last Glass Ceiling* (New York: Scribner's, 2000), p. 18.

10. "Coming Out," *Law Enforcement News*, July 31, 2003, p. 6.

11. Mara Stine, "Piluso to Lead Gresham Police," *Gresham Outlook*, Oct. 9, 2002, p. 1A; Stuart Tomlinson, "Gresham Chooses Piluso as Police Chief," *The Oregonian*, Oct. 9, 2002, n.p.

12. "Hand-Picked," *Law Enforcement News*, Feb. 28, 2002, p. 4; "Ziemba's Appointment Is the Right Move," *Cheektowaga Times*, Feb. 14, 2002, p. 6.

13. Linda Wirth, *Breaking Through the Glass Ceiling: Women in Management* (London: International Labour Office, 2001).

14. "Goddess with a Gun," *Palo Alto Weekly* (on-line ed.), Feb. 12, 2003, retrieved Nov. 15, 2003, from http://www.paloaltoonline.com/weekly/morgue/2003/2003_02_12.chieflynne6.html.

15. Heron Maques Estrada, "Diversifying Police Force Is a 'Long Slow Process'; Minority Candidate Pool Is Still Small," *Minneapolis Star Tribune*, Apr. 27, 1997, p. 1B; Conrad de Biebre, "Pioneer Police Officer to Head State Patrol," *Minneapolis Star Tribune*, Sept. 20, 1997, p. 1A.

16. Robert Whereall, "Inside Talk," *Minneapolis Star Tribune*, Feb. 1, 1999, p. 3B.

17. "Women in Policing: IACP, Gallup Assess Recruitment, Promotion, Retention Issues," *The Police Chief*, Oct. 1998, pp. 36–40. This research was an outgrowth of the IACP's Ad Hoc Committee on Women in Policing, of which the author was a member.

18. Arlie Hochschild & Anne Machung. *The Second Shift: Working Parents and the Revolution at Home* (New York: Viking, 1989). Indicative of the interest in how working women apportion their time, the book was updated and re-issued in paperback (New York: Penguin, 2003).

19. Nicholas J. Beutell & O. Carolyn Brenner, "Sex Differences in Work Values," *Journal of Vocational Behavior* 28 (1986): 29–41; Judith S. Bridges, "Sex Differences in Occupational Values," *Sex Roles* 29 (1989): 205–211; P.P. Scozzaro & Linda Mezydlo Sublich, "Gender and Occupational Sex-Type Differences in Job Outcome Factor Perceptions," *Journal of Vocational Behavior* 36 (1990): 109–119.

20. Thomas S. Whetstone & Deborah G. Wilson, "Dilemmas Confronting Female Police Officer Promotional Candidates: Glass Ceiling, Disenfranchisement or Satisfaction?" *International Journal of Police Science and Management* 2, no. 2 (Sept. 1999): 135–136.

CHAPTER 6

1. "Lady Sheriff an Unofficial Official," *The Hawk Eye* (Burlington, IA), July 23, 2003, retrieved June 3, 2004, from http://www.thehawkeye.com/columns/Hansen/2000/cha72300.html; B.J. Alderman, "The Story of 'Mrs. Sheriff,'" *American Western Magazine*, retrieved June 23, 2003, from. http://www.readthewest.com/MrsSheriff2003-04.html; Larry D. Ball, *Desert Lawmen: The High Sheriffs of New Mexico and Arizona 1864–1912* (Albuquerque: University of New Mexico Press, 1992), p. 292.

2. The case received wide publicity in Iowa newspapers. In addition to "A Jury of Her Peers," Susan Glaspell also wrote a one-act play, "Trifles," which was first performed in 1916. Both were forgotten until the 1970s, when "A Jury of Her Peers" was included in Lee R. Edwards & Arlyn Diamond, eds., *American Voices, American Women* (New York: Avon, 1973).

3. Kenneth E. Kerle, "The American Woman County Jail Officer," in Imogene L. Moyer, ed., *The Changing Roles of Women in the Criminal Justice System: Offenders, Victims, and Professionals* (Prospect Heights, IL: Waveland Press, 1985), p. 313.

4. After allegations that "Ma" and her husband had accepted bribes, there was an attempt to impeach her, but she survived. See "Nellie Tayloe Ross," retrieved Feb. 2, 2002, from http://www.unitedstates-on-line.com/wyoming/rossbio.htm; and "Ferguson, Miriam Amanda Wallace," in *The Handbook of Texas Online*, retrieved Feb. 2, 2002, from http://www.tsha.utexas.edu/handbook/online/artcles/view/FF/ffe6.html.

5. Irene Gladwin, *The Sheriff: The Man and His Office* (London: Victor Gollancz, Ltd., 1974), pp. 12, 15–26.

6. "History of Sheriffs," retrieved June 3, 2003, from http://www.geocities.com/vbenson_2000/history.htm; and "History of the Sheriff's Office (Sussex County, NJ)," retrieved June 3, 2003, from http://www.sussexcountysheriff.com/History.htm.

7. Harry C. Buffardi, *The History of the Office of Sheriff*, retrieved June 8, 2003, from http://www.hostpc/buffardi; "Maryland's Sheriffs...Chosen to Serve, Dedicated to Public Service," retrieved June 8, 2003, from http://www.mdle.net/mdsheriffs/histduties.html.

8. Kevin Bates, "Kansas 1st in Female Sheriffs," *Topeka Capital-Journal*, Aug. 7, 2000, p. 1-A.

9. "Maryland's Sheriffs"; "Banister, Emma Daugherty," in *The Handbook of Texas Online*, retrieved June 3, 2003, from http://www.tsha.utexas.edu/handbook/online/articles/view/BBfbacq.html.

10. John T. Felix & Cheryl Felix McClellan, "The First Female Sheriff," *Sheriff*, May–June, 1994, pp. 59–60.

11. Phillip L. Earl, "Law South of the Humboldt: Clara D. Crowell, Nevada's First Lady Sheriff 1919–1921," *North Central Nevada Historical Society Quarterly* 6, no. 2 (1983): 3–13; Craig MacDonald, "Nevada's First Woman Sheriff," *Historical Nevada Magazine* (1998): 25–27.

12. "Jesse and Ruth Lane Garfield," retrieved June 3, 2003, from http://www.rootsweb.com/~mtgolden/FirstSheriff.html.

13. Diane L. Griffith, *America's First Woman Sheriff Captures Kentucky's Barefoot Desperado* (Paducah, KY: Turner, 2000), p. 95. Griffith learned about Roach while researching a murder in Graves County that occurred before either Roach was sheriff. She incorrectly described Lois Roach as America's first woman sheriff, but provided details of Roach's tenure.

14. "Mrs. Holley Joins Search," *New York Times*, Mar. 4, 1934, p. 24; Kenan Heise, "Pioneering Female Sheriff Outlived Dillinger's Escape," *Chicago Tribune*, June 17, 1994, n.p.; "Dillinger—Public Enemy # 1—Escapes," *The Wire*, retrieved July 15, 2003, from http://wire.ap.org/APpackages/20thcentury/34dillinger.html.

15. Renée Montagne, "Word for Word/The Last Hanging: There Was a Reason They Outlawed Public Executions," *New York Times*, May 6, 2001, sec. 4, p. 5.

16. Perry T. Ryan, *The Last Public Execution in America*. The book is out of print, but was retrieved June 3, 2003, from http://www.geocities.com/lastpublichang/index.htm.

17. "Women in Criminal Justice Hall of Honor," retrieved July 9, 2003, from http://www.cj.msu.edu/%7eoutreach/azm/hof.html.

18. Nancy Beasley, "The Lace Curtain Jail," retrieved June 3, 2003, from http://www.dekalbcounty-il.com/dolder.html; "Women in Criminal Justice Hall of Honor"; and Martha Bergh Lantz, "Remembering the City of Bangor Wreck," retrieved July 15, 2003, from http://www.eagleharborweb.net/favorite.htm.

19. Beasley, "The Lace Curtain Jail."

20. "Women's Hall of Fame: Maude Charles Collins," Ohio Women's Hall of Fame, retrieved June 3, 2003, from http://www.state.oh.us/odjfs/women/halloffame.bio; "The First Lady Sheriff? Maude Collins of Vinton County," Regional History of Appalachian Ohio: Terra Incognita, retrieved June 3, 2003, from http://www.geocities/com/Athens/Olympus/5870/mc.html.

21. Dorothy Moses Schulz, "Married to the Job: Wisconsin's Women Sheriffs," *Wisconsin Magazine of History*, Spring 2003, pp. 22–37.

22. Charles Taylor, "In the Clink: Moore County Jail Museum Now Houses History, Not Prisoners," retrieved Nov. 15, 2003, from http://www.lynchburgtn.com/intheclink.html.

23. "New Sheriff Is on the Alert," *Barron County* (Wisconsin) *News*, Nov. 11, 1926, n.p.

24. *County of Washington v. Gunther*, 454 U.S. 161, 1981. The case was brought by four women who had been guards in the female section of the Washington County (Oregon) jail until it was closed and the inmates were transferred to another facility. Prior to Feb.1, 1973, female guards were paid between $476 and $606 per month, while male guards were paid between $668 and $853. Effective Feb.1, 1973, the females were paid between $525 and $668, while salaries for males ranged from $701 to $940. The women alleged that although the county had rated their posi-

tions at 95 percent parity with male officers, their pay was only at 70 percent parity. Although the District Count rejected the women's claim, the Court of Appeals reversed the District Court, which then appealed to the Supreme Court, which ruled 6 to 3 in their favor.

25. "Dorothy M. Lord" [obituary], *The Caledonia* (Minnesota) *Argus*, Mar. 31, 2003, retrieved Nov. 15, 2003, from http://www.ecm-inc.com/news/caledonia/2003/march/31DorothyM.Lord.htm.

26. Sheila Schmitt, "'Sheriff Mom': Women Are Gaining in Numbers in a Traditionally Male Post," *Law and Order*, Jan. 1996, p. 68.

27. John M.R. Bull, "Former Fayette Sheriff Fined for Nepotism," *Pittsburgh Post–Gazette*, June 1, 2000, retrieved Mar. 22, 2004, from http://www.postgazette.com; Matthew Junker, "Challengers Team Up to Take on Row Officers in County," *Pittsburgh Daily Courier*, May 10, 2003, retrieved Mar. 22, 2004, from http//www.pittsburghlive.com/x/dailycourier/news.

CHAPTER 7

1. Kelly Wolfe, "Saluting New Year, New Look," *Philadelphia Inquirer*, Jan. 3, 2001, n.p.

2. "Former Sheriff Guilty in Successor's Killing," *New York Times*, July 11, 2002, p. A16; "Ex-Sheriff Gets Life in Death of Successor," *New York Times*, Aug. 16, 2002, p. A14.

3. "Interviews in Sherwood: Councillor Joan Casson, the Sheriff of Nottingham: 2001–2002," retrieved June 3, 2003, from http://www.geocities.com/puckrobin/rh/casson.html.

4. "The Role of High Sheriffs," retrieved Nov. 15, 2003, from http://www.privy-council.org.uk; Ho Dillon, "Sheriffs Keep Their Badges in Old Boys' Club," *The Independent*, Feb. 11, 2003, retrieved Nov. 15, 2003 from http://www.obv.org.uk/reports/2001/rpt20010211f.html; "New Sheriffs to Ease Ban Burden," BBC News Online, UK: Scotland, retrieved Nov. 15, 2003, from http://www.news.bbc.co.uk/1/low/scotland/558290.stm.

5. See Beth Reingold, *Representing Women: Sex, Gender, and Legislative Behavior in Arizona and California* (Chapel Hill: University of North Carolina Press, 2000), pp. 13–18; Sue Thomas & Clyde Wilcox, eds., "Introduction," in *Women and Elective Office: Past, Present, and Future* (New York: Oxford University Press, 1998), pp. 1–14; Debra L. Dodson & Susan J. Carroll, *Reshaping the Agenda: Women in State Legislatures* (New Brunswick, NJ: Center for the American Woman and Politics, 1991).

6. Dodson & Carroll, *Reshaping the Agenda*; Michele L. Swers, "Are Women More Likely to Vote for Women's Issue Bills Than Their Male Colleagues?" *Legislative Studies Quarterly* 23 (1998): 435–448.

7. Kathleen Dolan & Lynne E. Ford, "Are All Women State Legislators Alike?", in Thomas & Wilcox, eds., *Women and Elective Office*, p. 83.

8. Reingold, *Representing Women*, pp. 13–17.

9. Zack Phillips, "Jailhouse Mothers Receive Holiday Visit," Arlington County in the News, Dec. 9, 2003, retrieved Apr. 30, 2004 from http://www.co.arlington/va/us/NewsDigestScripts.

10. Michelle Gaseau & Keith L. Martin, "Secrets Behind Bars: Sexual Misconduct in Jails," Corrections.com, Apr. 21, 2003, retrieved Apr. 30, 2004, from Stop Prisoner Rape, http://www.spr.org/en/sprnews/2003/0421.html.

11. Sheila Schmitt, "'Sheriff Mom': Women Are Gaining in Numbers in a Traditionally Male Post," *Law and Order*, Jan. 1996, pp. 62–69.

12. Ellen Swetts, "Woman behind the Badge: Travis County Sheriff Margo Frasier Is a Veteran at Being First," *Dallas Morning News*, Oct. 29, 1997, retrieved Apr. 30, 2004, from DallasNews.com.

13. Tony Plohetski, "Frasier Says She Won't Seek Re-Election," *American-Statesman*, Dec. 5, 2003; Tony Plohetski & Steven Kreytak, Frasier Tells of Reasons Not to Seek Re-Election," *American-Statesman*, Dec. 5, 2003, retrieved Apr. 30, 2004, from Travis County Sheriffs Law Enforcement Association, http://www.teslea.org/press_releases.php.

14. "Georgia: Class-Action on Behalf of Inmates," *New York Times*, Apr. 23, 2004, p. A18.

15. Shaila K. Dewan, "Sheriff Accepts Takeover of a Troubled Jail," *New York Times*, July 12, 2004; p. A12; "Georgia: Judge Picks a New Head of Jail," *New York Times*, July 15, 2005, p. A19.

16. Colin Campbell, "Who Will Take Lead to Shed the Sheriff?" *Atlanta Journal–Constitution*, Apr. 13, 2004, p. 2B; "The Sooner Barrett Quits, the Better for Fulton Jail," *Atlanta Journal–Constitution*, Apr. 19, 2004, p. 10A.

17. Jeffry Scott & Steve Visser, "Barrett Won't Run Again; Grand Jury Investigates Fulton Sheriff," *Atlanta Journal–Constitution*, Apr. 20, 2004, p. 1A; Ariel Hart, "Beleaguered Sheriff in Atlanta Area Will Leave Office Early," *New York Times*, July 17, 2004, p. A14.

18. "1996 General Primary—Our Choices," *Atlanta Inquirer*, July 6, 1996, p. 4.

CHAPTER 8

1. "Rights Fight Takes Cop to Top," *USA Today*, Jan. 25, 1985, n.p.

2. Penny Harrington, *Triumph of Spirit: An Autobiography* (Chicago: Brittany, 1999), pp. 266–267.

3. Ibid., p. 214.

4. Ibid., p. 110.

5. Harrington described the frenzy in ibid., pp. 182–188, which includes a copy of the *Downtowner* paper doll that appeared on Mar. 11, 1985.

6. Harrington's resignation received national press coverage. See Wallace Turner, "Under Fire, Woman Quits as Portland Police Chief," *New York Times*, June 3, 1986, p. A16; "Portland's Tarnished Penny; The Travails of a Crusading Woman Police Office," *Time*, Apr. 14, 1986, p. 26, and "First In—and Out; Portland's Woman Chief Quits," *Time*, June 16, 1986, p. 17.

7. "Portland's Tarnished Penny," p. 26; Harrington, *Triumph of Spirit*, p. 194.

8. Turner, "Under Fire," p. A16.

9. Lisa Belkin, "Woman Named Police Chief of Houston," *New York Times*, Jan. 20, 1990, p. 10.

10. "Pistol-Packin' Mama," *Time*, Feb. 19, 1990, p. 67.

11. Barbara Hustedt Crook, "*Cosmo* Talks to Elizabeth Watson: Houston's Pioneering Police Chief," *Cosmo*, Oct. 1990, pp. 116, 180; Walter Shapiro, "Reforming Our Image of a Chief," *Time*, Nov. 26, 1990, pp. 80–82.

12. "For She's a Jolly Good Fellow: Watson Leaves Austin PD for COPS Office Visiting Fellowship," *Law Enforcement News*, Feb. 14, 1997, p. 4.

13. Shapiro, "Reforming Our Image of a Chief," p. 80.

14. Deirdre Martin & Mark Levine, "From Matron to Chief: The Status of Women in Law Enforcement," *Law Enforcement Technology*, Feb. 1991, p. 52.

15. John Kirsh, "Few Women Reach the Rank of Top Cop," *Dallas–Fort Worth Star–Telegram*, Oct. 7, 2003, n.p.

16. Muriel L. Whetstone, "Atlanta's Top Cop," *Ebony*, Mar. 1995, pp. 92–95.

17. "Trail Blazer," *Law Enforcement News*, Nov. 30, 1994, p. 4.

18. "Atlanta's Police Chief Won More Than a Bet," *New York Times*, Nov. 30, 1994, p. C1; "First Black Woman to Run a Big City Police Force Cracks Down on Corruption," *Jet*, Oct. 2, 1995, pp. 8–13; "Beverly Harvard," *Current Biography*, Sept. 1997, pp. 11–14; James Booker, "Top Drawer Stuff," *Carib News*, week ending Sept. 3, 2002, p. 45.

19. "Trail Blazer," p. 4.

20. "Shooting Yields Procedural Change, but No Indictments," *Law Enforcement News*, Feb. 28, 1995, p. 5.

21. Curtis Wilkie, "Atlanta Chief Diffuses Tensions," *American Police Beat*, July/ Aug. 1997, p. 10.

22. "Corruption Scandal Surfaces in Atlanta—with Inside Help," *Law Enforcement News*, Oct. 31, 1995, p. 5.

23. "Do Atlanta's Numbers Add Up?" *Law Enforcement News*, Feb. 28, 1999, pp. 1, 9.

24. The report, commissioned by the Atlanta Police Foundation, a group of business leaders who raise money for police projects, received wide press coverage. See, for instance, Ariel Hart, "Report Finds Atlanta Police Cut Figures on Crime," *New York Times*, Feb. 21, 2004, p. A11; and Mark Neisse, "Audit: Atlanta Distorted Crimes," *Miami Herald*, Feb. 21, 2004, p. 7A.

25. Ernie Suggs, "Top Cop's Contract Totals $226,000 in Pay, Benefits," *Atlanta Journal–Constitution*, June 6, 2002, p. 1D.

26. "Land Baron," *Law Enforcement News*, Dec. 15, 1993, p. 4; "Around the Nation," *Law Enforcement News*, Feb. 28, 1995, p. 5; "Justice Delays: If SPD Chief John Harris Resigned, Why Is He Still Calling the Shots?" *Illinois Times*, June 12, 2003, retrieved July 7, 2003, from http://www.illinoistimes.com/gbase/Gyrostie/Content?oid%3A2244.

CHAPTER 9

1. Jesse Garza & Greg J. Borowski, "Hegerty Pick for Police Chief Praised: First Woman to Lead Department Wins 4–0 Vote," *Milwaukee Journal Sentinel*, Oct. 17, 2003, p. 1B.

2. Rebecca L. Warner, Brent S. Steele, & Nicholas P. Lovrich, "Conditions Associated with the Advent of Representative Bureaucracy: The Case of Women in Policing," *Social Science Quarterly* 70, no. 3 (Sept. 1989): 574–575.

3. Scott Williams, "Kruziki Gets Marshal Nomination; Quick Confirmation Likely, Senator's Aide Says," *Milwaukee Journal Sentinel*, Mar. 14, 2002, p. 1B.

4. Linda Babcock & Sara Laschever, *Women Don't Ask: Negotiation and the Gender Divide* (Princeton, NJ: Princeton University Press, 2003), p. 8.

5. Adrian Walker, "Right Choice in O'Toole," *Boston Globe*, Feb. 9, 2004, p. B1.

6. Garza & Borowski, "Hegerty Pick for Police Chief Praised," p. 1B.

7. "Black Out, Woman In," *Law Enforcement News*, Feb. 2004, p. 7.

8. "Days May Be Numbered for Milwaukee IAD," *Law Enforcement News*, Feb. 2004, p. 14.

9. Ben Schmitt, "Detroit's New Top Cop a Woman Who'll Keep the Hard Line: Interim Title a Formality; Oliver Charged with Misdemeanor in Gun Incident," *Detroit Free Press*, retrieved Nov. 11, 2003, from http://www.freep.com/news/locway/chief4_20031104.htm.

10. Darren A. Nicholas, "First Woman Chief Faces Harsh Glare of Scrutiny," *Detroit News*, Nov. 5, 2003, retrieved Nov. 7, 2003, from http://www.detnow.com/news/0311031201.html.

11. Donna Leinwand, "Lawsuits of '70s Shape Police Leadership Now," *USA Today*, Apr. 26, 2004, pp. 13A, 14A.

12. "Spate of Violence Brings Joint Effort Crime Crackdown," Associated Press, Feb. 9, 2004 (Lexis-Nexis Academic–Document, 2 pages).

13. Suzette Hackney & Jim Schaefer, "Native Detroiter Worked Her Way Up," *Detroit Free Press*, Nov. 4, 2003, n.p.

14. Lisa Leff, "In San Francisco, Public Safety Is Women's Work," Associated Press, Jan. 31, 2004 (Lexis-Nexis Academic–Document, 3 pages).

15. Dorothy Moses Schulz, *From Social Worker to Crimefighter: Women in United States Municipal Policing* (Westport, CT: Praeger, 1995), p. 145.

16. William Bratton with Peter Knobler, *Turnaround: How America's Top Cop Reversed the Crime Epidemic* (New York: Random House, 1998), pp.132–137.

17. Virginia O'Brien, *Success on Our Own Terms: Tales of Extraordinary, Ordinary Business Women* (New York: John Wiley, 1998), pp. 9, 29.

18. Babcock & Laschever, *Women Don't Ask*, pp. 138–140.

19. William E. Kirchhoff, Charlotte Lansinger, & James Burack, *Command Performance: A Career Guide for Police Executives* (Washington, DC: Police Executive Research Forum, 1999), pp. 23–25.

20. Fred W. Rainguet & Mary Dodge, "The Problems of Police Chiefs: An Examination of the Issues in Tenure and Turnover," *Police Quarterly* 4, no. 3 (Sept. 2001): 271.

CHAPTER 10

1. Brian A. Reaves & Matthew J. Hickman, *Sheriffs' Offices, 2000* (Washington, DC: U.S. Department of Justice, 2003).

2. Matthew J. Hickman & Brian A. Reaves, *Local Police Departments, 2000* (Washington, DC: U.S. Department of Justice, 2003), p. 1.

3. Matthew J. Hickman, *Tribal Law Enforcement, 2000* (Washington, DC: Department of Justice, 2003), pp. 1, 2.

4. Steven Krull, *What Criteria Will Be Used to Select Police Chiefs in Mid-Sized*

Agencies by the Year 2005 (Sacramento, CA: Command College Class XIX, Police Officer Standards and Training, 1995), p. 12.

5. For male chiefs' education levels, see Police Executive Research Forum, "Police Executive Survey" (1998), summarized in Marie Simonetti Rosen, "Getting Nice and Comfy? Don't," *Law Enforcement News*, Dec. 15/31, 1998, p. 2; and Robert Sheehan & Gary W. Cordner, *Police Administration*, 4th ed. (Cincinnati, OH: Anderson, 1999), p. 108.

6. "Again a First," *Law Enforcement News*, Feb. 2, 1995, p. 4; "Ivin B. Lee Named Dunbar, WV's First Female Police Chief," *Jet*, Jan. 15, 1966, p. 25.

EPILOGUE

1. Among the most prominent men who have led more than one major department are Kathleen O'Toole's mentor, William Bratton (five departments, including Boston, New York City, and Los Angeles), John Timoney (Philadelphia and Miami, after a career in New York City that included a number of top posts just below commissioner), Charles Moose (Portland, Oregon, and Montgomery County, Maryland), and Betsy Watson's mentor, Lee P. Brown (Multnomah County, Oregon; Altanta; Houston; and New York City), Ella Bully-Cummings's strong supporter, Jerry Oliver (Pasadena, California; Richmond, Virginia; and Detroit), and Richard Pennington, who replaced Beverly Harvard in Atlanta (New Orleans and Atlanta).

Selected Bibliography

A wealth of research went into writing this book. Interviews, unpublished sources, newspaper and short magazine articles, and Websites mentioned in the notes are not included here.

Alimo-Medcalfe, B. "An Investigation of Female and Male Constructions of Leadership and Empowerment." *Women in Management Review* 10, no. 2 (1995): 3–8.

Ashburn, Elizabeth A. *Motivation, Personality, and Work-Related Characteristics of Women in Male-Dominated Professions.* Washington, DC: National Association for Women Deans, Administrators, and Counselors, 1977.

Bartol, Curt B., George T. Bergen, Julie Seager Volckins, & Kathleen M. Knoras. "Women in Small-Town Policing: Job Performance and Stress." *Criminal Justice and Behavior* 19, no. 3 (Sept. 1992): 240–259.

Belnap, Joanne, & Edna Erez. "Redefining Sexual Harassment: Confronting Sexism in the 21st Century." *The Justice Professional* 10 (1997): 143–159.

Blount, Jackie M. *Destined to Rule the Schools: Women and the Superintendency, 1873–1995.* Albany: State University of New York Press, 1998.

Brown, Jennifer, & Frances Heidensohn. *Gender and Policing: Comparative Perspectives.* New York: St. Martin's Press, 2000.

Brown, Stephen M. "Male versus Female Leaders: A Comparison of Empirical Studies." *Sex Roles* 5, no. 5 (Oct. 1979): 595–611.

Brunner, C. Cryss. *Principles of Power: Women Superintendents and the Riddle of the Heart.* Albany: State University of New York Press, 2000.

Brunner, C. Cryss, ed. *Sacred Dreams: Women and the Superintendency.* Albany: State University of New York Press, 1999.

Burke, Ronald J., & Carol A. McKeen. "Do Women at the Top Make a Difference?: Gender Proportions and the Experiences of Managerial and Professional Women." *Human Relations* 49, no. 8 (Aug. 1996): 1093–1105.

Bushardt, Stephen C., Aubrey Fowler, & Regina Caveny. "Sex Role Behavior and Leadership: An Empirical Study." *Leadership and Organizational Journal* 8, no. 5 (1987): 13–16.

Carless, Sally A. "Gender Differences in Transformational Leadership: An Examination of Superior, Leader, and Subordinate Perspectives." *Sex Roles* 39, no. 11/12 (Dec. 1998): 887–902.

Carroll, Susan J., ed. *The Impact of Women in Public Office*. Bloomington: Indiana University Press, 2001.

Chambers, Veronica. *Having It All?: Black Women and Success*. New York: Doubleday, 2003.

Comptroller General of the United States. *Conflicting Congressional Policies: Veterans' Preference and Apportionment vs. Equal Employment Opportunity*. Washington, DC: General Accounting Office, 1977.

Crank, John P., Robert Regoli, & John D. Hewitt. "An Assessment of Work Stress among Police Executives." *Journal of Criminal Justice* 21, no. 4 (1993): 313–324.

Crank, John P., Robert Regoli, John D. Hewitt, & Robert G. Culbertson. "Institutional and Organizational Antecedents of Role Stress, Work Alienation, and Anomie among Police Executives." *Criminal Justice and Behavior* 22, no. 2 (June 1995): 152–171.

Dantzker, Mark L. "The Position of Municipal Police Chief: An Examination of Selection Criteria and Requisite Skills." *Police Studies* 19, no. 2 (1996): 1–7.

Dobbins, G. H. "Equity vs. Equality: Sex Differences in Leadership." *Sex Roles* 15, no. 9/10 (1986): 513–525.

Duerst-Lahti, Georgia, & Cathy Marie Johnson. "Gender and Style in Bureaucracy." *Women & Politics* 10, no. 4 (1990): 67–120.

Dye, Thomas, & Julie Strickland. "Women at the Top: A Note on Institutional Leadership." *Social Science Quarterly* 58, no. 2 (June 1982): 333–341.

Enter, Jack E. "The Rise to the Top: An Analysis of Police Chief Career Patterns." *Journal of Police Science and Administration* 14, no. 4 (1986): 334–346.

Equality Denied: The Status of Women in Policing, 1998. Los Angeles: National Center for Women and Policing, 1999.

Felkenes, George T., & Jean Reith Schroedel. "A Case Study of Minority Women in Policing." *Women & Criminal Justice* 4, no. 2 (1993): 65–89.

Ferber, Marianne, Joan Huber, & Glenna Spitze. "Preference for Men as Bosses and Professionals." *Social Forces* 58, no. 2 (Dec. 1979): 466–476.

Fleming, John H., & Charles Shanor. "Veterans' Preferences in Public Employment: Unconstitutional Gender Discrimination?" *Emory Law Journal* 26 (Winter 1977): 13–64.

Gerber, Gwendolyn L. "Leadership Roles and the Gender Stereotype Traits." *Sex Roles* 18, no. 11/12 (1988): 649–668.

Gertzog, Irwin N. *Congressional Women: Their Recruitment, Treatment, and Behavior*. New York: Praeger, 1984.

Grennan, Sean, & Robert Munoz. "Women as Police Officers in the Twenty-first Century: A Decade of Promotional Practices by Gender in Three Major Police Agencies." In Roslyn Muraskin and Albert R. Roberts, eds., *Visions for Change: Crime and Justice in the Twenty-first Century*, pp. 340–354. Upper Saddle River, NJ: Prentice-Hall, 1996.

Griffith, Diane L. *America's First Woman Sheriff Captures Kentucky's Barefoot Desperado*. Paducah, KY: Turner, 2000.

Gruhl, John, Cassia Spohn, & Susan Welch. "Women as Policymakers: The Case of Trial Judges." *American Journal of Political Science* 25, no. 2 (May 1981): 308–322.

Halford, Alison. *No Way up the Greasy Police*. London: Constable, 1993.

Harriman, Ann. *Women/Men/Management*, 2nd ed. Westport, CT: Praeger, 1996.

Harrington, Penny. *Triumph of Spirit: An Autobiography*. Chicago: Brittany, 1999.

Heimovics, Richard D., & Robert D. Herman. "Gender and the Attributes of Chief Executive Responsibility for Successful Organizational Outcomes." *Sex Roles* 18, no. 9/10 (1988): 623–635.

Hewlett, Sylvia Ann. *Creating a Life: Professional Women and the Quest for Children*. New York: Talk Miramax Books, 2002.

Huddy, Leonie, & Nayda Terkildsen. "The Consequences of Gender Stereotypes for Women Candidates at Different Levels and Types of Office." *Political Research Quarterly* 46, no. 3 (Sept. 1993): 503–525.

Jacobson, Aileen. *Women in Charge: Dilemmas of Women in Authority*. New York: Van Nostrand Reinhold, 1985.

Jamieson, Kathleen Hall. *Beyond the Double Bind: Women and Leadership*. New York: Oxford University Press, 1995.

Kahn, Kim Fridkin. "Does Gender Make a Difference: An Experimental Examination of Sex Stereotypes and Press Patterns in Statewide Campaigns." *American Journal of Political Science* 83, no. 1 (Feb. 1994): 162–195.

Kahn, Kim Fridkin. "Gender Differences in Campaign Messages: The Political Advertisements of Men and Women Candidates for U.S. Senate." *Political Research Quarterly* 46, no. 3 (Sept. 1993): 481–502.

Kanter, Rosabeth M. *Men and Women of the Corporation*. New York: Basic Books, 1977.

Karsten, Margaret Foegen. *Management and Gender: Issues and Attitudes*. Westport, CT: Praeger, 1994.

Kerle, Kenneth E. "The American Woman County Jail Officer." In Imogene L. Moyer, ed., *The Changing Roles of Women in the Criminal Justice System: Offenders, Victims, and Professionals*, pp. 301–318. Prospect Heights, IL: Waveland Press, 1985.

Kwolek-Folland, Angel. *Incorporating Women: A History of Women and Business in the United States*. New York: Twayne, 1998.

Maher, Karen J. "Gender-Related Stereotypes of Transformational and Transactional Leadership." *Sex Roles* 37, no. 3/4 (Aug. 1997): 209–226.

Martin, Susan E., & Nancy C. Jurik. *Doing Justice, Doing Gender: Women in Law and Criminal Justice Occupations*. Thousand Oaks, CA: Sage, 1996.

Nichols, Nancy A. "Whatever Happened to Rosie the Riveter?" *Harvard Business Review* (July–Aug. 1993): 54–62.

O'Brien, Virginia. *Success on Our Own Terms: Tales of Extraordinary, Ordinary Business Women*. New York: Wiley, 1998.

Owings, Chloe. *Women Police: A Study of the Development and Status of the Women Police Movement*. New York: Hitchcock, 1925.

Penegor, Janice K., & Ken Peake. "Police Chief Acquisitions: A Comparison of Internal and External Selections." *American Journal of Police* 11, no. 1 (1992): 17–32.

Price, Barbara R. "A Study of Leadership Strength of Female Police Executives." *Journal of Police Science and Administration* 2, no. 2 (1974): 219–226.

Rainguet, Fred W., & Mary Dodge. "The Problems of Police Chiefs: An Examination of the Issues in Tenure and Turnover." *Police Quarterly* 4, no. 3 (Sept.): 268–288.

Regoli, Robert, John P. Crank, & Robert G. Culbertson. "The Consequences of Professionalism among Police Chiefs." *Justice Quarterly* 6, no. 1 (1989): 47–67.

Regoli, Robert, Robert G. Culbertson, John P. Crank, & James R. Powell. "Career Stage and Cynicism among Police Chiefs." *Justice Quarterly* 7, no. 3 (1990): 593–614.

Reingold, Beth. *Representing Women: Sex, Gender, and Legislative Behavior in Arizona and California*. Chapel Hill: University of North Carolina Press, 2000.

Rosener, Judy B. "Ways Women Lead." *Harvard Business Review* (November–December 1990): 119–125.

Ryan, Perry T. *The Last Public Execution in America*. N.p: P. T. Ryan, 1992. Available at http://www.geocities.com/lastpublichang/index.htm. Accessed June 3, 2003.

Saltzstein, Grace Hall. "Female Mayors and Women in Municipal Jobs." *American Journal of Political Science* 30, no. 1 (Feb. 1986): 140–164.

Schulz, Dorothy Moses. *From Social Worker to Crimefighter: Women in United States Municipal Policing*. Westport, CT: Praeger, 1995.

Schulz, Dorothy Moses. "Law Enforcement Leaders: A Survey of Women Police Chiefs in the United States." *The Police Chief* (March 2002): 25–28.

Schulz, Dorothy Moses. "Married to the Job: Wisconsin's Women Sheriffs." *Wisconsin Magazine of History* (Spring 2003): 22–37.

Schulz, Dorothy Moses. "Women Police Chiefs: A Statistical Profile." *Police Quarterly* 6, no. 3 (Sept. 2003): 330–345.

Silvestri, Marisa. "Visions of the Future: The Role of Senior Policewomen as Agents of Change." *International Journal of Police Science and Management* 1, no. 2 (1998): 148–161.

Smulyan, Lisa. *Balancing Acts: Women Principals at Work*. Albany: State University of New York Press, 2000.

Steel, Brent S., & Nichlas P. Lobrich. "Fiscal Stress, Competing Values and Municipal Governance: What Fate Befell Affirmative Action in Municipal Police Departments?" *Journal of Urban Affairs* 15 (1986): 15–30.

Stivers, Camilla. *Gender Images in Public Administration: Legitimacy and the Administrative State*. Newbury Park, CA: Sage, 1993.

Thomas, Sue. "Why Gender Matters: The Perceptions of Women Officeholders." *Women & Politics* 17, no. 1 (1997): 27–53.

Thomas, Sue, & Clyde Wilcox, eds. *Women and Elective Office: Past, Present, and Future*. New York: Oxford University Press, 1998.

Valian, Virginia. *Why So Slow? The Advancement of Women*. Cambridge, MA: MIT Press, 1998.

Walker, Samuel. "Racial Minority and Female Employment in Policing: The Implications of Glacial Change." *Crime and Delinquency* 31 (1985): 555–572.

Warner, Rebecca L., Brent S. Steele, & Nicholas P. Lovrich, "Conditions Associated with the Advent of Representative Bureaucracy: The Case of Women in Policing," *Social Science Quarterly* 70, no. 3 (Sept. 1989): 562–578.

Whetstone, Thomas S., & Deborah G. Wilson. "Dilemmas Confronting Female Police Officer Promotional Candidates: Glass Ceiling, Disenfranchisement or Satisfaction?" *International Journal of Police Science and Management* 2, no. 2 (Sept. 1999): 128–143.

Witham, Donald C. *The American Law Enforcement Chief Executive: A Management Profile*. Washington, DC: Police Executive Research Forum, 1985.

Index

About the Author

DOROTHY MOSES SCHULZ is Professor of Law, Police Studies, and Criminal Justice Administration at the John Jay College of Criminal Justice (City University of New York). She was the first woman captain to serve with the Metro-North Commuter Railroad Police Department and its predecessor department, the Conrail Police Department. She is the author of *From Social Worker to Crimefighter: Women in United States Municipal Policing* (Praeger, 1995), and has published widely on historical and current issues involving women in policing. She is a member of numerous police and academic associations, and has spoken at conferences of the International Association of Women Police, Women in Federal Law Enforcement, the National Center for Women & Policing, the Senior Women Officers of Great Britain, and the Canadian Police College.